Rosie's BAKERY

ALL-BUTTER
FRESH CREAM
SUGAR-PACKED

No-Holds-Barred

BAKING BOOK

Rosie's BAKERY

ALL-BUTTER
FRESH CREAM
SUGAR-PACKED
No-Holds-Barred
BAKING BOOK

BY ♥ JUDY ♥ ROSENBERG

Written with Nan Levinson

Illustrations by Barbara Maslen

Workman Publishing
New York

Copyright ©1991 by Judy Rosenberg

Illustrations ©1991 by Barbara Maslen

Library of Congress Cataloging-in-Publication Data

Rosenberg, Judy,
Rosie's Bakery all-butter, fresh cream, sugar-packed, no-holds-barred baking book / Judy Rosenberg.
p.   cm.
Includes index.
ISBN 1-56305-126-5 (cloth) — ISBN 0-89480-723-4 (pap)
1. Baking. 2. Rosie's Bakery. I. Title. II. Title: All-butter, fresh cream, sugar-packed, no-holds-barred baking book.
TX763.R66 1991
641.8'65 — dc20 91-50380
CIP

Cover design by Ira Teichberg
Front cover photograph by Richard Feldman
Back cover photographs by Richard Feldman and Jim Scherer
Art direction by Lisa Hollander
Book design by Karen Trittipo
Illustrations by Barbara Maslen

Workman Publishing Company, Inc.
708 Broadway
New York, NY 10003

Manufactured in the United States of America

First printing October 1991
10 9 8 7 6 5 4 3 2

Dedication

—❖—

To my mother and father,

Debbie and Jack Rosenberg, for what they taught me

about quality and for their loving

encouragement, support, and guidance.

I love you both very much.

Rosie's

❖

What is cooking on Chestnut Hill?
Rosie is baking on Chestnut Hill!
Millions of mavens marvel and chatter,
"See all that butter go into the batter!"
Out of the oven pops her poppy-seed pound cake,
Her prize winning chocolate bound-to-astound cake,
The country's best brownies, on Chestnut Hill!

Why all the crowds on Chestnut Hill?
Groupies and gourmets on Chestnut Hill!
The aroma of baking tells where Paradise is,
Gluttony here is the nicest of vices,
So sample a sample, nibble a nibble,
Once you have tasted, how can you quibble?
Critics will praise her, poets will scribble,
"Rosie's is Heaven on Chestnut Hill!"

No one bakes bread on Chestnut Hill!
Let 'em eat cake on Chestnut Hill!
Let 'em eat cake and have it, too
For weddings, bar mitzvahs, a bris, a debut.
Rosie is ready, her pastries behind her,
Her fan clubs have met and almost enshrined her,
So follow your palate, your taste buds will find her
In Heaven at Rosie's on Chestnut Hill!

Mom and Dad

Special Thanks

—❖—

To my partner Eliot Winograd, who believed in my creativity and gave me the space to write this book while he bore the everyday stress and responsibility of running a business.

To Nan Levinson, whose humor, style, and good nature helped to make the book what it is.

To my agent Doe Coover, whose encouragement, enthusiasm, and warmth gave me the confidence to fulfill a dream.

To my editor Suzanne Rafer, who patiently awaited — and awaited — the manuscript while I carried and gave birth to twins and reared three children.

To Mimi Santini-Ritt, my righthand lady, who tested every recipe with patience and good humor, was a joy to work with, and showed undying enthusiasm over helping to create a wonderful cookbook.

To my darling husband Richard, who has loved me through the whole ordeal, endured my chaos and hysteria, typed most of the manuscript, and gained six pounds.

To Susan Donaghey and Ingrid Motsis, who also helped test recipes for a compulsive fanatic and who kept their cool.

To Jean and Jim Murray, whose dedication and competence gave me the freedom to be away from my business and still be a proud owner.

To Jake, Noah, and Maya, my children, for the love, inspiration, and *tsurus* they give me in my life.

To Viktoria Paulini, their nanny, who loved and nurtured them while I was working, and who helped me maintain sanity in my life.

To Lee Orloff, my oldest friend, whose love and support were ever present.

To all my friends and neighbors, who ate endless desserts in various stages of completion and assured me they were delicious, even when I knew they still needed work.

To all my wonderful employees, whose hard work and devotion help to make Rosie's so special.

Contents

—❖—

INTRODUCTION

Meet
Rosie

I can't say for sure that I came out of the womb on a diet, but it certainly wasn't long afterward that I was put on one. As far back as I can remember, it was a family ritual to climb on the scale each morning: first my father, blessed with a metabolism that burned up everything he ate; then my mother, with the will power to stay thin; and finally, me, their chubby child. No one would have guessed then that I'd end up a baker, least of all me.

We lived in a huge apartment in the middle of Manhattan. My mother was a theatrical agent, and my father quit teaching English to join her in the business. Our apartment was often full of people, all talking, making music, and eating. I heard the score for "A Funny Thing Happened on the Way to the Forum" way before anyone else. I remember Julie Andrews, Jean Stapleton, and Imogene Coca coming over for auditions. Rob Reiner was at my third birthday party, and, best of all, Marilyn Monroe lived in an apartment upstairs. It seemed ordinary to me.

It also seemed perfectly ordinary that my mother worked. I think of her as forever talking on the phone, making arrangements or organizing some event, so with all that, she didn't have a lot of time to spend in the kitchen. But that was never a problem. A master orchestrator, she'd go through cookbooks to pick out recipes for our housekeeper to make, and her instincts were unerring. Although my mother was anything but domestic, she knew exactly where to shop to get the best meats, the best fish . . . and the best desserts.

Sometimes, as a special treat for me, my mother baked brownies. It was the only thing she did bake, but her grandmother was reputed to have been a master baker in Czechoslovakia, so it may have been an inherited talent. In any event, those wonderful brownies were the stuff of my dreams from early childhood on. I still get a heightened physical reaction, a buzz, when I bite into a spectacular dessert, and lust is probably the only word that accurately describes my relationship to chocolate. So when people ask me how I came up with the name "Chocolate Orgasms" for Rosie's brownies, I don't know how to answer because it seemed the most obvious name in the world to me.

In the 1950s there weren't cookie shops or gourmet ice cream outlets on every corner, even in New York City, where you can get nearly anything you can imagine if you're willing to pay for it. But if you were as serious in your quest for the ideal dessert as I invariably was, you could be well rewarded. There were William Greenberg, Jr.'s, brownies made of that dense, not-too-sweet chocolate that I think of as pure American. There was Reuben's cheesecake, heavy enough to choke on if you didn't drink milk with it, and Seren-dipity's Frozen Hot Chocolate, which was so cold it gave me a headache, but so good I didn't care. Eclair made a chocolate cake with sour cherries, Ebinger's had rugalah, Bonte's madeleines would have inspired Proust to write another seven books, and even Schrafft's brownies were great in those days. On the home front, there were Hershey's Golden Almond Bars, which my mother hid in her stocking drawer for fear my father and I would consume them in a frenzy. A good number of my childhood memories, it seems, were chocolate-coated.

Majoring in Dessert

7 hings didn't change much as I grew older. When I went away to college at the Uni-versity of California at Berkeley in the late sixties, I continued my research into the ultimate dessert and added Crucheon's Fudge Pie, King Pin donuts, and See's candy to my pantheon. Officially I was studying French, but it was the era of the Free Speech move-ment, communes, and organic food, so I learned a lot of other things on the side. After gradua-tion I moved to Cambridge, Mass-achusetts, and looked for work. To no one's surprise, I gravitated toward food.

For a while, I waitressed in a coffeehouse in Harvard Square (which I loved and my parents hated), then I went back to school for another degree (which I hated and my parents loved), all of which qualified me to waitress at a classier restaurant and spend a year and a half at the Boston Museum of Fine Arts School (which, at last, pleased both my parents and me).

It was in those days that I developed my philosophy of food, an answer to every glutton's dream, because I figured out how to have my cake and eat it too. It all had to do with balance, a kind of Yin and Yang of calorie con-sciousness. I lived on a strict diet of brown bread, cheese, fruit, nuts, and vegetables — sensible, healthy, balanced eating. Then I'd polish the meal off with a fat slab of cheesecake from Jack and Mar-ion's, a now-departed Brookline delicatessen. After all, guilty plea-sures are still pleasures.

The Awakening

Then on Valentine's Day 1974, all those years of appetite and abstinence were vindicated. I was wondering about life after art school when it popped into my mind to create edible valentines. Until then I had done only the most basic baking: brownies and birthday cakes when the occasion demanded, not much more. Yet once I started, I found that this was how I loved spending the day: creating pastries that would delight the eyes as well as the belly.

I baked heart-shaped sugar cookies, glazed them in lavender and pink, and decorated them with velvet flowers, miniature angels, silver sugar pearls, and colored crystals. They were elaborately campy concoctions that could have been eaten, I suppose, although I thought of them more as romantic gifts to be saved and savored. I arranged them on trays lined with purple satin, and trotted off to present my wares to four Cambridge art galleries and

one food shop called Baby Watson Cheesecake.

The cookies were a hit, and Baby Watson called me early the next morning. "What else can you bake?" they demanded. I was on my way. There was the chocolate layer cake I made for birthdays, a carrot cake whose recipe had come from a friend's mother in California, and my own brownies, which I had perfected when I realized that I didn't want to go through life without a really good brownie recipe. Beyond that, I was starting from scratch. I began to investigate recipes, but I was seldom satisfied—too sweet, not chocolaty enough, too many additions. So I experimented and learned. I created Boom Booms, Harvard Squares, Chocolate Orgasms, Queen Raspberries . . . the names entered the Cambridge lexicon. I called them all my BabyCakes and went into the baking business.

I lugged hundred-pound bags of flour up to my second-floor apartment, where every doorknob was coated with chocolate. I learned to sleep with sugar in my bed and ignore that my floor crunched as I walked on it. I invested in a twenty-quart professional mixer and thirty-gallon trash cans to hold the sugar and flour. I woke at five in the morning and baked, took a quick run while the pastries cooled, then delivered them to Harvard Square, where customers were lined up in anticipation. I must have

been quite a sight, almost an emblem of the era, in my hot pants and platform shoes with a hairdo that stuck out about a foot from my head. I was having the time of my life.

Everything moved so quickly in the beginning that within six months I had outgrown the kitchen in my apartment. I built a new kitchen adjacent to Baby Watson, right in the heart of Harvard Square, and enclosed it in glass so that customers buying my goods could see the baking process. It was like a movie set, complete with custom-built cherry cabinets with cut-crystal knobs, an Art Deco lantern with satin shades, Edwardian botanical prints on the walls, and the insistent pulse of Toots and the Maytals in the background.

Hello Rosie's

*A*fter almost three years of working there and selling through Baby Watson, the next obvious step was to market my pastries myself; so I opened my own store in Inman Square in Cambridge and named it Rosie's as a declaration of independence. This new place was a full-range bakery where you could pick up a muffin and coffee on your way to work, a pie to take home for dinner, or a custom-made cake decorated for a special celebration. If you had the time, there were tables where you could indulge in a brownie and cup of tea while you discussed the soaps, a proposal for work, or the meaning of life. Over time Rosie's became the incongruous but appealing combination of a friend's kitchen, a neighborhood bar, and a thriving bakery.

In those first days, though, going from Harvard Square to Inman Square was a shock. The two neighborhoods are less than a mile apart, but when Rosie's arrived, Inman could be most charitably described as "funky." Since restaurants and jazz clubs were opening there, we did a lot of business late at night when people came from all over the city. During the day we were a neighborhood attraction and had our regulars. There was the professor who came in every morning to read his newspaper over coffee and a lemon poppy-seed muffin, and a guy writing his magnum opus—about what I never found out—in daily sessions at one of our tables. We had little kids counting out pennies to buy a treat, mothers with baby carriages converging every afternoon at about three o'clock, doctors and nurses from Cambridge City Hospital who never ordered less than twenty items for take-out, and the firemen of Cambridge Local 30 who gave us a plaque in appreciation of our hospitality and pastries after a particularly bad fire nearby.

Graduate students who had once gotten stoned to the strains of the Velvet Underground stood shoulder-to-shoulder with businessmen who had never heard of the rock group but hungered just as avidly for our dark chocolate cake of the same name. Genteel women ordered Chocolate Orgasms in elegant but unflinching tones, while our nonchocolate products developed equally loyal followings since rugalah, butter cookies, and shortbread seemed appropriate tributes to everyone's grandmother, no matter what her heritage.

In a neighborhood then short on decoration, our pink neon sign in the window drew people, and, once inside, they stayed, mostly for the goodies but also for the homey atmosphere. I had determined from the first that Rosie's would be a treat not just for the taste buds but for all the senses, so I painted and decorated, lugged in overstuffed furniture, and made sure we had fresh flowers every week.

Since those early years, Rosie's has grown larger and more established. What began as a whim in Harvard Square now occupies an entire building in Inman Square, a second store in suburban Chestnut Hill, and a new store in Boston's South Station. In the intervening years, my first customers have cut their hair, put on suits, acquired kids, mortgages, and life insurance, and ventured beyond the rarified atmosphere of "the Square." But they haven't changed their desire for a little something from Rosie's, and they still indulge it, even if that now means having to go out of their way.

So it's sometimes tempting to view Rosie's as an inevitability— you know, the hand of fate gently nudging me in that direction from birth, all that lust and denial as a rite of passage. Or maybe it was bred in the bone, this taking my chocolate very seriously and insisting on the best. Not that it matters, really. When you're having so much fun, it seems greedy to question fate.

CHAPTER ONE

Common Sense Baking

We all have certain conversations that get repeated so often we could conduct them in our sleep. Mine begins, "No kidding! You own Rosie's? Where did you study baking?" When I answer that I didn't but learned on my own, the response is often amazement. But what's amazing to me is that so many people don't believe it's possible. It makes me wonder who has been perpetuating this myth that baking involves a delicate chemical reaction that only the chosen few can control. And, more to the point, it makes me ask where all the hocus-pocus has gotten us. I mean, how many oh-so-stylish Baba au Hazelnut Tortes do we have to try before we admit that both Aunt Esther and our college roommate's mother could whip up better at a moment's notice?

I don't mean to denigrate expertise, but all this training business should be put in perspective. Baking does involve chemical reactions, but so does taking an aspirin. While you may not reach baker's heaven on your first try, if good food is important to you, if you like desserts, and if you can count, none of the recipes in this book is beyond you. It's as simple as that. Baking can also be fun; there are even those among us who find it more therapeutic than a hot bath or a session on the couch, and that's not even considering its more tangible rewards.

Now, about achieving those tangible rewards. Let's start with one basic rule I learned from my years on the baking front: Don't let yourself be intimidated. That may sound simple, but bear in mind that these are the words of a woman who used to panic whenever a recipe called for beaten egg whites. I was sure I had a genetic inability to tell if they were stiff or soft enough, and even if by some miracle I made it past that hurdle, who knew how gently I should be folding the stiff-soft whites into the batter? I had myself convinced that if I beat the egg whites one second too long, the entire enterprise would be a flop. And you know what? It often was, fear of failure being one of those things that fulfills itself with depressing regularity.

Only slightly daunted though, I remembered that old chestnut about learning from my mistakes, and I now stand before you a reformed egg beater. The moral of this story (and the trick with more than just egg whites) is to

Baking Temperatures and Times

—❖—

I can't emphasize enough how important it is to remember that oven temperatures vary greatly from oven to oven and sometimes even from week to week in the same oven. Consequently baking times will vary too. Don't take the times suggested in the book too literally; rely on the visual descriptions of the various stages and finished product, as well as the techniques suggested to test for doneness.

develop a feel for what you're doing and the confidence to make adjustments. That's where real creativity comes from, because when you're in control, you feel freer to experiment.

There's something to be said for serendipity, too. I've put too little flour in a cake only to find that it came out lighter, and the time I forgot to add the eggs to pumpkin bread, I ended up liking the texture better without them. Archimedes, on discovering the principle of displacement of water, was said to have run naked through the streets shouting, "Eureka! I have found it!" I merely file my discoveries in the back of my mind to use for future creations.

In addition to goofs, there are lots of factors that affect how a recipe comes out, and you can't

be aware of all of them before you start. Your oven may bake differently from mine, your apples may be less juicy, or your eggs larger. That's where adaptability and experience come in.

First you learn that time-honored baking ritual in which you take something out of the oven, hit yourself on the forehead, and say, "Darn, I should have thought of that!" Next you figure out how to adjust your oven temperature so that your cake layers don't have a crust or how much juice to add to keep your apple pies from drying out. One of the joys of baking is that problems have solutions, and they're often a matter of common sense.

Aside from the power of positive thinking and the incantation I chant over each batch of brownies that I'm not at liberty to disclose, I have a few suggestions that should help you avoid basic problems in baking and keep your frustration level within reason.

Method to the Madness

*S*oul and panache go a long way to making a good baker, but it helps to be organized and systematic, too, and I don't make that suggestion lightly. When I left home and my mother's compulsion for tidiness, I realized that by nature I'm a slob. So it wasn't until years later that I also realized my mother was on to something. Chaos makes baking twice as hard. I don't always practice what I preach, but nonetheless I'd like to pass on to you Rosie's Five Steps to Carefree Baking, Longer Life, and Gaining Permission to Use Your Mother's Kitchen.

1. First, read the entire recipe so that there are no surprises. It's a pain to discover halfway through that you're out of an essential ingredient and can't finish baking without a trip to the store.

2. Line up, pour, measure, and count out all your ingredients in advance, replacing boxes and containers as you go along to avoid confusion (as in: Uh oh, is that white mound in the batter baking soda or baking powder?).

3. Avoid distractions: chatty phone calls, drop-in visits, disgruntled children pulling at your apron strings, the soaps, or Oprah Winfrey. You may think you're concentrating, but sooner or later you will be rummaging through the garbage counting egg shells to figure out how many you've cracked.

4. Bake when you're not tense or in a hurry. Otherwise baking becomes a chore, not a pleasure, and you're more likely to make mistakes.

5. Make sure you understand basic baking techniques and try to become comfortable with the procedures explained in the recipes you use so that you can deepen your confidence and expand your creativity.

The Right Stuff

*W*hen you're stocking up on ingredients, keep in mind that it's hard to improve on nature when it comes to food, so you're on firm ground if you rely on fresh, pure items as much as possible. That doesn't mean that you have to buy the most expensive ingredients or that all things imported are heaven-blessed, despite what many gourmet shops would have us believe. But baking with second-rate ingredients is like playing a sonata on a kazoo; it's not the real thing and it's not as good.

Check the pantry box on the facing page for a list of all-important baking ingredients.

Rosie's Pantry

— ❖ —

Most of my recipes call for ingredients that your supermarket stocks regularly, but if you want to be able to bake from this cookbook with a degree of spontaneity ("I think I'll whip up a little chocolate mousse cake tonight in case this blizzard lasts another week"), here are the ingredients you should keep in good supply in your pantry.

— ❖ —

Unbleached
all-purpose flour

Cake flour (not self-rising)

Baking soda

Baking powder

Cornstarch

Granulated sugar

Brown sugar
(light and dark)

Confectioner's sugar

Molasses

Honey

Corn syrup (light and dark)

Unsalted butter

Unflavored gelatin

Fruit preserves

Raisins

Peanut butter
(salted or unsalted)

Instant espresso
or other good-quality
coffee powder

Pure vanilla extract

Almond extract

Salt

Spices: ground ginger,
cinnamon, nutmeg,
mace, allspice, cloves

Sweetened shredded
coconut

Semisweet
chocolate chips

Unsweetened
chocolate

Equipment

*A*s with ingredients, having the equipment you need on hand will make baking convenient and more spontaneous. It's easy to go overboard on kitchenware, though, what with those seductive displays at kitchen shops and all the fads. Remember fondue pots and yogurt makers, those necessities of the seventies? And before you make major purchases, I suggest you shop around, because prices can vary widely. You might start at a commercial kitchen supply store that usually offers a large selection, sturdy quality, and reasonable prices.

To make the recipes in this book easily and successfully wherever you acquire your tools, I recommend that, as much as possible, you equip your kitchen with the following items:

❖ *Electric mixer* with *paddle and whisk attachments* and *two mixing bowls.* If your budget allows, invest in a mixer mounted on a base, as opposed to a hand-

Some Notes on Ingredients

— ❖ —

BUTTER: Keep in mind as you follow these recipes that melted butter is not equal to solid butter in terms of measurement. For example, 6 tablespoons of melted butter equals approximately 5½ tablespoons of solid butter. Always remeasure the butter once it's melted to make sure you are using the correct amount.

CAKE FLOUR (not self-rising): This flour is lighter than all-purpose flour because it contains less gluten. Although the standard wisdom says that 1 cup of all-purpose flour equals 1 cup plus 2 tablespoons of cake flour, I find that when I substitute all-purpose flour, I often have to adjust other ingredients to avoid getting a powdery texture. So to make life simple, I recommend using cake flour when it's called for. Convenience stores and smaller markets don't usually stock it, but you'll find it at large supermarkets.

SUGAR: Granulated and light and dark brown sugar differ in moisture and mass, though they are the same in weight. This means that the drier granulated sugar tends to produce crunchier cookies and slightly drier cakes when it is substituted for equal amounts of brown sugar. Also, dark brown sugar has a higher molasses content than light brown sugar, so the equivalent cup measure weighs more. When you substitute dark for light, you need smaller amounts. You can make accurate substitutions if you have an ounce scale. In other words, 6 ounces of granulated sugar equals 6 ounces of light of light brown sugar equals 6 ounces of dark brown sugar.

CHOCOLATE: I've spent my lifetime thinking and dreaming about chocolate, and I still swear by Baker's when it comes to baking chocolate. The company began two centuries ago in Boston, so there may be a little chauvinism involved but not so much that I ignore the basic qualities. I find the taste of Baker's to be real, unadulterated, and exactly what I think chocolate should be. You'll find a lot of cookbooks and chefs who recommend imported chocolate, but I haven't found any that's better than our homegrown variety for baking and don't see the point of paying the higher price.

That said, I make two exceptions to the rule. For chocolate chips, I like Nestlé's. Whatever brand you buy, make sure that they're real chocolate, not "chocolate flavored." And for making glazes, I've found that the more expensive chocolates do have a smoother texture, so I use Lindt bittersweet chocolate.

held one, for the simple reason that it leaves your hands free. The extra bowl is essential for cakes that require beaten egg whites. The KitchenAid mixer is the absolute best.

❖ *Food processor*. Great for preparing pie crusts, chopping nuts and chocolate, making fillings for tarts or Bavarians, and on and on. I don't know what I did without one.

❖ *Two 8-inch layer cake pans* (2 inches deep) of heavy metal.

❖ *Two 9-inch layer cake pans* (2 inches deep) of heavy metal.

❖ *One 9-inch and one 10-inch springform pan*, although you can usually get away with only the smaller one.

❖ *Standard jelly-roll pan*, 15 × 10¼ inches.

❖ *Four square or rectangular pans*: 11 × 7 inches, 8 × 8 inches, 9 × 9 inches, and 13 × 9 inches.

❖ *Bundt or tube pan*, 10-inch diameter with a removable bottom.

❖ *Two loaf pans*: 8½ × 4½ × 2½ inches and 9½ × 5¼ × 3 inches.

❖ *Two standard pie plates*, 9 × 1½ inches.

❖ *Deep-dish pie plate*, 9 × 2 inches, usually made of Pyrex.

❖ *Two cookie sheets*, 15 × 12 inches, standard, heavy weight. I don't care for the new air-cushion cookie sheets — they tend to take the crunch out and leave the cookies soggy. I'd use them only for baking cake-like cookies.

❖ *Two cooling racks*.

❖ *Two baking dishes* for puddings and custards, preferably ceramic, 1½ quart and 2½ to 3 quart.

❖ *Double boiler*, 3-quart, heavy weight.

❖ *Saucepan*, 3-quart, heavy weight.

❖ *Three or four small bowls*, 2 cup and 4 cup, for cracking eggs, sifting dry ingredients, and measuring nuts. *One large bowl*, 12 to 14 cup, for sifting flour or folding ingredients together.

❖ *Two attractive bowls* for mousses, Bavarians, and puddings, 5 cup and 2 quart.

❖ *Two sets of graduated measuring cups*, ⅛ cup, ¼ cup, ⅓ cup, ½ cup, and 1 cup for dry ingredients. Metal ones with handles last longest.

❖ *Pyrex measuring cup*, 2-cup measure, for liquids.

❖ *Two sets of metal measuring spoons*.

Some Notes on Equipment

— ❖ —

ELECTRIC MIXERS: The recipes in this book were tested with a KitchenAid mixer, which is more powerful than a standard hand mixer, so your mixing times may vary from the ones noted. When you're mixing batters, use the paddle attachment, if you have one. Save the whisk for whipping cream and egg whites and yolks.

MICROWAVE OVENS: I'm crossing my fingers we won't discover someday that microwaves turn teeth green or make our great-grandchildren grow horns, because I use mine constantly in baking. It's wonderful for melting butter and chocolate; bringing eggs, cold butter, liquids, sour cream, or cream cheese to room temperature; and softening hard brown sugar. Test your microwave to find the best temperatures and times for the results you're looking for, since the ovens vary. But, for the most part, avoid all high temperatures.

❖ *Two sturdy, standard-size rubber spatulas,* 9½ inches long (even better, make your second one commercial-quality, 13½ inches long—available at a kitchen supply store). *One very small rubber spatula,* 2 × 17 inch.

❖ *Standard metal frosting spatula* 10 inches long and 1½ inches wide for leveling off dry ingredients in the measuring cups and for icing cakes.

❖ *Small hand whisk,* 8 inches long, and a standard *domestic-size whisk,* 12 inches long, for beating by hand.

❖ *Standard-size or larger rolling pin.*

❖ *Pie weights.*

❖ *Large wooden spoon* for mixing puddings and custards.

❖ *Timer* and a *clock or watch with a second hand.*

❖ *Pancake spatula* to remove cookies from cookie sheets.

❖ *Two strainers,* about 3 and 5 inches in diameter.

❖ *Two sharp cutting knives;* one thin, one sturdy.

❖ *10- or 12-inch pastry bag* with *writing tips* for decorating cakes.

❖ *Baking parchment* for lining

cookie sheets and cake pans (also consider parchment cake pan liners).

❖ *Plastic wrap* or *waxed paper* for rolling dough.

Bare Essentials

— ❖ —

Having listed what may appear to be enough equipment to outfit Buckingham Palace, let me say that I know many bakers who wouldn't be able to fit into their kitchen if they followed my suggestions to the letter. Never fear, there's no question that you can bake successfully without purchasing a whole battery of equipment.

Of course, with less equipment, you will have to make some common-sense recipe adjustments. For example, if a recipe calls for baking brownies in an 11 × 7-inch pan and you only have an 8-inch square pan, your brownies will be thicker and therefore should bake more slowly and at a temperature 25°F lower than the one called for. If you bake a recipe calling for 8-inch layers in a 9-inch layer pan, they will require a shorter baking time because the batter level will be lower. Use your judgment; if the results are less than

perfect, you'll know to make further adjustments next time.

If you want to start off easy, here are the important items to have on hand:

1 electric mixer, stationary or hand-held

2 round layer cake pans, 8 or 9 inches

1 springform pan, 9 or 10 inches

2 cookie sheets

1 standard pie plate, 9 × 1½ inches

1 set graduated measuring cups for dry ingredients

1 measuring cup (2 cup size) for liquid ingredients

1 set measuring spoons

1 set small, medium, and large mixing bowls

1 rubber spatula

1 hand-held whisk

1 wooden spoon

1 rolling pin

A Final Word

I confess that I began this book with grand ambitions. It was to be a cookbook that grew dog-eared and smudged with fingerprints from generations of use while the recipes wormed their way into family lore and got trotted out along with the old photos. You know: "I've still never run across anyone who can make brownies as scrumptious as my father's," or "Every time I visited my grandmother, she used to make this really incredible chocolate cake with raspberries."

I still hope for something like that. But, as I mentioned earlier, my more immediate goal is to demystify baking through common sense, because I'm convinced that that is the key to successful and happy baking. In an odd way I was lucky in my baking career. Lacking formal training, I learned what I know through passion, instinct, and trial and error, and these still seem to me to be the best teachers anyone — novice or pro — can find.

So my final advice is to trust my recipes but trust yourself as well. After all, the worst that can happen is that you make a mistake — and one of the joys of baking is that the majority of our mistakes are edible.

CHAPTER TWO

Piece
of Cake

In my teenage years, while my friends spent their Saturdays shopping for Villager outfits and Pappagallo loafers, I hung out in Doubleday's, poring over cookbooks with color photos of cakes. Who needed forbidden passages from *Peyton Place* when I could salivate over luscious pictures of double chocolate cakes?

I like to think I learned of the consolations of art early on, but even for those whose pleasures take a different form, cakes are an integral part of the way we celebrate. From birthday cakes adorned with plastic ballerinas or cowboys and Indians, to wedding cakes worthy of Claes Oldenburg, it's hard to imagine a proper anniversary or holiday as a cakeless event. So, early on, Rosie's started developing an array of cakes for every occasion.

I began with a little something chocolate, of course: Rosie's Famous Chocolate Sour-Cream Layer Cake which, when topped with ice cream, was cause for celebration in its own right. That was followed by the Snow Queen, inspired by the yellow cakes with white frosting and raspberry jam that are the perennial mark of an authentic birthday party among the under-ten crinoline set. Next came the Velvet Underground (as decadent as the group it was named after), the Mocha Cake, Queen Raspberry, Cold Fudge Sundae, and Texas Ruby Red, which have become the mainstays of Rosie's menu.

Theme and Variations

I learned quickly an old baker's strategy of taking a basic recipe and adding one or two things to make it into a whole new cake. For instance, once you've perfected a simple chocolate cake, you can layer it with fudge, preserves, whipped cream, mousse, fresh or frozen fruit, bananas and cream, or liqueur, and, *voilà!* have seven additional cakes in your repertoire. Then we have the humble pound cake which, like one of those make-overs in a fashion magazine, can appear plain at morning coffee, dressed tastefully with fruit for afternoon tea, or transformed into a rich layer cake for a ritzy dinner party. And you get to call the cake something different in each of its incarnations — naming is half the fun.

Since getting a cake just right can take some doing, you need something that comes easily at the beginning. Cake batters can be finicky, and a slight variation, such as the sequence in which ingredients are added, mixing technique, or baking time and temperature, can affect the outcome greatly.

Telling someone how to bake a cake gets complicated because nearly every rule has an exception. To try to simplify things in the following sections, I've identified basic rules. So unless you're fond of reading cookbooks cover to cover, I suggest that you glance through each section to find the category that applies to the cake you're making.

Preparing the Pan and the Batter

Layer Cakes

Do yourself a favor and line your baking pans with inserts made of baking parchment, which are larger versions of muffin papers and are usually available at kitchen stores. This way, you won't have to grease or flour your pans, and because the batter doesn't touch the sides of the pan, your cake edges come out moist and spongy. If you don't have ready-made liners, I recommend using parchment rather than waxed paper, which smokes as it heats.

To cut parchment circles from a larger roll, place the baking pan right side up on the paper and trace around the base of the pan with a pen or pencil. Cut out the shape with scissors just inside the outline and place the paper cutout in the bottom of the pan.

Regardless of whether you grease the pan or use parchment, it's best to cool all your cakes on a cooling rack and to leave the layer in the pan until you're ready to frost the cake. If you leave it for any length of time, cover it with plastic wrap after it has cooled.

When you use a pan insert, after the layer has baked and cooled, pick it up by the edge of the insert and lift it out of the pan onto a plate. When you've used circles cut out of parchment, after the cake has baked and cooled, run a frosting spatula around the edge to loosen it. Then turn the pan upside down at a 45° angle and allow the layer to drop onto your hand. Peel the parchment off with your other hand and flip the layer onto a plate.

If you have neither paper inserts nor baking parchment, use a small piece of paper towel or waxed paper to grease the pan lightly and thoroughly with butter or vegetable oil. Then, when the layer has cooled but is still slightly warm, run the spatula along the edge to loosen it, turn the pan over, and, holding the layer in place with your hand, tap the pan lightly on the counter as you rotate it. When the layer has loosened, let it fall onto your palm, then flip it over onto a plate.

Tube and Bundt Pans

Parchment doesn't work here, so grease these pans lightly with butter or oil, paying special attention to where the center tube meets the bottom of the pan because cakes tend to stick there. Pans without removable bottoms require particularly thorough greasing.

When the cake has cooled in the pan, run a flat frosting spatula around its sides. If the bottom is removable, lift it out, then run the spatula between the cake and the bottom of the pan and leave it under one side of the cake. Place a second spatula or a knife under the opposite side of the cake and use both to lift the cake off the pan bottom. (I sometimes press my chin against the top of the tube to help release the tube from the cake too.) Put the cake on a plate and cover it with plastic wrap until you're ready to frost or serve it.

For chiffon and angel food cakes, use a tube pan with a re-movable bottom and don't grease it because grease keeps them from rising. When cooling the cake, rest it upside down on the counter to prevent it from drop-ping back into the pan. If the tube pan isn't high enough to keep the top of the cake from touching the counter, stick a fun-nel or bottle into the hole of the pan, then turn it upside down and balance it on the funnel. Either way, after the cake cools for about 1½ hours, run a spatula around the sides and bot-tom and   remove it the same as you would above.

Springform Pans

This is an either/or situation vis-à-vis inserts or greasing. If you've greased the pan, when the cake has cooled, run a spatula around its edge, release the pan's lock, and remove the side of the pan. Then run a spatula between the cake and the bottom of the pan and use the spatula and your hand or two spatulas to lift the cake onto a plate.

If you have time to chill the cake for a minimum of 6 hours after baking, it will be sturdy enough to turn upside down, so use a parchment cutout. Chill the cake in the pan, then run a spatula around its edge and release the sides. Turn the cake upside down onto a plate or counter, peel off the paper, then flip the cake right side up, if necessary (depending on the type of cake, the bottom can be more attractive than the top and easier to frost).

Square and Rectangular Pans

If you plan to frost your cake in the pan and cut it into squares to serve, then it's best to grease the bottom and sides of the pan with butter or oil. If, however, you want to take the cake out of the pan in one piece and serve it on a plate, I'd go with a parchment liner. Let the cake cool, run a spatula around the edges, turn the pan over onto a plate, drop the cake out, and then remove the parchment. When you don't have parchment but want to remove the cake, grease the pan and remove the cake from the pan while it is still slightly warm with the assistance of your trusty spatula.

Batters with the Right Texture

So much depends on texture that, to me, it contributes as much to a cake's character as does its flavor. Not to panic though; a cake's texture depends largely on the way you mix the batter, and there are basic rules for mixing that will stand you in good stead.

I've found it useful to divide mixing techniques into six categories, and once again, I suggest you find the one that applies to the recipe you're making. This system is imperfect, however (too much order makes me nervous), and a few recipes in this chapter blithely defy all my categories. Where there are exceptions to the rules, I've noted in the recipe how to deal with them.

Before you begin to follow any of these methods, it's very important that all of your ingredients be at room temperature, unless the recipe specifies otherwise. This makes it easier to mix everything together thoroughly.

Creaming Method

This is a standard method for mixing cakes, such as Poppy-Seed Pound Cake and Breakfast Coffeecake, that have a high fat content (for example, eggs, butter, and margarine). You alternate adding liquid and dry ingredients so that the flour helps the butter absorb the liquid. These cakes have a sturdy texture, but vary in lightness and density.

1. Sift all the dry ingredients except for the sugar together into a small bowl.

2. Blend the butter and sugar with the paddle attachment of an electric mixer set on medium or medium-high speed until light and fluffy.

3. Add the eggs one at a time to the butter mixture (unless the recipe says otherwise) and beat at medium-low to medium speed until each one is distributed evenly. Scrape the bottom and side of the bowl with a rubber spatula once during the mixing. The mixture will not be smooth at this time.

4. Add the dry ingredients to the butter, sugar, and egg mixture, alternating with the liquid. To do this, set the mixer on low speed, add one-third of the dry ingredients, and mix just until they are blended. Scrape the bowl with a rubber spatula now and each time new ingredients are blended in. Next add half the liquid; blend and scrape. Follow this with another third of the dry ingredients; blend and scrape. Add the remaining liquid; blend and scrape. Then add the remaining dry ingredients and—do I sound like a caller at a square dance?—blend just until everything is incorporated and scrape again. If the recipe doesn't call for liquid, add the dry ingredients in two parts, mixing just until blended.

5. Use your rubber spatula to complete the blending by hand.

6. Pour the batter into the prepared pan and bake the cake immediately.

Creaming with Separated Eggs Method

This method is good for recipes such as Sour Cherry Fudge Cake and Pineapple Upside-Down Cake. Because the whites are beaten to a froth before being added to the batter, this method produces a lighter cake.

1. Follow the Creaming Method, but separate the egg yolks from the whites and set the whites apart in a grease-free bowl.

2. Add the yolks to the butter and sugar mixture and beat until incorporated, using the paddle attachment of an electric mixer set on medium-low speed.

3. Add the dry ingredients and liquid alternately as in the standard Creaming Method.

4. Whip the egg whites with the whisk attachment on medium speed until they are frothy.

Gradually add the sugar reserved for the whites over a span of about 20 seconds. Increase the speed to high and beat until they form firm but not dry peaks. Fold them into the batter gently with a rubber spatula.

5. Pour the batter into a prepared pan and bake the cake immediately.

Standard Sponge Method

These cakes, such as the Lemon-Strawberry Sponge Roll and Chocolate-Custard Sponge Roll, usually contain little or no butter or oil and get their sponginess from the air in the eggs. The mixing process begins by foaming the eggs, that is, beating air into them with a whisk or paddle. Sometimes the whole egg is foamed, other times the yolks are foamed separately from the whites, or just the whites are foamed.

1. Sift the dry ingredients together into a small bowl.

2. Separate the egg yolks from the egg whites, and set the whites aside in a grease-free mix-ing bowl. Put the yolks in a sepa-rate medium-size mixing bowl and, with the whisk attachment of an electric mixer, beat them with the sugar at high speed until they are thick and pale.

3. Sift the dry ingredients over the egg yolk mixture, then fold it in with a rubber spatula.

4. Whip the egg whites with the whisk attachment on medium-low speed until they are frothy. In-crease the speed to medium and gradually add the sugar reserved for the whites. Beat until they form firm but not dry peaks. Fold the egg whites into the batter gently by hand right away.

5. Pour the batter into the pre-pared pan and bake immediately.

Butter Sponge Method

These cakes are similar to the ones above but include melted butter, producing a cake that is somewhat denser and richer. De-sert Island Butter Cake, for exam-ple, uses this method.

1. Sift all the dry ingredients except for the sugar into a small bowl.

2. In a separate medium-size bowl, beat the eggs and sugar with the whisk attachment of an electric mixer at high speed until the mixture is thick and pale, 4 to 5 minutes.

3. While the eggs and sugar are beating, melt the butter.

4. Sift the dry ingredients a second time over the egg and butter mixture and fold them in carefully with a rubber spatula.

5. Fold the melted butter in with a rubber spatula.

6. Pour the batter into the prepared pan and bake immediately.

Two-Bowl Method

Batters containing a lot of sugar and more liquid (for example, eggs, milk, or juice) than usual use this method. The batter is usually runny before baking, and the texture of these cakes can vary considerably. Rosie's Famous Chocolate Sour-Cream Cake Layers and Lemon-Glazed Orange Chiffon Cake both use this method.

Some Notes on Procedures

TO SEPARATE AN EGG: Hold a raw egg over a bowl and crack its shell open around the middle with a knife. Gently separate the two halves of the shell, keeping the yolk in one half while letting the white run through your fingers into the bowl. Take care not to allow any of the yolk to get into the white, then slide the yolk into a separate bowl.

TO DIVIDE A YOLK IN TWO (when you want to halve a recipe): Follow the procedure for separating an egg, but rather than sliding the yolk into a bowl at the end, slide it into the palm of your hand. With a sharp knife — careful, now — slice through the yolk's center and push half off your hand into the cake batter. Save the other half to scramble into your kid's eggs.

TO MELT CHOCOLATE IN A DOUBLE BOILER: Place the chocolate in the top of a double boiler; the water in the bottom shouldn't touch the top pan. Cover the top pot and allow the water to simmer until the chocolate is about two-thirds melted — the shape will still be discernible but the chocolate will be soft. Turn the heat off and let the chocolate continue to melt completely.

TO MEASURE DRY INGREDIENTS: This includes flour, sugar, cocoa, confectioner's sugar and others. Use individual measuring cups (1 cup, $\frac{1}{2}$ cup, $\frac{1}{3}$ cup, $\frac{1}{4}$ cup, $\frac{1}{8}$ cup) and spoons (1 tablespoon, 1 teaspoon, etc.) Scoop the ingredients into the cup or spoon, then level the top by scraping off the excess with a frosting spatula.

TO LINE A LOAF PAN: Cut a piece of waxed paper or parchment big enough to overhang the sides and ends by a couple of inches when it is molded into the pan.

1. Sift the dry ingredients together into a medium-size mixing bowl, add the butter or oil, and mix on low speed, using the paddle attachment of an electric mixer.

2. If the recipe calls for melted chocolate, mix it in now.

3. Stir the eggs together with the liquid ingredients in a separate bowl and add the liquid in a stream to the dry ingredients, while mixing at low speed. Mix just until the batter is blended.

4. The batter will be thin, but pour it into the prepared pan and bake immediately.

On the Way to the Oven

*F*ew recipes I've come across pay attention to the steps between mixing the batter and getting it into the oven. Yet how the batter sits in the pan is crucial to the baking process. Pour loose (thin) batters directly into a prepared pan by tipping the mixing bowl at a sharp angle and using your trusty rubber spatula to direct the flow and to scrape the bowl clean. The batter needs to be distributed evenly in the pan to bake well, so rock the pan gently from side to side to achieve this. For a thicker batter, use a rubber spatula to scoop it from the bowl and to spread it evenly in the pan.

The tricky question though, and one my mother never really answered, is, when is enough enough? Layer, springform, and sheet cake pans should be between one-half and two-thirds full. Bundt and tube pans should be two-thirds full. This is important because too much batter in the pan can overflow, and, even if it doesn't, the edges of the cake will overcook before the center is done. With too little batter, however, the cake won't rise or brown properly. So if you don't have a large enough pan, put the right amount of batter in the one you have and make cupcakes from what's left over. If you don't have a small enough pan, borrow one from your neighbor.

Into the Oven

*S*o now you've got the properly mixed batter properly poured into the proper size pan, and all that's left is to get the cake into the oven—properly. But oven temperature and the position of your oven racks are crucial to attaining the proper taste and texture.

No matter what kind of cake you're baking, you want to place it in the center of a rack that is positioned in the center of your oven, where the heat is most even. When baking layer cakes, make sure that your pans are at least 1 to 1½ inches apart and arrange them on a slight diagonal so that they can both take advantage of this sweet spot in your oven.

The majority of cakes bake at 350°F, but several kinds require a slightly different temperature. When an oven is too hot, a cake rises too quickly, often forming an underdone mound at the center and a dark crust at the edges. When an oven is too cool, a cake, unlike the sun, never rises.

Sponge Rolls

I bake these cakes, Chocolate-Custard Sponge Roll and Lemon-Strawberry Sponge for example, at 400°F. Because there's usually less than an inch of batter in the pan, the cake can bake quickly and evenly without burning or drying out, even at this high temperature.

Flourless and Chiffon Cakes

These cakes, such as Chocolate Truffle Soufflé Cake and Lemon-Glazed Orange Chiffon Cake, contain a number of beaten egg whites and often call for an oven set between 300° and 325°F so that they will bake evenly and rise gently.

Cheesecakes

Because cheesecake batter is heavy and doesn't rise much anyway, I use a lower temperature, usually 300°F. In this cooler oven, cheesecake bakes slowly and evenly and its surface is less likely to crack. Try putting a shallow pan of hot water on the oven rack below; its steam will keep the cake moist. You can turn the oven off when the cake is done and leave it inside to set for 1 hour. By avoiding a quick change in temperature, you can often keep your cake from dropping or cracking. Or you can cool it on a wire rack. I've had success both ways.

And Out of the Oven

*O*vens vary; that's one of those truisms like fish swim and birds fly, only with fewer exceptions. It's for that reason that

I suggest you first look at your cake about ten minutes before the end of the baking time suggested in the recipe. To tell if it's done then, consider three indicators in the following order:

1. How the cake looks.

2. What the cake feels like when you touch it lightly.

3. If a tester inserted into the center comes out dry.

The cake's appearance and feel will vary, depending on your oven: layers will spring back to the touch; cheesecakes will feel firm; bundt cakes will have a rounded crisp top, and cakes baked in jelly-roll pans will be spongy in texture and almost level. Every recipe in this book describes what the finished cake should look like, but the most dependable test is to insert a cake tester or a long skewer in the center of the cake when you think it's done. (I don't use the time-honored toothpick because it's seldom long enough to get to the bottom of the cake.) If the tester comes out dry or with a few crumbs on it, the cake is done. If it comes out at all wet, the cake isn't done and needs to be baked a little longer, after which you should test it again. Don't remove the cake from the oven when performing this test, just slide the cake forward on the rack or gently slide out the rack.

The Eyes Have It

*O*n more than one occasion I have argued for an anatomical connection between the eyes and the appetite, but even if there isn't one, there is surely a sensual relationship. So how your cake looks can add to its appeal. I'm partial to decoration that enhances the taste and appearance of the cake without overwhelming the cake itself. I find desserts that proclaim "Look at me!" are about as appealing as people who do, and it's been my experience that gobs of over-the-top sugar frosting lose their allure shortly after one's tenth birthday.

The simplest decoration for a cake is frosting, although getting the frosting on evenly and neatly takes several steps. Before beginning make sure your cake has cooled to room temperature.

Frosting a Two-Layer Cake

1. To keep the plate clean, cut 4 strips of baking parchment or waxed paper, each 3 inches wide and 2 inches longer than the diameter of your cake. Arrange the strips around the edge of your cake plate to form a square with the ends of the strips overlapping. Put the plate on a turntable or lazy Susan, if you have one.

2. Place one layer right side up on the plate so that the strips of paper are under the outer edge of the cake with their ends sticking out.

3. Using a frosting spatula, spread frosting ¼ inch thick over the top of this layer and then stack the second layer on top.

5. Spread another layer of frosting, no more than a ¼ inch thick, over the sides of the cake and smooth it out with the long, thin edge of the spatula.

4. Apply a thin layer of frosting to the top and sides of the cake to form a base coat which seals the cake, contains the crumbs, and makes it easier to frost.

6. Spread the remaining frosting over the top of the cake, smooth it out, then glide the rounded tip of a frosting spatula across the top of the cake on a diagonal to form parallel ridges. Trim off excess frosting by passing the long edge of the spatula around the circumference of the cake's top.

If you have a cake wheel, you can add a swirl by centering the cake on the wheel and spinning the wheel slowly while holding the top of the spatula at a 45° angle to the cake and gliding it toward the center of the cake in a continuous stroke.

7. Pull the paper strips out carefully. If there are any frosting or finger smudges on the plate, wipe them off with a damp paper towel.

If you were working on a cake wheel, ease your spatula under-

neath the cake and gently lift it. Use both your free hand and the spatula to support the cake as you move it to a serving platter.

Frosting a Four-Layer Cake

Follow the steps above, but in step 2, carefully slice each layer through its middle (see the box below on splitting layers). In step 3, spread frosting between each of these new layers, then continue on to the next step.

Writing on a Cake

Use a number 14 or 15 star tip and a 10- or 12-inch pastry bag. All of the items needed for writing are available at a cake decorating store. Before beginning, write your

Splitting Layers

— ❖ —

To split each layer in two, put the full layers on a piece of waxed paper on a flat surface, such as a counter or table. Place the blade of a long, thin knife at the midpoint of the first layer. With your free hand resting lightly on the top of the layer, slice through the layer evenly, keeping the knife parallel to the flat surface. Repeat with the second full layer.

If you have a cake wheel, follow these instructions, but turn the wheel carefully for a full revolution as you cut through the middle of the layer.

message down on a piece of paper. Check the spelling of all words, especially names.

1. If the pastry bag is new, clip just enough of the tip off so that the plastic cone fits securely, and insert the cone. Put the metal writing tip over the end of the cone and secure it by screwing the ring in place.

2. Fold the top of the bag down once over your left hand and hold it there. With a rubber spatula, fill the bag one-third full with butter cream frosting, then pull the collar back into place.

3. Gather the top of the bag together with your right thumb and forefinger and squeeze out any air bubbles with your palm.

4. Use your left thumb and forefinger to support and guide the bag as you write. If you're left-handed, reverse these directions.

5. Again, practice writing on a piece of baking parchment or waxed paper before you tackle your cake; it's not erasable.

Making a Chain of Rosettes

Fit a 10- or 12-inch pastry bag with a large star tip. All the items needed to make rosettes are available at a cake decorating store.

1. Remove all parchment strips from under the cake.

2. Follow steps 2 and 3 for writing on cakes but fill the bag half full of frosting.

3. Hold the bag as you would for writing, but keep it at a 45° angle with the tip touching the outer edge of the top of the cake. Squeeze the bag enough for a single rosette, then slowly pull the bag away while releasing the pressure. Continue this rocking motion until you have a chain of rosettes around the edge of the entire cake.

4. Repeat this process around the base of the cake, pointing the tip at the edge where the cake meets the plate.

Fresh Flowers

Not all decorations have to be edible. When I first started adorning my cakes, I had no idea how to make those pink, sugary roses bakeries use, and I waited for someone to discover my secret and say, "And you call yourself a baker!" So in self-defense, I found the one lavender plastic orchid in a five-and-ten that didn't look tacky and stuck it on top of a chocolate sour-cream layer cake whose rich brown frosting showed it off to distinction.

Then it dawned on me that there is an alternative to plastic, and I began to decorate cakes with real flowers. I've learned how to make the bakery buds since then, but why bother when a bouquet of fresh flowers is so much prettier?

I generally opt for elegant flowers such as roses, orchids, tiger lillies, dendrobium orchids, freesia, and snapdragons. Delphiniums and sweet peas are lovely as well although they do not last more than a couple of hours. Statice, baby's breath, and any frilly or lacy flower and the like can cover stems and create texture between flowers and greens such as various ferns, fica leaves, palm spears, and ivy. The greens provide accent and structure to the bouquet. Look for variety in color, texture and shape when you're choosing your flowers and avoid lillies of the valley and the berries on holly leaves because of their toxicity.

It is essential when decorating with fresh flowers and leaves that they look fresh and crisp; slightly browned or wilted petals must be removed, frosting smudges or crumbs must be cleaned off, and placement should be such that these beauties of nature rise above the surface of the cake if only by a fraction of an inch.

Flowers stay fresh for a surprisingly long time on a cake, but still add them as close to serving time as possible.

The Center Bouquet: This bouquet should give the feeling that it is growing right out of the cake's center, bursting forth with freshness. The bouquet is most dramatic when a few primary flowers such as roses, tiger lilies or tulips are placed at slightly varying heights to form the center of the bouquet. To insert the flowers, make a fresh cut across the stems leaving 1½ to 3 inches to insert in the cake depending on placement and the desired height of each flower. After the primary flowers have been placed, secondary flowers such as Peruvian lilies and freesia

can be used to surround the primary flowers, once again imbedded at slightly different heights to make the bouquet more interesting. Next use statice or baby's breath to fill in some of the spaces between and around the base of the bouquet, and to add a more impressionistic texture that softens the bouquet.

Positioning the leaves is the next step; these darker accents can shoot out from the base of the bouquet as if to be almost supporting it and they can be placed inside the bouquet to contribute to the texture and color.

The Arched Bouquet: This bouquet is particularly nice for cakes that are going to have an inscription. The arch can span anywhere from one-quarter to halfway around the outer edge of the top of the cake on the right hand side (just inside the frosting rosettes if the cake has them). For this bouquet you generally need more flowers than for the center bouquet. Use primary flowers in the middle of the arch and smaller flowers tapering out to the ends or make the arch using only smaller delicate flowers and filler and dainty leaf accents.

Dotting with Statice: On frosted cakes that have been piped with rosettes and are going to be inscribed, I like to pinch off little pieces of statice and place them in between every 3 to 4 rosettes. Then I choose an inscription color that complements the statice.

Log Cakes, Bundt Cakes, and Loaf Cakes: These cakes can be decorated as well. On log cakes, such as Tom's Birthday Roll or the Lemon-Strawberry Roll, flowers can be placed in little whipped cream rosettes accented by leaves as well as at the base of the cake. Bundt and loaf cakes look lovely on paper lace doilies, surrounded at the base with greens and an occasional flower.

Fresh Fruit

Fruits in season (and, for some varieties, out of season) add decoration, taste, and extra freshness to your baking. Try strawberries or raspberries arranged around the top of a frosted cake (I'm partial to berries with chocolate), or intersperse flowers with fruit. For a special touch, you can dip the strawberry peaks in melted bittersweet chocolate, allow the chocolate to harden, and then arrange the strawberries point side up on top of the cake.

You can slice citrus fruits thin and press them along the sides of a frosted cake or at the base of a bundt cake. Or you can slit the slices up the center, twist them and place them on top of the cake to give it height. Put the fruit on the cake just before serving so it won't dry out.

Chocolate Shavings

Chocolate shavings are a perfect final touch for any cake with chocolate in it. Use an ounce of Baker's unsweetened chocolate or any other dark chocolate. Using the fine side of a standard kitchen grater, first dust the top of the cake with shavings, then accent it with coarser gratings. For a dramatic effect, shave larger flakes onto the cake from an ounce or bar of chocolate. Use a sharp thin knife and allow the flakes to fall randomly over the top or around the outer edge of the cake.

Salvaging

*E*ven the best of cooks goof on occasion; layers can come out overcooked and cakes sometimes crumble as you transfer them to a plate. That's when you revert to a salvage operation. You can slice a layer through the middle so that you have two layers half as thick, and then smother each half with frozen berries in juice and whipped cream. If that won't work, cut the layers into chunks, toss them with wet fruit—raspberries, strawberries, ripe peach cubes— maybe mix in some vanilla pudding or custard, and put the whole thing in custard cups, crowning it with a piece of fruit and a dollop of whipped cream. Because you need the liquid to moisten the cake, pour the fruit's juice over the chunks as early before serving as possible.

Serving

*P*resentation doesn't stop with what's *on* the cake but includes what the cake is *presented* on as well. I swear by decorative plates which I pick up everywhere from china shops to garage sales. I'm lavish with lacy paper doilies, but cutting a frosted cake on a paper doily can be a messy business, so I avoid it by putting the doily under the plate instead. Make sure that your doilies are crisp and clean, your flowers, berries, and nuts are fresh, and all your toppings are perched lightly *on* the cake, not imbedded in the frosting and looking like ships foundering at sea.

If it's theatricality you want, present your cake on a pedestal cake server and maybe add the circular straw or cloth placemat or a crocheted doily underneath. When you're serving several cakes at once, create tiers by putting one or two on a pedestal and

others on flat plates or baskets turned upside down.

Consider serving a bundt cake or a loaf cake in slices, or with half of it whole and the other half in overlapping slices like felled dominoes. If you're serving part of a bundt or tube cake, cut thin slices and arrange them in concentric circles on a round plate. Then dress them up by sprinkling confectioner's sugar over the top and strewing strawberries or flowers over all.

Cut frosted cakes with a sharp long, thin knife. To make each slice come out neatly, dip the knife in hot water and wipe it dry

Baking Cupcakes

You don't have to be a kid to love cupcakes, They're portion controlled, transportable, festive, and best of all, fun to eat.

You can make cupcakes from almost any cake recipe. If you're a cupcake fan, keep a couple of muffin tins and a package of muffin cup liners on hand. I find that the paper liners keep the outside of the cupcake moist and make life very easy when it comes to removing the cupcakes from the tin. I also love peeling the paper away as I eat the cupcake. If you don't have liners, just be sure that each muffin cup is well greased with vegetable oil before pouring in the batter.

I fill each muffin cup to the top of the paper liner or three-

quarters of the way up if I have no papers. This will produce a nice full cupcake. Bake them at the temperature called for in the cake recipe (usually 350°F) until the top is firm and a tester inserted in the center comes out dry, 30 to 35 minutes.

Cool the cupcakes in the pan. If you've used paper liners, the cupcakes should lift right out. If you've greased the pan, run a thin knife or spatula around the cupcakes and gently pick them up by their tops. Sometimes it's necessary to place the pan on an angle and tap it lightly on the counter to release the unpapered cupcakes.

Once cooled, frost the cupcakes, if desired, with a spatula.

before you make each cut. But if this means bringing a bowl of water to the table, just wipe the knife well after each cut.

Pound cakes, chiffon cakes, sponge cakes, and unfrosted bundt cakes, which are somewhat fragile, are best cut with a serrated knife, which puts less pressure on them. I find cake servers — slightly wedged-shaped spatulas — useful, especially for removing the first slice or when I'm serving frosted rectangular or square cakes from the pan.

Storing

*T*o keep a frosted cake that has been sliced, pat plastic wrap against the cut surfaces. The wrap will stick to the frosting and help keep the cake moist. If you plan to finish the cake in a day or two, keep it at room temperature, preferably under a cake dome. Longer than that, a cake needs to be refrigerated, but bring it to room temperature before you serve it again. (Cold cakes usually taste dry and bland.)

Unfrosted cakes don't have a built-in sealer, so they should be kept under a cake dome or covered completely with plastic wrap. Most unfrosted cakes will stay moist for two or three days if they're well covered.

You can freeze any cake (although a cake that's been frozen won't taste as fresh or flavorful), but you have to seal it from the air. Tupperware dome containers work best placed over cakes wrapped in plastic. But if your generation missed out on Tupperware parties, you can wrap your cake in a layer of plastic wrap, followed by a layer of aluminum foil. Finally, put it in a heavy plastic bag and use one of those twisty things to close it up tight.

Relaxing

*A*ll these directions and admonitions — do this, don't do that — may leave you reeling and wondering why anyone in his or her right mind would bother. Bring on the Hostess Twinkies, you say, but the truth is that much of baking becomes second nature quickly.

Perhaps that's why, more than any other class of desserts, cakes seem to bear the individual stamps of their creators. Each has its own style and each has a mystique which I'd be the last to try to analyze. Instead I recommend that you follow these recipes with care, unleash your imagination when the cake comes out of the oven, and then flash a Mona Lisa smile as everyone asks you how you did it.

Rosie's Famous Chocolate Sour-Cream Cake Layers

I've read that chocolate contains a chemical similar to the one our bodies produce when we fall in love. This doesn't surprise me because I've never had any doubt that chocolate has transcendent powers. I wish my readers all the love they need, but in a pinch I offer this recipe. Baking the layers a bit below 350°F keeps them moist. In my well-considered opinion, these are the perfect chocolate layers: dark and not too sweet compared to other chocolate cakes, quintessentially American. The variations that follow match them up with rich fillings and frostings for unbeatable delicious layer cakes.

INGREDIENTS

4 ounces unsweetened chocolate
2 cups sugar
1½ cups sifted all-purpose flour
¾ teaspoon baking soda
½ teaspoon salt
1 cup hot strong brewed coffee or 5 teaspoons instant coffee powder dissolved in 1 cup hot water
½ cup sour cream, at room temperature
½ cup vegetable oil
2 large eggs, lightly beaten with a fork, at room temperature

1. Preheat the oven to 345°F. Lightly grease two 8-inch layer cake pans with vegetable oil or butter, or line them with parchment circles or inserts.

2. Melt the chocolate in the top of a double boiler placed over simmering water, then turn off the heat.

3. Sift the sugar, flour, baking soda, and salt together into a large mixing bowl.

4. In a separate bowl, blend the hot coffee, sour cream, and vegetable oil with a whisk.

5. With the mixer on low speed, add the coffee mixture in a stream to the dry ingredients and mix until blended, about 35 seconds. Stop the mixer to scrape the bowl several times with a rubber spatula.

6. Add the eggs one at a time and mix on medium-low speed after each addition until smooth, about 15 seconds. Scrape the bowl each time. Add the chocolate and mix until the batter is uniform in color, about 10 seconds more.

7. Divide the batter evenly between the prepared pans and place them on the center rack of the oven.

8. Bake until the cake springs back to the touch and a tester inserted in the center comes out dry (do not wait for a crust to form), 35 to 38 minutes.

9. Cool the layers in the pans on a rack before frosting.

Makes 12 to 16 servings when frosted

Fudge Cake

*T*wo layers and one terrific frosting stack up to the simplest and dreamiest of the chocolate cakes. It's the ultimate at birthday time — copacetic with ice cream — need I say more?

INGREDIENTS

1 recipe Rosie's Famous Chocolate Sour-Cream Cake Layers (recipe precedes)
1 recipe Fudge Frosting (page 83)

Follow the procedure for frosting a two-layer cake on page 27.

Makes 12 to 16 servings

Velvet Underground Cake

A deep dark inside of layers of chocolate cake and hot fudge concealed by a velvety buttercream.

INGREDIENTS

1 recipe Rosie's Famous Chocolate Sour-Cream Cake Layers (facing page), split into 4 layers (page 29)
1 recipe Hot Fudge Filling (page 87)
About 1½ cups Rosie's or Mocha Buttercream (page 85 or 86)
1 ounce dark chocolate for shaving

1. Following the procedure for frosting a four-layer cake (page 29), spread all interior layers with fudge filling, and the outside of the cake with the buttercream.

2. Shave the dark chocolate over the surface of the cake with a fine grater, then use the knife method of shaving (page 33) to make darker accents on the top of the cake.

Makes 12 to 16 servings

Queen Raspberry Cake

*A*n elegant cake which combines chocolate and raspberries with mocha or vanilla buttercream. I decorate it very simply: a dab of raspberry preserves on the center of the top and chocolate shavings around the top edge.

1 recipe Rosie's Famous Chocolate Sour-Cream Cake Layers (page 36), split into 4 layers (page 29)

²/₃ cup raspberry preserves, plus 1 teaspoon for garnish

¹/₃ recipe (¼ cup) Hot Fudge Filling (page 87)

About 1½ cups Rosie's or Mocha Buttercream (page 85 or 86)

1 ounce dark chocolate for shaving

1. Following the procedure for frosting a four-layer cake, spread the preserves, fudge filling, and buttercream as follows: cake layer, ⅓ cup preserves, layer, fudge filling, layer, ⅓ cup preserves, layer, buttercream on the top and sides.

2. Using the knife method for shaving chocolate (page 33), shave a wreath of dark chocolate around the top edge of the cake and place the remaining 1 teaspoon preserves in the center before serving.

Makes 12 to 16 servings

Cold Fudge Sundae Cake

I like to serve this cake — a new twist on the classic soda fountain treat — for celebrations, New Year's Eve for instance, accompanied by Champagne. It's particularly festive looking because the sides are not frosted and the whipped cream ruffles out like crinolines between the dark chocolate layers.

1 recipe Rosie's Famous Chocolate Sour-Cream Cake Layers (page 36), split into 4 layers (page 29)

1 recipe Hot Fudge Filling (page 87)

1 double recipe Whipped Cream (page 86)

1½ cups frozen raspberries (optional)

1 ounce dark chocolate for shaving

12 fresh raspberries

1. Following the procedure for frosting a four-layer cake (page 29), spread the fudge filling, whipped cream, and raspberries (if using) as follows: cake layer, ¼ cup fudge filling, ½ cup frozen raspberries (leave a ½-inch border of plain fudge to prevent raspberry juice from dripping down the sides of the cake), ½ cup whipped cream (it should extend just beyond the edge of the cake), layer, ¼ cup fudge filling, ½ cup frozen raspberries, ½ cup whipped cream, layer, remaining ¼ cup

fudge filling, remaining frozen raspberries, ½ cup whipped cream, layer, and
the remaining whipped cream on top.
As you stack each layer, press down
lightly with your hand so that the
whipped cream is squeezed out from
between the layers a little.

2. Shave the dark chocolate over the
top of the cake and crown it with the
fresh raspberries.

Makes 12 to 16 servings

Texas Ruby Red Cake

*L*ayers of chocolate cake,
raspberry preserves, and
fudge frosting make this a very
rich choice.

INGREDIENTS

*1 recipe Rosie's Famous Chocolate
Sour-Cream Cake Layers
(page 36), split into 4 layers
(page 29)*
⅔ cup raspberry preserves
1 recipe Fudge Frosting (page 83)
½ pint fresh raspberries (optional)
1 recipe Whipped Cream (page 86)

1. Following the procedure for frosting a four-layer cake (page 29), spread
the preserves and frosting as follows:

cake layer, ⅓ cup preserves, layer, ½
cup fudge, layer, remaining ⅓ cup
preserves, layer, remaining fudge on
top and sides.

2. Crown the cake with fresh
raspberries and serve each slice with
a dollop of whipped cream.

Makes 12 to 16 servings

Snowball Cake

*R*emember those soft fluffy
pink and white mounds covered with coconut? Well, this is a
more sophisticated version, but
we only make it in white!

INGREDIENTS

*1 recipe Rosie's Famous Chocolate
Sour-Cream Cake Layers (page 36)*
1 recipe Rosie's Buttercream (page 85)
2 cups shredded coconut

1. Following the procedure for frosting a two-layer cake (page 27), frost
the chocolate layers with buttercream.

2. Pat the coconut gently around the
sides of the cake and sprinkle it generously over the top.

*Makes
12 to 16
servings*

Mocha Cake

*T*he wonderful combination of chocolate cake, fudge filling, and mocha buttercream produces one of our all-time favorite cakes at Rosie's.

INGREDIENTS

1 recipe Rosie's Famous Chocolate Sour-Cream Cake Layers (page 36), split into 4 layers (page 29)
1 recipe Hot Fudge Filling (page 87)
1 recipe Mocha Buttercream (page 86)

1. Following the procedure for frosting a four-layer cake (page 29), spread the fudge filling and buttercream as follows: cake layer, ¼ cup fudge filling, layer, ½ cup plus 2 tablespoons buttercream, layer, ¼ cup fudge filling, layer, remaining buttercream on top and sides.

2. Heat the remaining ¼ cup fudge filling until it's syrupy but not hot and drizzle it over the cake with a spoon or a pastry bag fitted with a fine tip.

Makes 12 to 16 servings

Chocolate Buttermilk Cake

A light chocolate cake that I like to frost with Marshmallow Frosting.

INGREDIENTS

4 ounces unsweetened chocolate
¾ cup plus 2 tablespoons cake flour
¼ cup all-purpose flour
¾ teaspoon baking soda
12 tablespoons (1½ sticks) unsalted butter, at room temperature
1¼ cups sugar
1 teaspoon vanilla extract
2 large eggs, at room temperature
¾ cup buttermilk, at room temperature
1 recipe Marshmallow Frosting or German Chocolate Topping (page 83 or 84)

1. Melt the chocolate in the top of a double boiler placed over simmering water, then set aside.

2. Preheat the oven to 350°F. Grease an 11 × 7-inch baking pan lightly with vegetable oil or butter.

3. Sift both flours and the baking soda together into a small bowl.

4. Cream the butter, sugar, and vanilla in a medium-size mixing bowl with an electric mixer on medium-high speed until light and fluffy, about 2 minutes. Stop the mixer once or twice to scrape the bowl with a rubber spatula.

5. Add the eggs one at a time and mix on medium speed after each addition, about 10 seconds. Scrape the bowl each time.

6. Add the chocolate on medium-low speed and mix until blended, about 8 seconds. Scrape the bowl.

7. With the mixer on low speed, add the dry ingredients in three additions alternating with the buttermilk in two additions, starting and ending with the dry ingredients. Beat for 2 or 3 seconds after each addition except the last and scrape the bowl. After the last addition, beat the batter till everything is well blended, about 5 seconds.

8. Spoon the batter into the prepared pan and spread it evenly. Bake the cake on the center oven rack until the top is firm and a tester inserted in the center comes out dry, 30 to 35 minutes. Allow the cake to cool completely before frosting.

Makes 12 servings

Sour Cherry Fudge Cake

*A*n odd combination of tastes, you say? Not once you try it. The tartness of the cherries contrasts wonderfully with the sweetness of the chocolate, and all together it makes a dense substantial cake. You can make it for Passover by substituting matzoh cake flour for the all-purpose flour in the recipe.

INGREDIENTS

8 ounces semisweet chocolate chips
4 ounces unsweetened chocolate
¼ cup water
1 cup (2 sticks) unsalted butter, at room temperature
2 cups sugar
2 teaspoons vanilla extract
6 large eggs, separated, at room temperature
1 cup all-purpose flour, sifted
2 cups canned or frozen sour red cherries, drained well and patted dry with a paper towel

1. Preheat the oven to 300°F. Lightly grease the bottom of a 9-inch springform pan with butter or vegetable oil.

2. Melt both chocolates with the water in the top of a double boiler placed over simmering water. Set aside to cool to room temperature.

3. Cream the butter, 1½ cups of the sugar, and the vanilla in a medium-size bowl with an electric mixer on medium speed until light and fluffy, about 2 minutes. Stop to scrape the bowl several times with a rubber spatula.

4. Using a whisk, stir the egg yolks into the chocolate and add this mixture to the butter mixture. Beat on medium speed until smooth, about 2 minutes, stopping to scrape the bowl once or twice.

5. With the mixer on low speed add the flour and mix until incorporated, about 20 seconds.

6. Beat the egg whites in another mixing bowl until frothy, about 30 seconds. Gradually add the remaining ½ cup sugar and continue beating until the whites form soft peaks, about 45 seconds more.

7. Whisk one-third of the whites into the chocolate mixture to loosen it, then fold the remaining egg whites into the batter with a rubber spatula. Place the cherries evenly over the surface of the batter and fold them in very gently with several slow strokes of the spatula.

8. Pour the batter into the prepared pan. Bake the cake on the center oven rack until it has risen and set and a tester inserted in the center comes out with a moist crumb, about 2 hours 10 minutes. Cool in the pan.

Makes 12 to 16 servings

Note: The cake will form a crust on top while baking; when the cake cools it will drop and the crust will crack. If you are bothered by its appearance, spread a layer of whipped cream on top and sprinkle chocolate shavings over the whipped cream or just sprinkle confectioner's sugar over the cake and eat it plain.

Chocolate Mousse Cake

*A*fter indulging in my first piece of chocolate mousse cake on a visit to New York several years ago, I decided that Rosie's could go no longer without our own version. By definition, the cake is rich and a little piece goes a long way, so I aimed to balance its richness with a deep semisweet chocolate flavor. A thin base of flourless cake supports a thick layer of mousse, which I accent with rum (though brandy or framboise will work too), then it's topped off with a veneer of whipped cream. The result looks very fancy, making this a perfect dessert for a dinner party or any celebration. Because this cake is made with uncooked eggs, be sure to prepare the mousse quickly and to refrigerate it while the base is baking.

INGREDIENTS

8 ounces semisweet chocolate
3 ounces unsweetened chocolate
1 cup (2 sticks) unsalted butter
5 large eggs, separated
¼ cup rum
1 teaspoon vanilla extract
⅓ cup plus 1 teaspoon sugar
1¾ cups heavy (whipping) cream, chilled
1 ounce dark chocolate for shaving

1. Preheat the oven to 350°F. Line the bottom of a 9-inch springform pan with a parchment or waxed paper circle.

2. Melt both chocolates and the butter in the top of a double boiler placed over simmering water.

3. Transfer the chocolate mixture to a large mixing bowl and allow it to cool to room temperature.

4. Add the egg yolks, rum, and vanilla to the chocolate mixture and whisk briskly until blended, 5 seconds.

5. Beat the egg whites in a medium-size mixing bowl with an electric mixer on medium-high speed until frothy, about 30 seconds. Gradually add ⅓ cup sugar and continue beating just until the peaks are stiff but not dry, about 1 minute more.

6. Add one-third of the egg whites to the chocolate mixture and whisk

gently to lighten this batter. Add the rest of the egg whites and whisk until blended.

7. To form the cake base, spread one-third of the chocolate mixture evenly in the prepared pan with a rubber spatula. Refrigerate the rest immediately.

8. Bake the base until it rises and then drops, 18 to 20 minutes. Cool it in the pan in the refrigerator, 15 minutes.

9. Meanwhile whip 1 cup of the cream until stiff in a medium-size mixing bowl with an electric mixer on medium-high speed. Fold the cream into the remaining chocolate mixture using a rubber spatula.

10. Scoop the chocolate mixture onto the cooled base and smooth the surface with a spatula. Stretch a piece of plastic wrap over the top of the pan and place the cake in the freezer overnight.

11. The next morning run a frosting spatula around the sides of the springform pan and remove the side.

12. Place a large plate upside down on the top of the cake and flip the cake onto the plate. Remove the bottom of the pan and the paper. Then flip the cake right side up onto a second large plate.

13. Beat the remaining ¾ cup of cream with 1 teaspoon sugar in a mixing bowl with an electric mixer on medium-high speed until stiff peaks are formed.

14. Spread half the whipped cream gently over the top of the mousse cake.

15. Place the remaining whipped cream in a pastry bag fitted with a decorative tip. Pipe rosettes of whipped cream around the top edge of the cake.

16. Shave the dark chocolate over the top of the cake and refrigerate it for 8 hours.

17. Remove the cake from the refrigerator 1 hour before serving.

Makes 16 servings

Chocolate Nut Torte

*T*his is a luxuriously rich cake which I often garnish with whipped cream, although, on its own, it is dark and moist and glazed with bittersweet chocolate. You can substitute matzoh cake flour for the all-purpose flour in the recipe and have an elegant Passover cake. Have all the ingredients prepared before starting because the chocolate starts to harden immediately when added to the egg yolks.

CAKE
8 ounces semisweet chocolate
4 ounces unsweetened chocolate
1½ cups (3 sticks) unsalted butter
1 cup ground almonds (about 1⅓ cups slivered almonds ground in a food processor)
¼ cup slivered almonds for the top
9 large eggs, separated, at room temperature
1½ cups sugar
½ cup sifted all-purpose flour

GLAZE
6 ounces semisweet chocolate
3 ounces unsweetened chocolate
4 tablespoons (½ stick) unsalted butter
1½ tablespoons light corn syrup
1 teaspoon boiling water

1. Preheat the oven to 350°F. Lightly grease a 10-inch springform pan with butter or vegetable oil.

2. For the cake, melt both chocolates and the butter in the top of a double boiler placed over simmering water. Let cool slightly.

3. Place the ground almonds on half of a cookie sheet and place the slivered almonds on the other half. Toast them in the oven until they are golden, about 10 minutes. Leave the oven on.

4. Beat the egg yolks and 1 cup of the sugar with an electric mixer on medium-high speed until they are thick and lemon colored, 4 minutes.

5. Beat the egg whites in another mixing bowl on medium-high speed until frothy, 45 seconds to 1 minute. Gradually add the remaining ½ cup sugar and continue beating until the whites have soft peaks, about 45 seconds more. Set them aside.

6. Add the chocolate mixture to the egg yolks and mix on low speed until blended, 5 to 8 seconds. Scrape the bowl with a rubber spatula and mix on low speed again until blended, about 5 seconds more. Transfer the mixture to a large bowl.

7. Combine the ground almonds and the flour and sprinkle them on top of the chocolate mixture.

8. Place the beaten whites on top of the nuts and flour and with gentle strokes of a rubber spatula, fold everything together.

9. Pour the batter into the prepared pan. Bake the cake on the center oven rack until the top springs back to the touch, about 1 hour. Allow the cake to cool in the pan.

10. When the cake has cooled, prepare the glaze. Melt both chocolates and the butter in the top of a double boiler placed over simmering water.

11. Dissolve the corn syrup in the boiling water and stir this into the chocolate mixture.

12. Turn the cake upside down on a cutting board or plate and pour the glaze over the cake. Use a frosting spatula to spread the glaze to the edge of the top so it can drip down the sides of the cake.

13. Crush the toasted slivered almonds in your hand or chop them and sprinkle them around the top edge of the cake. Allow the glaze to set before slicing the cake.

Makes 12 to 16 servings

Chocolate Fruitcake

*S*ince chocolate is a hallmark of Rosie's, I decided to take the traditional fruitcake recipe and gussy it up a little. Like its forebears, this is a dense cake aged in liquor, but the chocolate and unsweetened dried fruits (not those cloying candied ones) make it stand out even in the special category of fruitcakes.

INGREDIENTS

**2 cups chopped mixed dried fruits,
such as apricots, dates, prunes,
pears, and raisins (½-inch pieces)**

**6 tablespoons Grand Marnier or other
orange liqueur**

2 tablespoons Cognac

3 ounces unsweetened chocolate

**½ cup plus 1 tablespoon all-purpose
flour**

½ teaspoon baking powder

**8 tablespoons (1 stick) unsalted butter,
at room temperature**

1 cup sugar

3 large eggs, at room temperature

**½ cup chopped walnuts, almonds, or
pecans**

¼ cup Cognac for brushing the cake

1. Combine the dried fruits, Grand
Marnier, and Cognac in a small bowl
or container and allow it to sit covered
for 24 hours. Toss the fruit occasionally to ensure that it is completely
saturated.

2. The next day melt the chocolate
in the top of a double boiler placed
over simmering water. Let it cool.

3. Preheat the oven to 325°F. Line a
9½ × 5½ × 2-inch baking pan with a
piece of greased waxed paper that overhangs both long sides of the pan by 2
inches.

4. Sift the flour and baking powder
together into a small bowl and set aside.

5. Beat the butter and sugar in a
medium-size mixing bowl with an
electric mixer on medium speed until
light and fluffy, about 2 minutes.

6. Add the chocolate to the butter
mixture and beat on medium speed until
completely blended, about 10 seconds.
Scrape the bowl with a rubber spatula.

7. Add the eggs one at a time and
mix on low speed after each addition
for 10 seconds. Scrape the bowl each
time. Increase the speed to medium
and mix 15 seconds more.

8. Add the flour mixture and mix on
low speed just until blended, about 8
seconds. Scrape the bowl.

9. Stir the fruit (and any remaining
liquid) and the nuts in by hand with a
wooden spoon.

10. Spoon the batter into the prepared pan. Bake on the center oven
rack until a tester inserted in the
center comes out with a moist crumb,
1 to 1¼ hours.

11. Allow the cake to cool in the
pan, then remove it from the pan.
Remove the paper.

12. Using a pastry brush, brush
some of the Cognac over all surfaces
of the cake. Wrap the cake in cheesecloth or a light cotton cloth and brush
the cloth with the liqueur.

13. Place the cake in a container or
Ziploc bag and refrigerate it. If you
plan to keep it for several weeks or
months, brush it with more Cognac
when the cloth is dry. The cake gets
better and better as it ages.

Makes 12 to 14 servings

Golden Cake Layers

***R**emember the beautiful slice of cake on the box of Betty Crocker cake mix? I used to look at it and think that I could never make anything quite so perfect, but this cake not only looks good, it tastes a whole lot better. Although all-purpose flour can, in most cases, be substituted for cake flour (1 cup all-purpose equals 1 cup plus 2 tablespoons cake), I highly recommend using cake flour in this recipe — it greatly contributes to the delicacy of texture.*

INGREDIENTS

2¼ cups plus 3 tablespoons sifted cake flour (measure after sifting)
¾ teaspoon baking soda
¾ teaspoon baking powder
½ teaspoon salt
1 cup plus 2 tablespoons (2 sticks plus 2 tablespoons) unsalted butter, at room temperature
1¼ cups plus 1 tablespoon sugar
2 teaspoons vanilla extract
4 large yolks, at room temperature
1 large whole egg, at room temperature
¾ cup sour cream, at room temperature

1. Preheat the oven to 350°F. Lightly grease two 8-inch square layer pans with vegetable oil or butter, or line them with parchment circles or inserts.

2. Resift the flour with the baking soda, baking powder, and salt into a small bowl.

3. Cream the butter, sugar, and vanilla in a medium-size mixing bowl with an electric mixer on medium-high speed until light and fluffy, about 2 minutes. Stop the mixer twice to scrape the bowl with a rubber spatula.

4. Add the yolks one at a time, blending for 5 seconds on medium-low speed after each addition. Scrape the bowl each time. Then add the whole egg and mix until blended, 10 seconds.

5. Add one-third of the dry ingredients to the butter mixture by stirring them in lightly with the rubber spatula so that the liquid is absorbed. Then turn the mixer on low to blend partially, about 5 seconds. Scrape the bowl.

6. Add half of the sour cream and blend in with several broad strokes of the spatula. Then fold in one-third more dry ingredients by hand, followed by the remaining sour cream, then the rest of the dry ingredients. Turn the mixer to low and blend until the batter is velvety in texture, 10 seconds.

7. Divide the batter evenly between the prepared pans and place them on the center rack of the oven.

8. Bake until the layers are golden in color and spring back to the touch, and a tester inserted in the center comes out dry, 35 minutes.

9. Cool the layers in the pans on a rack before frosting.

Makes 12 to 16 servings when frosted

Summertime Cake

*T*his delicately light cake is one of my favorites. It combines the tartness of lemon filling with the sweetness of buttercream icing.

INGREDIENTS
---

1 recipe **Golden Cake Layers** (page 47), split into 4 layers (page 29)

1 recipe **Lemon Custard Filling** (page 88)

About 1½ cups **Rosie's Buttercream** (page 85)

1 lemon for garnish

1. Following the procedure for frosting a four-layer cake (page 29), spread the lemon custard over all interior layers.

Frost the outside of the cake with the buttercream. The custard may cause the layers to slip from side to side, so I suggest placing one hand on the top of the cake while you frost the sides using the base coating method on page 28.

2. Refrigerate the cake after the base coat and allow the custard to set for an hour before completing the frosting.

3. Cut thin slices of lemon and place them on top of the frosted cake as suggested on page 32.

Makes 12 to 16 servings

Snow Queen Cake

*T*his is a golden butter cake layered with raspberry preserves. Probably because I'm getting sentimental in my old age, it tickles me to see that it's the dream cake of both the 10-year-old birthday girl and the bride planning her wedding feast. There will be those with quite different ideas of how to celebrate momentous occasions, I know, but keep in mind that this is the cake those fat little birds were busy festooning in Disney's *Sleeping Beauty*. And who am I to argue with Walt Disney?

*1 recipe Golden Cake Layers
(page 47), split into 4 layers
(page 29)*
⅔ cup raspberry preserves
*1 recipe Rosie's Buttercream
(page 85)*

Following the procedure for frosting a four-layer cake (page 29), spread preserves and buttercream as follows: cake layer, ⅓ cup preserves, layer, buttercream, layer, remaining preserves, layer, and the remaining buttercream on the top and sides.

Makes 12 to 16 servings

Harvard Mocha Cake

*P*eople who like their chocolate in moderation love this cake, which gives them four layers of golden cake layered with mocha buttercream and frosted all over with fudge. I'm not sure why I named it after Harvard.

INGREDIENTS

*1 recipe Golden Cake Layers
(page 47), split into 4 layers
(page 29)*
2 cups Mocha Buttercream (page 86)
1 recipe Fudge Frosting (page 83)

Following the procedure for frosting a four-layer cake (page 29), spread ½ cup buttercream over each interior layer. Frost the top and sides of the cake with fudge frosting and crown the cake with mocha buttercream rosettes (page 30).

Makes 12 to 16 servings

Boston Cream Pie Cake

*M*ore Boston than baked beans (which seem to exist mostly in cans around here), this cake creates the taste of Boston cream pie with layers of golden cake iced with a rich vanilla custard. It's frosted with a dark fudge, and, since Boston is the home of America's first chocolate factory, you can't get more authentic than that.

INGREDIENTS

*1 recipe Golden Cake Layers
(page 47), split into 4 layers
(page 29)*
1 recipe Fudge Frosting (page 83)
*1 recipe Vanilla Custard Filling
(page 87)*

1. Following the procedure for frosting a four-layer cake (page 29), spread the frosting and custard as follows:

cake layer, half the custard, layer, ½ cup fudge, layer, remaining custard, layer, remaining fudge on top and sides. The custard may cause the layers to slip from side to side, so I suggest placing one hand on the top of the cake while you frost the sides using the base coating method on page 28.

2. Refrigerate the cake after the base coat and allow the custard to set for an hour before completing the frosting.

Makes 12 to 16 servings

Pineapple Upside-Down Cake

I wonder about the mind that first conceived of an upside-down cake, although something is right side up about it, since I've yet to meet an American who hasn't tasted a pineapple upside-down cake. It was a staple of dorm food during my college years, but I don't hold that against it. This version is a light yellow cake topped with pineapple chunks that have caramelized in brown sugar and butter.

INGREDIENTS

TOPPING

¾ cup (lightly packed) light brown sugar

½ teaspoon salt

3 tablespoons unsalted butter, melted

1½ cans (20 ounces each) pineapple chunks, drained, patted dry with paper towels, then wrapped in more paper towels, and set in a bowl for several hours

CAKE

1 cup all-purpose flour

½ teaspoon baking soda

½ teaspoon baking powder

¼ teaspoon salt

6 tablespoons (¾ stick) unsalted butter, at room temperature

1 cup granulated sugar

1½ teaspoons vanilla extract

2 large eggs, separated, at room temperature

½ cup buttermilk, at room temperature

1. Preheat the oven to 350°F.

2. For the topping, mix the brown sugar, salt, and butter in a medium-size bowl with a spoon. Add the pineapple and toss the chunks in the mixture.

3. Spread the topping evenly in an 8-inch square pan and set aside.

4. For the cake, sift the flour, baking soda, baking powder, and salt together into a small bowl.

5. Cream the butter, ¾ cup of the granulated sugar, and the vanilla in a medium-size mixing bowl with an electric mixer on medium speed until light and fluffy, about 2 minutes. Stop the mixer once or twice to scrape the bowl with a rubber spatula.

6. Add the egg yolks and beat the mixture on low speed until they are incorporated, about 30 seconds. Scrape the bowl.

7. With the mixer on low speed, add half the dry ingredients to the butter mixture and blend just until incorporated, about 10 seconds. Scrape the bowl. Add the buttermilk and mix on low speed for about 8 seconds. Scrape the bowl. Fold in the rest of the dry ingredients by hand, then turn the mixer to low for several spins. Scrape the bowl.

8. In another medium-size mixing bowl, whisk the egg whites on medium-high speed until frothy, about 15 seconds. Gradually add the remaining ¼ cup sugar and continue beating the whites to soft peaks, about 15 seconds more.

9. Stir one-third of the whites into the batter with a wooden spoon, to loosen the mixture. Fold in the remaining whites with a rubber spatula.

10. Spread the batter evenly over the pineapple and place the pan on a rack in the oven just below the center. The higher heat allows the topping to caramelize better. Bake the cake until the top is golden and springs back to the touch, and a tester inserted in the center comes out dry, about 50 minutes.

11. Remove the cake from the oven and allow it to cool for about 2 hours. Run a frosting spatula around the sides and turn the pan upside down onto a plate.

Makes 9 to 12 servings

Carrot-Pineapple Layer Cake

*7*his is a wonderfully moist, fruity cake, delicious plain or frosted with a Cream Cheese Frosting.

INGREDIENTS

2 cups all-purpose flour
2 teaspoons baking powder
1½ teaspoons baking soda
1 teaspoon salt
2 teaspoons ground cinnamon
½ teaspoon ground cloves
½ teaspoon ground allspice
½ teaspoon ground mace
1 cup drained crushed pineapple
2 cups grated carrots (about 4 carrots)
½ cup chopped walnuts
1¾ cups sugar
1½ cups vegetable oil
1 teaspoon vanilla extract
4 large eggs, at room temperature
1 recipe Cream Cheese Frosting
  (optional; page 85)

1. Preheat the oven to 350°F. Lightly grease two 9-inch layer cake pans with butter or vegetable oil or line them with parchment inserts.

2. Sift the flour, baking powder, baking soda, salt, and spices together into a small bowl and set aside.

3. Pat the pineapple dry and place it in a medium-size bowl. Add the grated carrots and the nuts to the pineapple and mix them together.

4. Mix the sugar, oil and vanilla together in a medium-size mixing bowl using an electric mixer on medium speed until completely blended, 20 seconds. Stop the mixer to scrape the bowl twice with a rubber spatula.

5. Add the eggs one at a time and mix on medium speed after each addition until blended, 10 seconds. Scrape the bowl each time.

6. Add the dry ingredients and beat on low speed for 5 seconds. Scrape the bowl, then mix the batter by hand until the dry ingredients are incorporated.

7. Blend in the pineapple mixture with several turns of the mixer at low speed.

8. Pour the batter into the prepared pans and bake on the center rack until the top is golden and springs back to the touch, and a tester inserted in the center comes out dry, about 45 minutes. Place the cake on a rack to cool completely.

9. Eat as is or frost with Cream Cheese Frosting.

Makes 8 to 12 servings

Bittersweet Orange Cake with a Lemon Glaze

*I*f a cake can contradict itself, this one does: It combines the bite of the citrus fruits with the sweetness of the raisins, the crunch of the nuts with a moist texture. To me, though, that's what makes this cake special.

I N G R E D I E N T S

CAKE
3 cups all-purpose flour
1½ teaspoons baking soda
1½ teaspoons baking powder
¾ teaspoon salt
*1½ oranges with rind, cut into
    chunks and seeds removed*
1½ cups raisins
¾ cup walnut pieces
*12 tablespoons (1½ sticks) unsalted
    butter, at room temperature*
1½ cups sugar
1 tablespoon grated lemon zest
3 large eggs, at room temperature
1½ cups buttermilk, at room temperature

GLAZE
½ cup fresh lemon juice
¼ cup fresh orange juice
5 tablespoons sugar

1. Preheat the oven to 350°F. Generously grease a 10-inch bundt pan with vegetable oil or butter.

2. Sift the flour, baking soda, baking powder, and salt together into a small bowl and set aside.

3. Put the oranges and raisins in a food processor and process with short pulses until the ingredients are chopped but not puréed, about 30 pulses. Add the nuts and pulse 6 more times.

4. Cream the butter, sugar, and lemon zest together in a medium-size mixing bowl with an electric mixer on medium speed until light and fluffy, about 1½ minutes. Stop the mixer once or twice to scrape the bowl with a rubber spatula.

5. Add the eggs one at a time and mix on medium speed after each addition until blended, 8 seconds. Scrape the bowl each time.

6. Fold the orange mixture in by hand. The batter will appear curdled.

7. Fold in the dry ingredients by hand alternating with the buttermilk as follows (to prevent overmixing, do not completely blend each addition): one-third of the dry ingredients, half the buttermilk, another third of the dry ingredients, the remaining buttermilk, and then the rest of the dry ingredients. Mix on low speed just until blended, several seconds.

8. Pour the batter into the prepared pan. Bake the cake on the center oven rack until the top is a deep golden color and a tester inserted in the center comes out dry, about 1¼ hours. Allow the cake to cool completely in the pan on a wire rack.

9. Meanwhile prepare the glaze: Whisk both juices and the sugar together in a small bowl until blended.

10. When the cake has cooled, remove it from the pan, put it on a plate, and poke holes over the entire surface with a fork. Then use a pastry brush to baste the glaze repeatedly over the surface of the cake until all the glaze has been absorbed. (You can also pour the glaze over the entire cake, reusing the excess that has dripped onto the plate to pour onto the cake again.)

Makes 12 to 16 servings

Apple Cake

*S*ince apples taste best in fall or winter, this cake is a seasonal treat and one that can be stored nearly forever—if it makes it as far as the fridge.

INGREDIENTS

3 cups all-purpose flour
2 teaspoons ground cinnamon
1 teaspoon baking soda
1 teaspoon salt
1 cup (2 sticks) unsalted butter,
    at room temperature
1/4 cup vegetable oil
2 cups sugar
2 teaspoons vanilla extract
3 large eggs, at room temperature
4 cups apples (3 to 4 large apples),
    peeled, cored, and cut into
    1/2-inch cubes
1 teaspoon cinnamon mixed with
    1 tablespoon sugar for topping

1. Preheat the oven to 350°F. Lightly grease a 10-inch tube pan with a removable bottom with butter or vegetable oil.

2. Sift the flour, cinnamon, baking soda, and salt into a small bowl.

3. Cream the butter, oil, sugar, and vanilla in a medium-size mixing bowl with an electric mixer on medium speed until the ingredients are blended, about 2 minutes. Stop to scrape the bowl twice with a rubber spatula.

4. Add the eggs one at a time, and mix on medium-low speed after each addition until blended, 10 seconds. Scrape the bowl each time. Once the eggs are added, mix again for 10 seconds.

5. Add half the dry ingredients and blend on low speed for 15 seconds. Scrape the bowl, add the rest of the dry ingredients, and mix on low speed until blended, about 5 seconds more.

6. Add the apples with a few turns of the mixer or by folding them in by hand with a wooden spoon.

7. Spoon the batter into the pan and sprinkle the cinnamon-sugar over the top. Bake the cake on the center oven rack until the top is firm and golden and a tester inserted at the cake's highest point comes out dry, about 1 hour 5 minutes.

Makes 12 to 16 servings

Applesauce-Raisin Cake

*D*ark and hearty, this cake is a great fall and winter treat. I like to use unsweetened applesauce because the cake doesn't need the extra sweetness.

I N G R E D I E N T S

CAKE

2 cups all-purpose flour
1½ teaspoons baking soda
½ teaspoon salt
8 tablespoons (1 stick) unsalted butter,
    at room temperature
1 cup granulated sugar
½ cup (lightly packed) light brown
    sugar
1½ teaspoons ground cinnamon
1½ teaspoons ground nutmeg
1 teaspoon ground cloves
½ teaspoon ground ginger
½ teaspoon ground allspice
3 tablespoons unsweetened cocoa
    powder
2 large eggs, at room temperature
1½ cups applesauce, at room
    temperature
¾ cup raisins
¾ cup chopped walnuts or pecans

GLAZE

1½ cups sifted confectioner's sugar
1 tablespoon ground allspice
2 teaspoons ground ginger
1 teaspoon ground cinnamon
6 tablespoons (¾ stick) unsalted
    butter
3 tablespoons heavy (whipping)
    cream

1. Preheat the oven to 350°F. Generously grease a 10-inch bundt pan with
vegetable oil or butter.

2. For the cake, sift the flour, baking
soda, and salt together into a small
bowl.

3. Cream the butter, both sugars,
the spices, and cocoa together in a
medium-size mixing bowl with an
electric mixer on medium-high speed

until light and fluffy, about 2 minutes.
Stop the mixer once or twice to scrape
the bowl with a rubber spatula.

4. Add the eggs one at a time and
mix on medium-low speed after each
addition until blended, 8 to 10 seconds. Scrape the bowl each time. After
the final scraping mix again on
medium speed, about 10 seconds.

5. Add the applesauce and blend it in
with a rubber spatula. Turn the mixer
to medium for 2 complete spins.

6. Fold in the dry ingredients by
hand with the spatula until they are
almost incorporated. Then turn the
mixer to medium speed and blend the
ingredients until the batter is well
mixed, about 8 seconds.

7. Fold in the raisins and nuts by
hand with the rubber spatula.

8. Pour the batter into the prepared
pan. Bake the cake on the center oven
rack until the top is firm to the touch
and a tester inserted in the center
comes out dry, about 1 hour 10
minutes.

9. Allow the cake to cool completely
in the pan.

10. To make the glaze, sift the confectioner's sugar and spices together
into a small bowl.

11. Melt the butter in a small saucepan over low heat, add the cream
when the butter has melted, and cook
just until the cream is hot.

12. Stir the butter mixture vigorously into the dry ingredients with a whisk until they are absorbed. There will be lumps.

13. Pour the glaze into an electric blender and blend on medium speed until smooth, about 20 seconds.

14. Remove the cake from the pan and place it on a cake plate. Pour the glaze over the top of the cake, allowing it to run down the outer sides and down the center hole. Allow the glaze to set for an hour before cutting the cake.

Makes 12 to 16 servings

Banana Cake

*B*anana cake par excellence: a sheet cake that's perfect in flavor, delicate and moist in texture, and delicious plain or with Cream Cheese Frosting.

INGREDIENTS

2¼ cups sifted cake flour
5 tablespoons all-purpose flour
1½ teaspoons baking soda
½ teaspoon salt
1 cup plus 2 tablespoons buttermilk,
*   at room temperature*
¾ cup mashed banana
*   (about 2 very ripe bananas,*
*   skin should be brown)*
10 tablespoons (1¼ sticks) unsalted
*   butter, at room temperature*
6 tablespoons vegetable oil
¾ cup (lightly packed) light brown sugar
¾ cup granulated sugar
1 teaspoon vanilla extract
3 large eggs, at room temperature
1 recipe Cream Cheese Frosting
*   (optional; page 85)*

1. Preheat the oven to 350°F. Grease a 13 × 9-inch baking pan lightly with butter or vegetable oil.

2. Sift both flours, the baking soda, and salt together into a small bowl and set aside.

3. In a second small bowl, stir the buttermilk into the mashed banana and set aside.

4. Cream the butter, oil, both sugars, and vanilla in a medium-size mixing bowl with an electric mixer on medium speed until light and fluffy, about 2 minutes. Scrape the bowl with a rubber spatula.

5. Add the eggs one at a time to the butter mixture and mix on medium speed after each addition until blended, about 10 seconds. Scrape the bowl each time.

6. Add one-third of the dry ingredients with the mixer on low speed, and mix for 8 seconds. Scrape the bowl. Add half the banana mixture, mix 10 seconds, and scrape the bowl. Add the rest of the dry ingredients and the rest of the banana mixture and mix for 10 seconds. Scrape the bowl and stir the batter several times by hand to mix thoroughly.

7. Pour the batter into the prepared pan. Bake on the center oven rack until the top is golden, springs back to the touch, and a tester inserted in the center comes out dry, 30 to 35 minutes. Place the cake on a rack to cool completely.

8. Eat as is or frost with Cream Cheese Frosting.

Makes 12 to 18 servings

Mustard Gingerbread

*I*n my opinion this is the classic American gingerbread: dark, moist, sharp in flavor, and not gummy the way some gingerbreads are. Serve it hot with whipped cream or vanilla ice cream.

2½ cups sifted cake flour
1¼ teaspoons baking soda
½ teaspoon salt
¾ teaspoon mustard powder
2 tablespoons plus 2 teaspoons ground ginger
2 teaspoons ground cinnamon
¼ teaspoon ground allspice
10 tablespoons (1¼ sticks) unsalted butter, at room temperature
⅓ cup (lightly packed) light brown sugar
2 large eggs, at room temperature
¾ cup unsulphured molasses, at room temperature
1 cup strong brewed coffee

1. Preheat the oven to 350°F and lightly grease a 10-inch springform pan with butter or vegetable oil.

2. Sift the flour, baking soda, salt, mustard powder, and spices together into a medium-size bowl.

3. Cream the butter and sugar together in a medium-size mixing bowl with an electric mixer on medium speed until light and fluffy, about 2 minutes. Stop the mixer twice to scrape the bowl with a rubber spatula.

4. Add the eggs one at a time to the butter mixture and mix on medium speed after each addition until the eggs are blended but not smooth, 8 to 10 seconds. Scrape the bowl each time.

5. Add the molasses with the mixer on medium-low speed and mix for 5 seconds. The batter will look very separated.

6. Add half the dry ingredients to the batter with the mixer on low speed and mix just until they have absorbed the liquid but are not thoroughly blended, about 10 seconds. Add half the coffee and fold it into the mixture with a rubber spatula.

7. Add the remaining dry ingredients on medium-low speed and blend until they are almost incorporated, 10 seconds. Pour in the remaining coffee, then fold it in by hand with a rubber spatula. Turn the mixer to low and blend until the batter is smooth, 5 seconds.

8. Pour the batter into the prepared pan. Bake the cake on the center oven rack until the top springs back to the touch and a tester inserted in the center comes out dry, about 45 minutes. Cool slightly in the pan before serving.

Makes 12 to 16 servings

Coconut-Pecan Oatmeal Cake

*T*his is a hearty cake, almost more of a fall or winter snack than a dessert. Be careful not to let the oatmeal stand or it

will coagulate. Serve this cake soon after it has baked — it's great warm.

INGREDIENTS

CAKE
1¹⁄₃ cups all-purpose flour
1 teaspoon baking soda
¹⁄₂ teaspoon baking powder
1 teaspoon salt
¹⁄₂ teaspoon ground cinnamon
1 cup quick-cooking oats
8 tablespoons (1 stick) unsalted butter,
*   at room temperature*
1 cup plus 3 tablespoons sugar
2 teaspoons vanilla extract
2 large eggs, at room temperature
1¹⁄₃ cups boiling water

TOPPING
6 tablespoons (³⁄₄ stick) unsalted
*   butter, at room temperature*
1 cup (lightly packed) light brown sugar
¹⁄₄ cup light cream, half and half, or milk
1 teaspoon vanilla extract
¹⁄₂ cup chopped pecans
¹⁄₂ cup shredded coconut

1. Preheat the oven to 350°F. Lightly grease an 11 × 7-inch broiler-proof baking pan with butter or vegetable oil.

2. For the cake, sift the flour, baking soda, baking powder, salt, and cinnamon together into a small bowl. Place the oats in a medium-size bowl.

3. Cream the butter, sugar, and vanilla together in a second medium-size mixing bowl with an electric mixer on medium speed until light and fluffy, about 2 minutes. Stop the mixer twice to scrape the bowl with a rubber spatula.

4. Add the eggs one at a time to the

butter mixture and mix on medium speed after each addition until blended, 10 seconds. Scrape the bowl each time.

5. Pour the boiling water over the oatmeal and stir several times with a wooden spoon. Add the oatmeal to the egg mixture and mix on medium speed until blended, about 6 to 7 seconds.

6. Partially fold in the dry ingredients by hand with the spatula, using several broad strokes. Then mix on medium speed until all the ingredients are blended, about 10 seconds. Scrape the bowl.

7. Pour the batter into the prepared pan. Bake the cake on the center oven rack until the top is golden and springs back to the touch, 25 to 30 minutes. Remove the cake from the oven and allow it to cool for 15 minutes.

8. Meanwhile prepare the topping. Put all the ingredients in a medium-size mixing bowl and stir vigorously with a whisk until they are blended.

9. Preheat the broiler.

10. Spread the topping over the cake with a spatula, then place the cake on a cookie sheet (to catch any drips). If your broiler is part of your oven, place the cake on the center rack of the oven. If you have a separate broiler unit, place the cake as far as possible from it. With the oven or broiler door open, broil, rotating the pan several times, until the topping bubbles to a deep golden color, 5 to 6 minutes. Watch it carefully.

Makes 12 servings

Breakfast Coffeecake

A classic sour-cream coffeecake layered and topped with a sweet, crunchy pecan mixture.

INGREDIENTS

TOPPING
1¹/₃ cups (lightly packed) light brown
    sugar
1 tablespoon ground cinnamon
1¹/₂ cups chopped pecans
8 tablespoons (1 stick) unsalted
    butter, cool but not cold

CAKE
2²/₃ cups all-purpose flour
1¹/₄ teaspoons baking powder
1 teaspoon baking soda
¹/₂ teaspoon salt
12 tablespoons (1¹/₂ sticks) unsalted
    butter, at room temperature
1 cup plus 2 tablespoons granulated
    sugar
2 teaspoons vanilla extract
4 large eggs, at room temperature
1¹/₃ cups sour cream,
    at room temperature

1. Preheat the oven to 350°F. Grease a 9-inch springform pan lightly with butter or vegetable oil.

2. For the topping, combine the brown sugar, cinnamon, and pecans in a medium-size bowl and rub the butter into this mixture with your fingertips until it is incorporated. Set aside.

3. For the cake, sift the flour, baking

powder, baking soda, and salt into a small bowl.

4. Cream the butter, sugar, and vanilla in a medium-size mixing bowl with an electric mixer on medium speed until light and fluffy, about 2 minutes. Stop the mixer twice to scrape the bowl with a rubber spatula.

5. Add the eggs one at a time to the butter mixture and mix on medium-low speed after each addition until blended, 5 seconds. Scrape the bowl each time.

6. By hand add the dry ingredients in 4 additions alternately with the sour cream in 3 additions, beginning and ending with the dry ingredients. Do not blend each addition in fully before adding the next. When everything has been added, turn the mixer on low and blend until smooth, 5 seconds.

7. Spread half of the batter in the prepared pan and distribute half the topping over it. Spoon the remaining batter on top, smooth it out evenly, and distribute the remaining topping over the top.

8. Place a piece of foil or a cookie sheet on the bottom oven rack, then place the cake on the center rack. Bake the cake until the top turns golden, about 40 minutes. Gently place a piece of aluminum foil over the top of the cake (do not mold it) and continue to bake the cake until a tester inserted in the center comes out dry, about 40 minutes more. Serve warm or at room temperature.

Makes 12 to 16 servings

Fresh Blueberry-Muffin Breakfast Cake

*T*his is really a blueberry muffin masquerading as a cake, which makes it perfect for brunch or snacking — anytime you want something to accompany a cup of tea or coffee or a glass of milk. The cake should be served quite warm, soon after it comes out of the oven, and I especially like my piece with a thin veneer of sweet butter. Cranberries can be substituted for blueberries when they are in season.

INGREDIENTS

CAKE
2 cups all-purpose flour
2 teaspoons baking powder
¾ teaspoon salt
*10 tablespoons (1½ sticks)
    unsalted butter, at room
    temperature*
1½ cups granulated sugar
1½ teaspoons vanilla extract
2 large eggs, at room temperature
¾ cup milk, at room temperature
1¾ cups fresh blueberries

TOPPING
*8 tablespoons (1 stick) unsalted
    butter, cut into 8 pieces,
    at room temperature*
¼ cup all-purpose flour
½ cup granulated sugar
*½ cup (lightly packed) light brown
    sugar*
¼ teaspoon ground cinnamon
Pinch of salt

1. Preheat the oven to 350°F. Grease a 9-inch square baking pan lightly with butter or vegetable oil.

2. For the cake, sift the flour, baking powder, and salt together into a small bowl.

3. Cream the butter, sugar, and vanilla in a medium-size mixing bowl with an electric mixer on medium speed until the mixture is light and fluffy, about 2 minutes. Stop the mixer once or twice to scrape the bowl with a rubber spatula.

4. Add the eggs one at a time to the butter mixture and mix on medium speed after each addition until blended, 8 to 10 seconds. Scrape the bowl each time.

5. Fold one-third of the dry ingredients in by hand just until they have absorbed the liquid but are not thoroughly blended. Fold in half the milk by hand with several strokes, then the rest of the dry ingredients, folding just until they are absorbed. Add the rest of the milk and fold it in just until the batter is smooth.

6. Fold the blueberries in gently.

7. Pour the batter into the prepared pan. Bake the cake on the center oven rack until the top is just set but not golden, 25 to 30 minutes.

8. Meanwhile prepare the topping: Place all the ingredients in a food processor and pulse until blended, about 10 pulses. Or mix all the dry ingredients in a small bowl and rub the butter into the mixture with your fingers.

9. When the top of the cake is set, cover the surface with spoonfuls of topping and return the cake to the oven until the topping spreads and begins to get crunchy, 15 to 20 minutes.

10. Remove the cake from the oven and serve it hot. It is good eaten plain or buttered like a muffin.

Makes 9 to 12 servings

Cream Cheese Pound Cake

I dedicate this dessert to my sister-in-law Laura, who is such a fan that when she first tasted it, she devoured nearly the entire cake. The cream cheese combines with the other ingredients to make it velvety and moist, but it doesn't overpower the flavor of the butter.

INGREDIENTS

3 cups cake flour
1½ cups (3 sticks) unsalted butter, at room temperature
1 package (8 ounces) cream cheese, at room temperature or warmed lightly in a microwave
3 cups sugar
1 tablespoon vanilla extract
6 large eggs, at room temperature

1. Preheat the oven to 325°F. Lightly grease a 10-inch tube pan with butter or vegetable oil.

2. Sift the cake flour into a small bowl and set aside.

3. Cream the butter, cream cheese, sugar, and vanilla in a medium-size mixing bowl with the mixer on medium-high speed until light and fluffy, about 2 minutes. Stop the mixer once or twice to scrape the bowl with a rubber spatula.

4. Add the eggs one at a time to the butter mixture and mix on medium speed after each addition until blended, about 10 seconds. Scrape the bowl each time. When all the eggs are added, mix 30 seconds more.

5. Stir the flour gently into the batter with a rubber spatula. Then mix on low speed 5 seconds, scrape the bowl, and blend until the batter is smooth and even, 5 to 10 seconds.

6. Pour the batter into the prepared pan. Bake the cake on the center oven rack until golden and firm to the touch, and a tester inserted in the center comes out dry, about 1 hour 35 minutes.

7. Allow the cake to cool completely in the pan before unmolding and serving.

Makes 12 to 16 servings

Almond Pound Cake

H ere is a simple butter pound cake with a distinctive almond taste. I top it with an almond glaze and crushed almonds.

CAKE

1½ cups plus 3 tablespoons cake flour
¾ teaspoon baking powder
½ teaspoon baking soda
¼ teaspoon salt
10 tablespoons (1½ sticks) unsalted
    butter, at room temperature
¾ cup granulated sugar
2 teaspoons almond extract
1 teaspoon vanilla extract
3 large eggs, at room temperature
½ cup plus 1 tablespoon sour cream

GLAZE

1 cup confectioner's sugar, sifted
2¼ teaspoons almond extract
2 tablespoons hot water
¼ cup chopped slivered almonds

1. Preheat the oven to 350°F. Grease an 8½ × 4½ × 2½-inch loaf pan lightly with butter or oil.

2. For the cake, sift the cake flour, baking powder, baking soda, and salt together into a small bowl.

3. Cream the butter, sugar, and both extracts in a medium-size mixing bowl with an electric mixer on medium speed until light and fluffy, about 2 minutes. Stop the mixer once or twice to scrape the bowl with a rubber spatula.

4. Add the eggs one at a time to the butter mixture and mix on medium speed after each addition until blended, 10 seconds. Scrape the bowl each time. The eggs will not be fully mixed into the batter at this point.

5. Add half the dry ingredients and mix on low speed for 10 seconds. Add half the sour cream and mix for 5 seconds. Add the remaining dry ingredients and mix 5 seconds, then add the remaining sour cream and mix another 5 seconds. The batter should be velvety.

6. Pour the batter into the prepared pan. Bake on the center oven rack until the top is firm and golden, and a tester inserted in the center comes out dry, about 50 minutes. The top will crack slightly. Let the cake cool completely.

7. Prepare the glaze: Stir the confectioner's sugar, almond extract, and water together in a small bowl with a small whisk until the sugar is completely dissolved.

8. Remove the cake from the pan and place it on a cookie sheet. Pour the glaze over the cake slowly so that it covers the top and drips down the sides. Sprinkle the almonds over the top immediately. When the glaze hardens, transfer the cake to a pretty serving plate.

Makes 8 to 12 servings

Poppy-Seed Pound Cake

---

*P*ound cakes got their name because originally they were made with a pound of each ingredient. For this recipe, I kept the name but changed the weight to come up with a remarkably versatile cake. It's ideal sliced thin as a tea cake, as a chunk cut for an after-school snack, served with fresh fruit as dessert, or dunked into coffee in place of a breakfast doughnut. That probably accounts for its popularity, although the crunchiness of the whole poppy seeds also has something to do with it. You can also substitute 1¼ cups blueberries, cranberries, chocolate chips, or nuts for the poppy seeds, and have an equally scrumptious cake.

INGREDIENTS

4 cups all-purpose flour
2 teaspoons baking soda
1 tablespoon baking powder
½ teaspoon salt
1 cup (2 sticks) unsalted butter, at
    room temperature
2 cups sugar
1 tablespoon vanilla extract
4 large eggs, at room temperature
2 cups sour cream, at room
    temperature
½ cup plus 1½ tablespoons poppy seeds

1. Preheat the oven to 350°F. Lightly grease a 10-inch tube pan with vegetable oil or butter.

2. Sift the flour, baking soda, baking powder, and salt together into a medium-size bowl.

3. Cream the butter, sugar, and vanilla in a large mixing bowl with an electric mixer on medium speed until light and fluffy, about 2 minutes. Stop the mixer once or twice to scrape the bowl with a rubber spatula.

4. Add the eggs one at a time to the butter mixture and mix on medium-low speed after each addition until blended, 5 seconds. Scrape the bowl each time. When all the eggs are added, beat the mixture for 10 seconds. It will not appear smooth at this point.

5. Add one-third of the dry ingredients to the egg mixture and fold them in lightly with a rubber spatula so that the liquid is absorbed. Mix on low speed 5 seconds until partially blended. Scrape the bowl.

6. Add half the sour cream, and mix on low speed for 5 seconds until partially blended. Mix the batter with several broad strokes of the spatula and scrape the bowl. Add another third of the dry ingredients, the remaining sour cream, and then the remaining dry ingredients with this same procedure. Mix the batter on low speed until it is velvety, about 15 seconds.

7. Add ½ cup of the poppy seeds on low speed and mix just until blended.

8. Pour the batter into the prepared pan and sprinkle the remaining poppy seeds over the top.

9. Bake the cake on the center oven rack until it is high and golden, about 1 hour 10 minutes. A cake tester inserted at the highest point should come out clean.

10. Remove the cake from the oven and allow it to cool in the pan on a rack for several hours before unmolding and serving.

Makes 12 to 16 servings

Poppy-Seed Chocolate-Chip Cake

*T*he name is complicated, but the cake is a straightforward butter cake embroidered with chocolate and poppy seeds, a surprisingly complementary combination.

INGREDIENTS

2½ cups all-purpose flour
2 teaspoons baking powder
1 teaspoon baking soda
¼ teaspoon salt
1 cup (2 sticks) unsalted butter,
    at room temperature
1 cup plus 4 tablespoons sugar
2 teaspoons vanilla extract
1 teaspoon ground cinnamon
4 large eggs, separated,
    at room temperature
1 cup buttermilk, at room
    temperature
1 cup semisweet chocolate chips,
    coarsely chopped by hand
1½ ounces unsweetened chocolate,
    grated
¼ cup poppy seeds
Confectioner's sugar for garnish

1. Preheat the oven to 350°F. Grease a 10-inch bundt pan with butter or vegetable oil.

2. Sift the flour, baking powder, baking soda, and salt together into a small bowl.

3. Beat the butter, 1 cup plus 1 tablespoon of the sugar, the vanilla, and cinnamon in a medium-size mixing bowl with an electric mixer on medium speed until blended, about 2 minutes. Stop the mixer once or twice to scrape the bowl with a rubber spatula.

4. Add the egg yolks to the butter mixture and beat on medium speed until blended, about 10 seconds. Scrape the bowl once during the mixing and again at the end. The batter will not be smooth at this point.

5. Fold in one-third of the dry ingredients with a rubber spatula. Then fold in half the buttermilk, another third of the dry ingredients, the remaining buttermilk, and the remaining dry ingredients. Do not fully blend in the ingredients after each addition until the end.

6. Beat the egg whites in another medium-size mixing bowl with an electric mixer on medium-high speed until frothy, about 30 seconds. Gradually add the remaining 3 tablespoons sugar and continue beating until the whites form soft peaks, about 30 seconds more. Stir one-third of the whites into the batter to loosen it, then fold in the rest of the whites with a rubber spatula. Fold in the chocolate chips, grated chocolate, and poppy seeds.

7. Scoop the batter into the pan and distribute it evenly. Bake the cake on the center oven rack until it is golden and a tester inserted in the center comes out dry, about 1 hour.

8. Let the cake cool completely in the pan. Sift confectioner's sugar over the top before serving.

Makes 12 to 16 servings

Desert Island Butter Cake

*7*his cake got its name because it would be my choice if I were stranded on a desert island and could have only one sweet. (How come no one ever gets stranded on a desert island?) This cake is unbelievably easy and quick to make with a flavor and texture halfway between a sponge and a pound cake. You can gussy it up with strawberries or cut off a chunk to eat plain with an occasional dunk in your coffee.

I N G R E D I E N T S

1 cup (2 sticks) unsalted butter
3 large eggs, at room temperature
1 cup sugar
1 cup sifted all-purpose flour
Frozen strawberries, thawed, or fresh
*   strawberries, hulled and lightly*
*   sugared to make a juice,*
*   for serving (optional)*

1. Preheat the oven to 350°F. Lightly grease an 8-inch springform pan with butter or vegetable oil.

2. Melt the butter in a saucepan over low heat.

3. Beat the eggs and sugar in a medium-size mixing bowl with an electric mixer on high speed until the mixture is thick and pale, about 4 minutes.

4. Resift the flour over the egg mixture and fold it in gently with a rubber spatula.

5. When the flour is almost but not completely incorporated, slowly fold in the melted butter with gentle strokes.

6. Pour the batter into the prepared pan. Bake the cake on the center oven rack until the center of the top puffs up and then falls level with the outer edges, 35 to 40 minutes. The center will drop slightly as the cake cools to room temperature.

7. For the best flavor, serve the cake the next day with the strawberries, if desired.

Makes 12 to 15 servings

Fresh Berry Sponge Cake

*W*henever I make this dessert for Passover, people are always surprised that a cake made with matzoh flour could taste so wonderful. The lemony sponge cake makes a lovely change from the usual berry shortcake.

INGREDIENTS

6 tablespoons potato starch
10 tablespoons matzoh cake flour
½ teaspoon salt
6 large eggs, separated,
    at room temperature
2 tablespoons water
1¼ cups plus 1 tablespoon sugar
2 tablespoons fresh lemon juice
1 tablespoon grated lemon zest
2 teaspoons vanilla extract
1½ cups hulled, sliced fresh or
    frozen strawberries, or raspberries, thawed if frozen
1 double recipe Whipped Cream
    (page 86)
12 fresh whole strawberries or
    24 fresh whole raspberries
    for garnish

1. Preheat the oven to 350°F. Line two 8-inch layer pans with waxed paper or parchment circles or inserts.

2. Sift the potato starch, matzoh flour, and salt together into a small bowl.

3. Beat the egg yolks, water, 1 cup plus 1 tablespoon sugar, the lemon juice and zest, and vanilla in a medium-size mixing bowl with an electric mixer on medium speed until blended, about 10 seconds. Scrape the bowl with a rubber spatula.

4. Blend the dry ingredients into the egg yolk mixture on low speed until incorporated, about 10 seconds. Scrape the bowl.

5. Beat the egg whites in another mixing bowl on medium-high speed until frothy, about 30 seconds. Gradually add the remaining ¼ cup sugar and continue beating the whites to firm peaks, about 90 seconds more.

6. Stir one-third of the egg whites into the batter to loosen it, then gently fold the remaining egg whites into the batter. Divide the batter evenly between the prepared pans. Shake the pans gently to level off the batter.

7. Bake the layers on the center oven rack until they are a rich golden color, spring back to the touch, and a tester inserted in the center comes out dry, about 25 minutes.

8. Cool the layers completely in the pans on a wire rack.

9. Remove the layers from the pan and remove the paper liners. Place one layer right side up on a cake plate. Slice it horizontally through the middle so that you have 2 layers. Spread ½ cup of the berries over the bottom layer, leaving a ½-inch border at the edge.

10. Put one-third of the whipped cream around this outer edge, like a wreath, and gently spread the cream toward the center of the layer with a frosting spatula. (This keeps the berries and the juice from dripping down the sides of the layer as you spread the cream.) Cut the other cake in half as well. Place 1 layer over the cream and continue layering the cake with the remaining berries and another one-third of the cream.

11. Place the last layer on the cake. Before frosting the top, press down

lightly on the top layer with your hand to make the whipped cream between each layer ooze out a little and form a ruffle. Then frost the top layer with the rest of the whipped cream. Stud the top of the cake decoratively with the 12 fresh strawberries or 24 fresh raspberries.

Makes 12 to 14 servings

Lemon-Glazed Orange Chiffon Cake

*7*his bundt cake is light and spongy with an orange flavor and a refreshing lemon glaze. I like to serve it with fresh or frozen strawberries.

I N G R E D I E N T S

CAKE
2¼ cups cake flour
2 cups granulated sugar
1 tablespoon baking powder
½ teaspoon salt
6 large eggs, separated,
    at room temperature
1 tablespoon grated orange zest
¾ cup orange juice
½ cup vegetable oil

GLAZE
9 tablespoons unsalted butter
2¼ cups confectioner's sugar
4½ tablespoons hot water
5½ tablespoons fresh lemon juice
    (1½ to 2 lemons)

*Frozen strawberries, thawed, or fresh
    strawberries, hulled and lightly
    sugared to make a juice,
    for serving (optional)*

1. Preheat the oven to 325°F. Have ready a 10-inch tube pan with a removable bottom. Do not grease it.

2. For the cake, sift the flour, 1½ cups of the sugar, the baking powder, and salt together into a large bowl.

3. In a small bowl, whisk the egg yolks, orange zest and juice, and oil together until blended.

4. Add the egg mixture to the dry ingredients and mix with an electric mixer on low speed until the batter is smooth, 1½ to 2 minutes, stopping the mixer once to scrape the bowl. Do not overmix.

5. Beat the egg whites in a medium-size bowl with an electric mixer on medium-high speed until frothy, about 30 seconds. Gradually add the remaining ½ cup sugar and continue beating until the whites form firm peaks, about 1 minute more. Stir one-third of the egg whites into the batter, then fold in the remaining whites with a rubber spatula.

6. Pour the batter into the tube pan and bake on the center oven rack until the top of the cake is golden and springs back to the touch, 1 hour.

7. Cool the cake upside down on a funnel or bottle (page 20).

8. Meanwhile prepare the glaze: Melt the butter in a small saucepan over low heat and transfer it to a small bowl.

9. Add the confectioner's sugar and water and whisk until blended. Add the lemon juice and whisk again. Pour the mixture through a strainer into a second small bowl.

10. When the cake has completely cooled, remove it from the pan and place it upside down on a cake plate. Pour half the glaze over the top of the cake so that it drips down the outside and down the inside of the hole. Allow this to set 30 minutes.

11. Whisk the remaining glaze in the bowl and pour it over the cake for a second coating. Eat the cake that day accompanied by strawberries, if desired.

Makes 12 to 14 servings

Tom's Birthday Roll

*M*y neighbor Tom can always be counted on to stop by and sample the results of whatever recipe I've been working on, so he's tasted my desserts in every stage from batter and scraps to *pièce de résistance*. I made this cake especially for his birthday, and it seems only appropriate that after all the leftovers he's consumed, he should get something special named for him. Made without flour, this moist chocolate cake is rolled into a log with a coffee whipped cream filling.

I N G R E D I E N T S

CAKE
4 ounces semisweet chocolate
2 ounces unsweetened chocolate
3 tablespoons strong brewed coffee
5 large eggs, separated, at room temperature
½ cup plus 2 tablespoons sugar

FILLING
5 teaspoons instant coffee powder
1 tablespoon water
1 tablespoon sugar
1 cup heavy (whipping) cream, chilled

2 tablespoons unsweetened cocoa powder for sprinkling
Fresh strawberries or raspberries for garnish

1. Preheat the oven to 350°F. Grease a jelly-roll pan (15 × 10 inches) with vegetable oil or butter, line it with waxed paper, and grease the paper.

2. For the cake, melt both chocolates with the coffee in the top of a double boiler placed over simmering water. Cool until tepid.

3. Beat the egg yolks with ½ cup sugar in a medium-size bowl with an electric mixer on medium speed until thick and yellow in color, 3 to 4 minutes. Add the chocolate mixture and blend thoroughly, for about 10 seconds, stopping the mixer to scrape the bowl with a rubber spatula.

4. In a deep mixing bowl beat the egg whites to soft peaks, about 30 seconds. Add the remaining 2 tablespoons sugar, and continue beating until the whites are stiff but not dry, about 30 seconds more. Carefully fold the egg whites into the chocolate mixture with a rubber spatula.

5. Pour the batter into the prepared pan and spread it evenly. Bake the cake on the center oven rack until the surface is spongy and the cake springs back to the touch, about 15 minutes. Remove the pan from the oven and cover it with a damp kitchen towel for 1 hour.

6. Ten minutes before the hour is up, prepare the filling: In a medium-size mixing bowl, dissolve the instant coffee in the water. Add the sugar and cream and beat with an electric mixer on medium speed until firm peaks form.

7. Sprinkle the cocoa over a sheet of waxed paper or a damp kitchen towel (not terrycloth) that is 4 inches longer than the cake.

8. Remove the towel from the cake pan. Run a thin knife around the edge of the cake to loosen it. Flip the pan upside down onto the waxed paper. Carefully peel off the waxed paper lining from the bottom of the cake.

9. Spread the whipped cream filling over the cake, leaving a ½-inch strip uncovered along the length of one long side.

10. Roll up the cake, starting from one long side toward the clean strip, using the waxed paper to help. There will be cracks in the cake, but they give the surface an interesting texture. Twist the ends of the waxed paper like a hard candy wrapper and refrigerate the cake a minimum of 3 hours.

11. When ready to serve, remove the cake from the refrigerator and unwrap it. Trim the edges if they appear irregular or unattractive. Place it on an oval or rectangular platter that has been covered with a white lace doily, and garnish with green leaves at the base and fresh strawberries or raspberries if desired.

Makes 12 to 16 servings

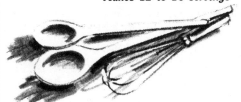

Chocolate Custard Sponge Roll

*T*his is a moist chocolate sponge cake rolled with custard and finished with whipped cream, which you can spread over its surface like icing or serve as a garnish with each slice.

INGREDIENTS

CAKE
3 tablespoons cake flour
2 tablespoons all-purpose flour
¼ cup unsweetened cocoa powder
¾ teaspoon baking soda
¼ teaspoon salt
4 large eggs, separated, at room temperature
½ cup plus 1 tablespoon (9 tablespoons) sugar
1 teaspoon instant espresso powder
1 teaspoon water

FILLING
2 tablespoons cornstarch
1 cup milk
2 ounces unsweetened chocolate, chopped
½ cup sugar
1 large egg yolk

TOPPING
1 recipe Whipped Cream (page 86)
1 ounce unsweetened chocolate for shaving or 12 fresh raspberries for garnish

1. Preheat the oven to 400°F. Line a jelly-roll pan (15 × 10 inches) with waxed paper that has been greased lightly with vegetable oil.

2. For the cake, sift both flours, the cocoa, baking soda, and salt together in a medium-size bowl.

3. Beat the egg yolks with ¼ cup sugar in a medium-size mixing bowl with an electric mixer on medium-high speed until light in color, 3 to 4 minutes.

4. Dissolve the espresso powder in the water and add it to the egg yolk mixture on medium speed. Beat until it is incorporated, 10 seconds.

5. Beat the egg whites in another mixing bowl on medium-high speed until frothy, about 30 seconds. Gradually add 3 tablespoons of the remaining sugar and continue beating to medium-firm peaks, about 1 minute more. Fold the whites gently into the yolks. *Do not overmix!*

6. Sift the dry ingredients (again) over the egg mixture and fold them in gently until the batter is uniform in color.

7. Pour the batter into the prepared pan and tip the pan gently back and forth so that the batter is evenly distributed. Bake the cake on the center oven rack until it springs back to the touch but has not formed a crust, about 12 minutes.

8. Allow the cake to cool for 10 min-utes, then sprinkle the remaining 2 tablespoons of sugar over a sheet of waxed paper or a damp kitchen towel that is 4 inches longer than the cake.

9. Run a thin knife around the edge of the cake to loosen it. Flip the pan upside down onto the waxed paper. Carefully peel off the waxed paper lining from the bottom of the cake.

10. Roll up the cake in the waxed paper, starting from one long side, using the waxed paper to help. The cake should never roll onto itself. Twist the ends of the waxed paper like a hard candy wrapper and refrigerate the cake a minimum of 3 hours.

11. Meanwhile prepare the filling: Dissolve the cornstarch in ¼ cup of the milk and set aside.

12. Heat the remaining milk with the chopped chocolate over medium-low heat in a small saucepan until the chocolate is completely melted, about 5 minutes. Stir the mixture vigorously with a whisk for the last few minutes to ensure that the mixture is uniform in color and all specks of chocolate are gone.

13. Vigorously whisk the sugar and the dissolved cornstarch into the chocolate, then whisk in the egg yolk.

14. Heat, stirring or whisking constantly, over low heat until the mixture begins to boil, 3 to 4 minutes. Remove it from the heat, stir it several times in the pan and pour it into a small bowl. Allow it to sit for 20 min-utes, stirring it gently several times to release steam. Then cover the surface directly with plastic wrap and refrigerate until it is cool.

15. When you're ready to fill the cake, remove it from the refrigerator and unroll it on a counter so that it is lying on the waxed paper in which it was rolled.

16. Spread the filling over the cake but leave a ½-inch strip along one side uncovered. Starting from the opposite side, roll up the cake, using the waxed paper to help. The roll should end up resting on its seam.

17. Rewrap the roll in the waxed paper and refrigerate it for several hours.

18. Just before serving, prepare the whipped cream. Unwrap the cake and place it on an oval or rectangular serving platter. Frost the cake with the cream and grate chocolate shavings over the top or use the whipped cream as a side garnish with fresh raspberries.

Makes 16 servings

Lemon-Strawberry Sponge Roll

I don't know any blues singers paying tribute to my sweet lemon jelly roll, but maybe that's because they haven't tasted this one yet. It's a springy roll, with tart lemon custard and strawberries substituted for the jelly inside. Then it's frosted with whipped cream. Try it in the spring or summer.

INGREDIENTS

CAKE
3 whole large eggs, at room temperature
3 large eggs, separated, at room temperature
15 tablespoons granulated sugar
2 teaspoons grated lemon zest
1½ teaspoons vanilla extract
2 tablespoons fresh lemon juice
¾ cup plus 3 tablespoons all-purpose flour
1 rounded tablespoon sifted confectioner's sugar for sprinkling

FILLING
4 large egg yolks
⅓ cup plus 1½ tablespoons sugar
¼ teaspoon unflavored gelatin powder
¼ cup plus 3 tablespoons fresh lemon juice
4 tablespoons (½ stick) unsalted butter, cut into small chunks
8 to 10 fresh strawberries, sliced ¼ inch thick

TOPPING
1 recipe Whipped Cream (page 86)
6 whole fresh strawberries

1. Preheat the oven to 350°F. Line a jelly-roll pan (15 × 10 inches) with waxed paper that has been greased lightly with butter or vegetable oil.

2. For the cake, mix the whole eggs and the 3 yolks in a medium-size mixing bowl with an electric mixer on medium-high speed until blended.

3. Add 11 tablespoons sugar and the lemon zest and beat the mixture on high speed until it is pale and thick, about 3½ minutes. (It may be necessary to hold a dish towel around the bowl to contain splatters until the mixture thickens.) Stop the mixer several times to scrape the bowl with a rubber spatula. Beat in the vanilla and the lemon juice.

4. Fold in the flour with a rubber spatula until it is incorporated.

5. Beat the egg whites in another mixing bowl with the mixer on medium-high speed until frothy, about 30 seconds. Gradually add the remaining 4 tablespoons sugar and continue beating just to soft peaks, about 30 seconds more. Fold the whites into the batter.

6. Pour the batter into the prepared pan and tip the pan gently back and forth so that the batter is evenly distributed. Bake the cake on the center oven rack until it is light golden and spongy and springs back to the touch, about 16 minutes.

7. Allow the cake to cool for 10 minutes. Sprinkle the confectioner's sugar over a sheet of waxed paper or a damp kitchen towel (not terrycloth) that is 4 inches longer than the cake.

8. Run a thin knife around the edge of the cake to loosen it. Flip the pan upside down onto the waxed paper.

Carefully peel off the waxed paper lining from the bottom of the cake.

9. Roll up the cake in the waxed paper, starting from one long side, using the waxed paper to help. The cake should never roll onto itself. Twist the ends of the paper like a hard candy wrapper and refrigerate the cake a minimum of 3 hours.

10. Meanwhile prepare the filling: In a small saucepan mix the egg yolks and the sugar with a whisk until they are blended. Warm the lemon juice slightly in another small saucepan. Add the gelatin to the lemon juice and stir to blend.

11. Add the gelatin mixture to the egg yolk mixture and cook over medium heat, stirring constantly with a wooden spoon, until the mixture thickens, about 3 minutes. When you run your finger across the wooden spoon, it should leave a path in the mixture.

12. Remove the lemon curd from the stove and strain into a small bowl. Add the butter, and stir until blended.

13. Allow the lemon curd to cool for 20 minutes, stirring occasionally. Puncture a piece of plastic wrap in several places, and use it to cover the surface of the filling. Allow the filling to set at room temperature until it is of spreading consistency, 30 to 40 minutes.

14. When the filling is set, remove the cake roll from the refrigerator and unroll it.

15. Spread the filling evenly over the cake but leave a 1-inch strip along one long side uncovered. Distribute the sliced strawberries evenly over the filling. Roll the cake toward the clean strip, peeling the waxed paper off as you roll. Put the roll in a fresh piece of waxed paper or plastic wrap and refrigerate it for several hours.

16. Just before serving, transfer the cake to a long serving tray and frost it with the whipped cream. Place the whole strawberries, points up, on top of the log. For a special look, arrange ferns around the base of the log.

Makes 16 servings

Lemon Pudding Cake

A layer of light lemon cake sitting atop a layer of tart lemon pudding, this dessert is wonderful served warm right out of the oven or at room temperature. But it is just as delicious cold on day two when its texture has become like that of a cheesecake.

I N G R E D I E N T S

½ cup plus 4 tablespoons sugar
¼ cup all-purpose flour
⅛ teaspoon salt
3 tablespoons melted unsalted butter
1 tablespoon plus 2 teaspoons grated lemon zest
6 tablespoons fresh lemon juice
3 large eggs, separated, at room temperature
1½ cups heavy (whipping) cream, at room temperature

1. Preheat the oven to 350°F. Have ready an 8-inch square baking pan and a larger baking pan in which the smaller pan fits comfortably.

2. Whisk ½ cup plus 1 tablespoon of the sugar, the flour, and salt together in a medium-size mixing bowl. Add the butter and lemon zest and juice to the flour mixture.

3. In a small bowl, whisk the egg yolks and cream until blended.

4. Add the yolk mixture to the flour mixture and blend with an electric mixer on medium-low speed until the batter is velvety, about 15 seconds. Set aside.

5. Whisk the egg whites at medium-high speed in a medium-size mixing bowl until frothy, about 30 seconds. Gradually add the remaining 3 tablespoons sugar and continue beating the egg whites to firm peaks, 45 seconds more. Gently fold them into the flour mixture.

6. Pour the batter into an 8-inch

square baking pan. Place the pan in the larger baking pan. Pour water into the larger pan to come about halfway up the sides of the smaller pan. Place on a rack in the center of the oven.

7. Bake the cake until the top is golden and springs back to the touch, 35 to 40 minutes. Spoon it immediately onto individual dessert plates or allow to cool to room temperature before serving.

Makes 9 servings

Lemon Icebox Cake with Fresh Strawberries

*Y*ou've invited people over for dinner on what turns out to be the hottest day of the year, and you avoid turning on your oven by barbecuing. Great, now what do you do about dessert?

You make this cake: light from the egg whites and whipped cream, tart from the lemon, and fresh out of the fridge with no baking involved. It's good after a heavy meal on a cooler day, too, when you want a strong flavor but not a lot of heft in your dessert.

INGREDIENTS

CAKE
About 30 (when split) ladyfingers
2 envelopes unflavored gelatin powder
3/4 cup plus 5 tablespoons fresh lemon juice (5 to 6 lemons)
3/4 cup water
4 large eggs, separated, at room temperature
1 cup sugar
1 1/4 cups heavy (whipping) cream, chilled

TOPPING
1 quart fresh strawberries, hulled and sliced
1/4 to 1/3 cup sugar

1. Line the bottom and sides of a 9-inch springform pan with the ladyfingers.

2. Combine the gelatin and 5 tablespoons lemon juice in a small bowl and let it soften, 1 to 2 minutes.

3. Bring the water to a boil and add it along with the remaining 3/4 cup lemon juice to the gelatin mixture.

4. Beat the egg yolks and 3/4 cup of the sugar in a medium-size mixing bowl with an electric mixer on medium speed until thick and light, about 3 minutes. Blend the gelatin mixture into the egg mixture on low speed.

5. Place the bowl of gelatin mixture in a larger bowl that is filled one-quarter full with cold water and a couple of ice cubes. Stir the mixture intermittently until it resembles a thick syrup, about 10 minutes. (It is important to keep a close eye on this. If the mixture stays in the ice water too long it will get lumpy.)

6. While the gelatin mixture is thickening, beat the cream in another mixing bowl with an electric mixer on medium speed to soft peaks and set aside (see Note).

7. Beat the whites in another mixing bowl with an electric mixer on medium-high speed until frothy, about 30 seconds. Gradually add the remaining ¼ cup sugar and continue beating the whites to soft peaks, about 30 seconds more.

8. Remove the bowl with the gelatin mixture from the ice water. Fold the cream, then the whites, into the lemon mixture with a rubber spatula.

9. Pour the mixture into the springform pan lined with the ladyfingers. Place the pan in the refrigerator to set overnight.

10. For the topping, toss the strawberries with the sugar several hours before serving the cake and set aside.

11. To remove the cake from the pan, run a frosting spatula between the sides of the pan and the cake, then release the sides.

12. To serve, top each slice with a generous helping of the strawberries.

Makes 12 to 14 servings

Note: This recipe requires several mixing bowls. If you do not have enough, transfer the whipped cream to a small bowl, thoroughly wash and dry the mixing bowl, and use it for the egg whites.

Traditional Cheesecake à la Reuben's

*W*hen I was a kid in New York City, a Sunday treat was lunch at Reuben's: a to-die-for corned beef sandwich topped off with a fat slice of cheesecake. Their cake was so creamy, it stuck to the roof of my mouth until I washed it down with several gulps of milk. Frankly, I think Reuben's broke the mold when they created their cheesecake, but I've tried with this recipe to recreate both the cheesecake and my childhood memory. (You're on your own with the milk.)

INGREDIENTS

CRUST

1¼ cups vanilla wafer crumbs

1 tablespoon sugar

6 tablespoons (¾ stick) unsalted
   butter, melted

½ cup ground almonds, walnuts, or
   pecans (optional)

CAKE

3 pounds cream cheese, at room
   temperature or warmed slightly in
   the microwave

1½ cups sugar

2 teaspoons vanilla extract

3 whole large eggs, at room
   temperature

2 large egg yolks, at room temperature

1 tablespoons fresh lemon juice

1. Preheat the oven to 375°F.

2. For the crust, place the cookie crumbs, sugar, melted butter, and nuts, if using, in a small bowl and toss them lightly with a fork until they are well blended.

3. Press this mixture firmly over the bottom of a 10-inch springform pan. Bake it on the bottom oven rack until crisp and golden, about 15 minutes. Remove it from the oven and cool.

4. Reduce the oven heat to 300°F and place a roasting pan or baking dish filled with hot water on the bottom rack of the oven to create moisture.

5. Meanwhile prepare the cake filling: Beat the cream cheese, sugar, and vanilla in a medium-size mixing bowl with an electric mixer on medium speed until light and fluffy, 30 to 60 seconds, depending on the temperature of the cream cheese. Scrape the bowl with a rubber spatula, then beat 45 seconds more.

6. Lightly whisk the whole eggs and egg yolks together and add them to the cream cheese mixture with the lemon juice. Mix on low speed until they are incorporated and the batter is velvety, about 30 seconds. Scrape the bowl with a spatula, then mix at medium-high speed for 10 seconds more.

7. Pour the filling over the crust. Bake the cake on the center oven rack until it appears golden, set, and a tester inserted in the center comes out dry, about 1¼ hours.

8. Cool the cake in the pan on a wire rack. When it is cool, refrigerate it overnight in the pan and serve it the next day.

Makes 12 to 16 servings

Pumpkin Cheesecake

I was weaned on Reuben's cheesecake, and, as a result, I remained an uncompromising purist when it came to variations on the theme. Let them keep their Kahlua, Amaretto, Grand Marnier variations, I scoffed; real cheesecake is dense and creamy and unadulterated. Then in 1985 I tasted Pam Ososky's (a former Rosie's baker) pumpkin cheesecake and relented. I bid farewell to pumpkin pie at Thanksgiving and replaced it with this rich and flavorful concoction, which I top with sour cream and pecans. I serve it on a large round cake plate or platter lined with a white paper lace doily, garnished with bits of holly or evergreen and topped with whole cranberries for a festive holiday look.

I N G R E D I E N T S

CRUST
2 cups gingersnap crumbs
   (35 Nabisco gingersnaps)
3 tablespoons sugar
6 tablespoons (¾ stick) unsalted
   butter, melted
¼ cup pecans, finely chopped

CAKE
1½ cups canned pumpkin purée
1 tablespoon plus 1½ teaspoons
   ground cinnamon
1 tablespoon ground ginger
2½ teaspoons ground cloves
2½ teaspoons ground nutmeg
1 teaspoon ground allspice
2½ pounds cream cheese, at room
   temperature
1⅓ cups sugar
1 teaspoon vanilla extract
5 whole large eggs, at room
   temperature
2 large egg yolks, at room temperature

TOPPING
1 cup sour cream, at room temperature
3 tablespoons sugar
¼ cup pecans, finely chopped
14 pecan halves

1. Preheat the oven to 375°F.

2. For the crust, place the gingersnap crumbs, sugar, butter, and nuts in a small bowl and toss lightly with a fork until well blended.

3. Press this mixture firmly over the bottom of a 10-inch springform pan. Bake it on the bottom oven rack until golden, 5 to 7 minutes. Remove it from the oven and cool.

4. Reduce the oven heat to 300°F and place a roasting pan or baking dish filled with hot water on the bottom rack of the oven to create moisture.

5. For the cake filling, lightly whisk together the pumpkin and spices in a small bowl until blended. Set aside.

6. Beat the cream cheese, sugar, and vanilla in a medium-size mixing bowl with an electric mixer on medium speed until light and fluffy, about 30 seconds. Scrape the bowl with a rubber spatula, then beat 30 seconds more.

7. Add the whole eggs, then the egg yolks, one at a time to the cream cheese on low speed. Blend each egg until incorporated, about 30 seconds. Scrape the bowl after each addition.

8. Add the pumpkin mixture to the

cream cheese batter and blend on medium speed until the mixture is velvety, about 1 minute. Scrape the bowl and beat another minute.

9. Pour the filling over the crust. Bake the cake on the center oven rack until the top is set and a tester inserted in the center comes out dry, about 1 hour 40 minutes. Turn off the oven and leave the cake in the oven for an additional hour. Remove the cake from the oven, place it carefully on a wire rack, and let cool for several hours.

10. While the cheesecake is cooling, prepare the topping: Mix the sour cream and sugar together in a small bowl.

11. Preheat the oven to 350°F.

12. Spread the sour cream mixture evenly over the surface of the cake with a spatula and sprinkle the chopped pecans on top. Evenly space the pecan halves around the top edge of the cake.

13. Bake the cheesecake in the oven for 5 to 7 minutes to set the topping. Remove the cheesecake from the oven and refrigerate before serving.

Makes 14 to 16 servings

Brownie Cheesecake

*I*ntroduced to me by my neighbor Susan, this brownie cheesecake is a direct translation of dark, fudgy brownies into cheesecake—how's that for truth in advertising? I like this cake in a vanilla crust, but it's also good with a chocolate cookie crust or a graham cracker crust.

INGREDIENTS

CRUST
1¼ cups vanilla wafer crumbs
    (about 30 cookies)
1 tablespoon sugar
6 tablespoons (¾ stick) unsalted
    butter, melted
½ cup chopped walnuts or pecans

CAKE
12 ounces semisweet chocolate chips
½ cup hot very strong brewed coffee
1 pound cream cheese, at room
    temperature
1 cup sugar
2 teaspoons vanilla extract
¼ teaspoon salt
4 large eggs, at room temperature

1. Preheat the oven to 350°F.

2. For the crust, place the wafer crumbs, sugar, butter, and nuts in a small bowl and toss them together with a fork. Press this mixture over the bottom of a 9-inch springform pan and bake for 10 minutes. Remove it from the oven and cool.

3. Reduce the oven heat to 300°F and place a roasting pan or baking dish filled with hot water on the bottom rack of the oven to create moisture.

4. For the cake filling, melt the chocolate in the coffee in the top of a double boiler placed over simmering water.

5. Cream the cream cheese, sugar, vanilla, and salt in a medium-size mixing bowl with an electric mixer on medium speed until light and fluffy, about 2 minutes. Stop the mixer once or twice to scrape the bowl with a rubber spatula.

6. Add the eggs and beat the mixture on medium-high speed for 30 seconds. Scrape the bowl and beat on medium speed 30 seconds longer.

7. Add the chocolate mixture to the egg mixture and beat on medium speed for 15 seconds. Scrape the bowl and then mix until the batter is smooth and uniform in color, about 10 more seconds.

8. Pour the filling over the crust. Bake the cake on the center oven rack until it is set and a tester inserted in the center comes out clean, about 1 hour 25 minutes.

9. Allow the cake to cool completely on a wire rack, then refrigerate the cake overnight.

Makes 12 to 16 servings

Caramel-Topped Pecan Cheesecake

*Y*ou might call this the southern cousin of traditional New York cheesecake, its creaminess interrupted by a generous helping of nuts.

INGREDIENTS

CRUST
1¼ cups graham cracker crumbs
6 tablespoons (¾ stick) unsalted
    butter, melted
3 tablespoons granulated sugar

CAKE
1½ pounds cream cheese, at room
    temperature
1¼ cups (lightly packed) light brown
    sugar
3 large eggs, at room temperature
1½ teaspoons vanilla extract
2 tablespoons all-purpose flour
1 cup chopped pecans

TOPPING
½ cup (lightly packed) light brown
    sugar
¼ cup heavy (whipping) cream
¾ teaspoon unsalted butter, melted

1. Preheat the oven to 375°F.

2. For the crust, place the cracker

crumbs, butter, and sugar in a small bowl and toss them together with a fork. Press this mixture over the bottom of a 9-inch springform pan. Bake the crust until it is crisp and golden in color, about 10 minutes. Let cool.

3. Reduce the oven heat to 300°F. Place a roasting pan or baking dish filled with hot water on the bottom rack of the oven to create moisture.

4. For the cake filling, cream the cream cheese in a medium-size mixing bowl with an electric mixer on medium speed for 1 minute. Scrape the bowl with a rubber spatula.

5. Add the brown sugar and beat on medium-high speed until the cream cheese is fluffy, about 1 minute. Scrape the bowl.

6. Add the eggs and the vanilla and beat the mixture on medium-low speed until smooth, about 45 seconds. Scrape the bowl.

7. Add the flour and mix on low speed for 5 seconds. Add the pecans and mix to blend, 15 to 20 seconds.

8. Pour the filling over the crust. Bake the cake on the center oven rack until the top is set and a tester inserted in the center comes out dry, about 1¾ hours.

9. Remove the cake from the oven, allow it to cool on a wire rack for 1½ hours, then refrigerate it overnight.

10. Two hours before serving the cake, prepare the topping: Place the brown sugar, cream, and butter in a small saucepan over medium heat and stir until the sugar is dissolved. Bring the mixture to a boil and continue to boil for 1½ minutes, stirring occasionally. The mixture will look like a thick golden syrup.

11. Remove the pan from the heat and pour the topping into a small bowl to stop the cooking process. When it stops bubbling, pour it over the cheesecake. Tip the springform pan from side to side so that the topping coats the cake evenly. Keep the cake at room temperature until ready to serve.

Makes 12 to 16 servings

Fudge Frosting

*I*f Rosie's house is built on chocolate, this frosting is the foundation—or is it the roof? Whatever the metaphor, it's the perfect frosting: dark and glossy and it looks as good as it tastes on any layer cake or brownie.

INGREDIENTS

4 ounces unsweetened chocolate
¾ cup evaporated milk
1 cup sugar

1. Melt the chocolate in the top of a double boiler placed over simmering water. Cool slightly.

2. Blend the evaporated milk and sugar in a blender on medium speed for 2 seconds.

3. Add the chocolate to the sugar mixture in the blender and blend on high speed until the frosting is thick and shiny, 1 to 1½ minutes. The mixer's sound will change when the frosting has thickened.

4. Spoon the frosting into a bowl and allow it to set at room temperature for 30 minutes. Then cover the bowl with plastic wrap and allow the frosting to set for 1 hour more before frosting. Do not refrigerate the frosting, even if you don't plan to use it for several days.

Makes 1¾ cups, enough to fill and frost a two-layer cake

Note: This recipe can only be made in a blender.

Marshmallow Frosting

*T*his is a frosting that takes me right back to childhood and that much coveted jar of Marshmallow Fluff! Use the back of a spoon to form little peaks in the frosting once it is on the cake. Note: This recipe can be easily doubled to frost a two-layer cake.

**2 large egg whites, at room
temperature**
¼ cup plus 2 tablespoons sugar
3 tablespoons light corn syrup
½ teaspoon vanilla extract

1. Put the egg whites, sugar, and
corn syrup in the top of a double
boiler placed over rapidly boiling water
and beat with a hand-held mixer (electric or rotary) until soft peaks form,
about 4 minutes.

2. Transfer the mixture to a
medium-size mixing bowl. Add the
vanilla and beat with an electric mixer
(whisk attachment, if possible) on
medium-high speed until soft peaks
form, about 30 seconds. Use immediately.

*Makes 1²/₃ cups, enough to frost
an 11 × 7-inch sheet cake*

German Chocolate Topping

My friends Susan and Stanley were visiting from
Seattle when I was working on
this topping, and they were so
enamored of it that they insisted
that it accompany every dessert I
served them. An extreme reaction,
perhaps, but not wholly improba-
ble. This topping is creamy,
strong on butterscotch, and full
of coconut and pecans. In addition to keeping Susan and Stanley
happy, I use it to frost Rosie's
Famous Chocolate Sour-Cream
Layer Cake and Chocolate Buttermilk Cake (see Index).

**1 tablespoon plus 1 teaspoon
cornstarch**
1 cup evaporated milk
½ cup granulated sugar
**½ cup (lightly packed) light
brown sugar**
**6 large egg yolks,
at room temperature**
**4 tablespoons (½ stick)
unsalted butter**
⅛ teaspoon salt
¾ teaspoon vanilla extract
⅓ cup chopped walnuts
1 cup shredded coconut

1. Dissolve the cornstarch in the
milk.

2. Place the cornstarch mixture, both
sugars, the egg yolks, butter, and salt
in a medium-size saucepan over
medium-low heat. Cook, stirring constantly, until the mixture thickens and
just starts to bubble, about 7 minutes.

3. Transfer the mixture to a blender
and blend on medium-low speed for 7
seconds. Scrape the sides of the blender with a rubber spatula and blend
several more seconds.

4. Transfer the mixture to a medium-size bowl and stir in the vanilla. Put a piece of plastic wrap directly over the surface and allow it to cool to room temperature or refrigerate it. When the mixture is cool, stir in the nuts and coconut.

Makes about 2 cups, enough to fill and frost a two-layer cake (not including the sides)

Cream Cheese Frosting

A fluffy white frosting that's sweet yet slightly tart.

INGREDIENTS

10 ounces cream cheese, at room temperature
3/4 cup confectioner's sugar
2 tablespoons unsalted butter, at room temperature
1/4 cup plus 1 tablespoon heavy (whipping) cream, at room temperature

1. Cream the cream cheese, sugar, and butter in a medium-size mixing bowl with an electric mixer on medium speed until light and fluffy, 3 to 4 minutes. Scrape the bottom and side of the bowl with a rubber spatula.

2. With the mixer on low speed, add the cream in a stream and mix until it is incorporated. Scrape the bowl.

3. Increase the speed to medium-high and beat the frosting until it is light and fluffy, 5 to 10 minutes. Stop to scrape the bowl several times with a rubber spatula. Keep the frosting at room temperature until you are ready to frost the cake, a maximum of 1 hour.

Makes 2 cups, enough to fill and frost a two- or four-layer cake

Rosie's Buttercream

A fluffy white frosting not overly sugary, this recipe is one you'll use often. It lasts for several days out of the refrigerator, but will require rewhipping after it sits for a while to restore its fluffy texture.

8 tablespoons (1 stick) unsalted butter, at room temperature
1¼ cups confectioner's sugar
¾ cup plus 2 tablespoons heavy (whipping) cream, chilled

1. Place all the ingredients in a food processor and process until light and fluffy, about 5 minutes. Stop the machine several times to scrape down the sides of the bowl with a rubber spatula.

2. Transfer the buttercream to a medium-size mixing bowl and, using the paddle attachment of an electric mixer, continue to beat on medium-high speed, until the buttercream is white and fluffy, 15 to 20 minutes. Stop the mixer to scrape the bowl several times with a rubber spatula. (If you do not have a paddle attachment, you can use the whisk.) Use the buttercream for frosting within an hour or it will need rewhipping.

Makes 2 to 2¼ cups, enough to fill and frost a two- or four-layer cake

Mocha Buttercream

*F*lavored lightly with coffee, this variation on Rosie's Buttercream has a lovely café au lait color.

¼ cup instant coffee powder
4½ teaspoons water
8 tablespoons (1 stick) unsalted butter, at room temperature
1¼ cups confectioner's sugar
¾ cup plus 2 tablespoons heavy (whipping) cream, chilled

Dissolve the coffee in the water and place all the ingredients in a food processor. Proceed as directed for Rosie's Buttercream (recipe precedes).

Makes 2 to 2¼ cups, enough to fill and frost a two- or four-layer cake.

Whipped Cream

*W*hipped cream may be rich, but it's not too sweet and is the perfect accent to so many desserts. Be sure not to overwhip the cream, you want it to have a fluffy texture.

1 cup heavy (or whipping) cream, chilled
1 to 2 tablespoons granulated or confectioner's sugar

Using the whisk attachment (if possible) of an electric mixer, beat the cream and the sugar on high speed until soft peaks (1 minute) or firm peaks (1 minute 15 seconds) are formed. This will vary depending on the recipe.

Makes just over 2 cups

Hot Fudge Filling

*7*radition has it that the hot fudge sundae was invented in Boston at Bailey's, which puts this recipe in honored company. It's a wonderful bittersweet filling for layer cakes, be they chocolate or golden, and it's great ladled warm over ice cream.

INGREDIENTS

2 ounces unsweetened chocolate
2 tablespoons unsalted butter
5 tablespoons plus 1½ teaspoons sugar
6 tablespoons hot water
½ teaspoon vanilla extract

1. Place all the ingredients except the vanilla in the top of a double boiler placed over simmering water and cook uncovered, stirring occasionally, until the chocolate is melted and the sugar

is dissolved, 30 minutes. The mixture will be smooth and velvety.

2. Pour the fudge into a small bowl, stir in the vanilla, and refrigerate until the mixture is thick and of spreading consistency, 2 hours.

Makes ¾ cup, enough to fill a four-layer cake

Vanilla Custard Filling

A thick, creamy filling for layer cakes and tarts, this is also delicious spooned over a bowl of fresh berries.

INGREDIENTS

10 tablespoons milk
¾ cup heavy (whipping) cream
6 tablespoons sugar
2 tablespoons cornstarch
1 large egg yolk
1 teaspoon vanilla extract

1. Scald 4 tablespoons of the milk, the cream, and the sugar in a medium-size saucepan over medium-low heat.

2. Dissolve the cornstarch in the remaining 6 tablespoons milk.

3. Add the egg yolk to the cornstarch mixture and stir it rapidly with a fork or whisk. Add this mixture to the scalded cream mixture and whisk over medium-low heat constantly until it thickens, 1½ to 2 minutes, and then for 30 seconds more.

4. Remove the custard from the heat, stir in the vanilla, and pour it into a ceramic or plastic bowl. Allow it to cool for 10 minutes, stirring it gently several times.

5. Put a piece of plastic wrap that has been punctured several times directly over the surface of the custard and refrigerate until completely chilled or overnight.

Makes 1¼ cups, enough to fill
a four-layer cake

Lemon Custard Filling

I put this thick custard filling between layers of cakes because I like the way its tartness contrasts with a sweet buttercream frosting.

INGREDIENTS

3 tablespoons cornstarch
1 cup water
2 large eggs
11 tablespoons sugar
⅛ teaspoon salt
5 tablespoons fresh lemon juice

1. Dissolve the cornstarch in ½ cup of the water in a small bowl. Add the eggs and whisk until blended.

2. Heat the remaining water, the sugar, and the salt in a medium-size saucepan over medium-low heat until the sugar dissolves and the mixture is hot, about 2 minutes.

3. Add the cornstarch mixture to the hot liquid, whisking constantly. Add the lemon juice and continue to cook, whisking constantly, until the mixture thickens, 3 to 4 minutes, and then for 30 seconds longer.

4. Pour the custard into a small bowl. Allow it to cool for 10 minutes, stirring it gently several times.

5. Put a piece of plastic wrap that has been punctured several times directly over the surface of the custard and refrigerate for at least 6 hours.

Makes about 1½ cups, enough to fill
a four-layer cake

CHAPTER THREE

Smart Cookies

Cookies may be a Dutch invention, but to me, they are quintessentially American. Even the word calls up memories of a steamy kitchen on a wet November afternoon with a treat fresh out of the oven and a glass of milk standing by. Never mind if your November afternoons weren't like that. The image is a part of the collective nostalgia, and cookies remain a way of reliving the wonderful innocence of eating till you think you're about to burst.

When I was a kid, cookies mostly came in packages from Keeblers or Nabisco; they were all the same size and shape and, not knowing any better, we took their uniformity for a sign of quality. One of my favorite tricks was to stroll down the aisle of the grocery store looking for open packages of cookies to sample. I was never bold enough to open one myself, but if there were cookies just sitting there waiting to be thrown away, far be it from me to let them go to waste. I told myself it was a way to deepen my expertise.

All these years later, I can still conjure up the taste of the cookies I liked best just by reciting their names: Lorna Doones, Social Teas, Vienna Fingers, Pecan Sandies, and Nutter Butters. But my favorites were Oreos because I could be magnanimous and let someone else have the white icing while I hoarded the chocolate wafers for myself.

Still, the cookies that were worth making a fuss over were those baked fresh, and my fondest cookie memories come from William Greenberg's in New York City where Mr. Greenberg made sure you got a free cookie whenever you bought something at one of his shops. I still remember the thrill of complicity when he leaned over the counter to hand one down to me. Maple cookies rolled in sugar, linzer cookies — two big, spicy cookies sandwiched together with jam and covered with confectioner's sugar — elegantly thin and crisp chocolate cookies. Just thinking about them makes me want to catch the next plane to New York.

Then came the day the cookie world finally caught up with my craving when chains such as David's and Mrs. Fields arrived to usher in our current cookie craze. As with any commodity that's hot, the quality of these designer cookies varies, and some aren't worth crossing the aisle of a shopping mall for. But even the crummy ones haven't stopped

Americans from devouring cookies in overwhelming abundance over the past decade.

It probably has something to do with how portable they are and the pleasure of noshing on the run. Whatever, cookies are our first treats and often our first word, and they remain among the easiest pastries to make so that the desire for a cookie is never too far from the satisfaction.

Cookies in General

*T*he cookie recipes in this book fall into six categories; each type has different characteristics, so each has its own requirements. But cookies are democratic creatures, and on some levels, they're all created equal. Hence, before we specialize, here are a few general principles.

Preparing Cookie Sheets: Baking parchment is a wonderful invention that saves you the time and bother of greasing your cookie sheets. On top of that—or on bottom, to be accurate—lining the sheets with this paper protects the bottoms of the cookies from overcooking. If you don't have parchment, grease your cookie sheets lightly with butter or oil. Very buttery cookies like shortbread are the exception;

their pans don't need any greasing.

When you drop or place your dough on the cookie sheets, rest the sheets on a counter or table, not on a hot stove. If the dough melts before it goes into the oven, it can affect the baking time.

Oven Temperatures: Although the oven temperature varies from cookie to cookie, a few simple measures apply in most cases. First, it's always a good idea to have your oven preheating for at least 15 minutes before you put your cookies in.

Second, if you have any question about your oven's dependability, test its temperature against the one recommended in the recipe by baking a couple of cookies for the time called for before you do the whole batch. If the suggested temperature is off, you can adjust it for the remainder before it's too late.

Third, baking time will vary depending on the size of the cookies, large cookies obviously taking more time than small ones. If you choose to make your cookies a different size from the one suggested in the recipe, remember to adjust the baking time accordingly.

Finally, I never bake more than one cookie sheet at a time because the center rack of the oven is the only place that bakes evenly in a domestic oven. It takes longer, but it's worth it.

Handling the Dough: Generally, cookie doughs are hardier than batters for cakes or pastries, so, in most cases, mixing them requires much less caution. The less moisture a dough has, the longer you can beat it without having to worry about your cookies coming out tough or dry, especially when the recipe doesn't use eggs. Rosie's Butter Cookies and Chocolate-Dipped Pecan Logs, for example, can be beaten for a long time.

Classic cookies like chocolate chip or oatmeal, which contain eggs and a bit more liquid, need more delicate beating. But the cookies that require the greatest caution are cakelike cookies because they use a substantial amount of liquid and come out tough and rubbery, just like cake, if they're beaten too long.

Storing Cookies: All cookies should be stored in airtight containers. If you plan to eat them within two days, you can leave them at room temperature. Otherwise, they should be refrigerated.

To keep chewy cookies moist, I have a great trick. I place the cookies in the container, spreading parchment or waxed paper between the layers. Then I moisten a sponge or crumpled-up paper towel and place it on a piece of plastic wrap in the container with the cookies, but not lying directly on them, and snap on the lid.

When you want to restore the crunch in crisp cookies that have gone soggy, place them in a 275°F oven for 10 to 15 minutes. This works especially well for shortbread cookies.

Freezing works very well with all cookies, but frozen cookies need to be kept at room temperature for several hours before eating to allow their flavor to come out. If you don't have that much time, pop them into a 200°F oven until they're warm or microwave them lightly.

Cookie Types

*B*eyond these generalizations, it's every cookie for itself, so I suggest that you find the category that applies to the recipe you're making and read it through before you begin.

Traditional Drop Cookies

Drop cookies form the bedrock of cookiedom: chocolate chip, oatmeal, peanut butter, gingersnaps. You make them by dropping dollops of dough (usually made from the standard butter, sugar, egg, leavening, flour mixture) onto the cookie sheet. They're easy and quick to whip up. Texture can vary from thin and crispy like the Oatmeal Lace Cookies to thick and chewy in the center like the Chocolate Chips.

Oven Temperature: A cookie that's chewy at the center and slightly crunchy around the edges requires an oven temperature of between 350° and 375°F, with the exception of meringues, which bake at a lower heat. I find that in some cases it's best to chill the dough before baking so the cookie flattens out less and stays thick and chewy at its center. Crisp cookies like Oatmeal Lace and Crispy Orange Oatmeal Wafers bake faster with a higher oven temperature of 400°F.

Pan Preparation: Line cookie sheets with baking parchment or grease them lightly with butter or oil.

Shaping: Scoop a heaping teaspoon or tablespoon or a level ice cream scoop of dough from the bowl. Drop the spoonful of dough onto the cookie sheet, using your index finger or another spoon to loosen it. The cookies should be 1½ to 2 inches apart, depending on the size of the spoonful.

I prefer most drop cookies to be large so they can have that combination of crunchy outside and chewy middle (small cookies bake quicker and more uniformly). It also makes it easier to fool yourself into thinking that you're eating less by having only one. But if you prefer these classic cookies to be crisp through and through, flatten the dough with the palm of your hand after you've dropped it onto the cookie sheet. If you do this, remember to space the cookies farther apart on the cookie sheet. Bake the cookies at 350°F until the centers drop and the tops are uniform in color.

Testing for Doneness: The edges of these cookies will be the first to bake and change color, followed by the center, which will puff up but remain lighter colored. If you like a chewy center, remove the cookies from the oven at this point. If the cookies bake longer, their centers will drop in the oven and darken like the edges and the cookie will be crunchy throughout.

Cooling: Cooling these cookies on the sheet contributes to a crisp bottom, but they cool well on a rack too.

Eating: As soon as they're cool enough to put in your mouth, pour yourself a glass of milk and indulge. They're equally good later that day or the next, but are best eaten within two days of baking.

Storing: When they are completely cooled, store these cookies in a plastic container or an airtight plastic bag. You can freeze or refrigerate them but bring them to room temperature again before eating, maybe popping them in the toaster oven or regular oven to give them a just-baked aura. The batter can be stored for 4 to 5 days in the refrigerator or it can be frozen.

Cakelike Drop Cookies

These cookies, such as Lemon Cake Cookies and Butter-Glazed Nutmeg Mounds are appropriately named because they have the airier texture of cakes.

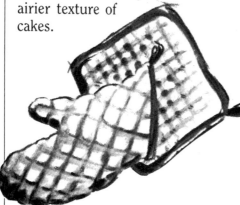

Oven Temperature: The oven is usually set high, around 375° to 400°F, so that the cookie rises. Bake the batter right after mixing so that the cookie achieves the right texture.

Pan Preparation: These cookies bake best on parchment, which protects them just enough from the heat of the pan and keeps them from getting crusty. Air-

cushion pans work beautifully too because they never get as hot, so the cookie doesn't develop a crust on the bottom.

Shaping: This thick, wet batter drops easily in generously rounded tablespoons onto a cookie sheet. Leave 2 inches between cookies.

Testing for Doneness: Remove the cookies from the oven when they are firm and spring back to your touch like a cake or when a cake tester inserted in the center comes out dry. Make sure that they don't cook long enough to form a hard crust.

Cooling: If these cookies sit on a hot surface after they're baked, their bottoms will continue cooking, so I remove them from the baking sheet immediately with a pancake spatula and place them on a cooling rack.

Eating and Storing: Cakelike cookies taste delicious the first day but can also be stored in an airtight plastic container overnight. Place a piece of parchment or waxed paper between layers of cookies, and if they are glazed, be sure that the glaze has hardened completely before you stack them. On the second day, the cookies will be more moist and, to my way of thinking, even better. This batter cannot be stored, though, because its leavening will get overactive in the moisture.

Log Cookies

Log cookies, such as Pecan Crunchies and Butterscotch-Cinnamon Icebox Cookies, are made of a stiff dough that is rolled, chilled, sliced, and then baked. They hold their shape well during baking and come out of the oven nice and crunchy.

Oven Temperature: Log cookies usually call for a low temperature (between 275° and 325°F) so the cookies bake evenly and get crisp.

Pan Preparation: Line cookie sheets with baking parchment or grease them lightly with butter or oil.

Shaping: When the dough is mixed, form it into logs about 2 inches in diameter. (You may want to dip your hands in flour before molding so that the dough doesn't stick to them.) Place a log near the edge of a piece of waxed paper that has been cut slightly longer than the log. Roll the log inside the waxed paper and twist the paper ends like a hard candy wrapper.

Chill the log for 2 hours, then while it is still in its waxed paper wrapping, roll it gently back and forth on a counter with the palms and fingers of your hands until it forms a smooth cylinder. Return the log to the fridge for several hours more. Finally, cut the log into slices ¼ to ⅜ inch thick and place them about 1½ inches apart on a cookie sheet.

Testing for Doneness: Log cookies are done when they are lightly golden and crisp to the touch. Because they need to bake throughout, I take one from the oven and break it in two to make sure that it's done. A doughy strip in the cookie's middle means that it needs to bake longer.

Cooling: These cookies can cool on the sheet or a cooling rack since they are sturdy and can be transferred easily.

Eating: Let the cookies cool completely before you eat them or, better yet, wait until the next day. They can taste a little doughy when they're warm, but that disappears soon.

Storing: Log cookies stored in an airtight plastic container remain fresh and can be stacked on each other if they're not frosted or adorned with jam. If they get soggy, simply put them in a pre-heated 275°F oven for 10 minutes to restore their crispness. These cookies freeze well too but taste best at room temperature. The unbaked logs can be stored for 4 to 5 days in your refrigerator, or they can be frozen for up to several weeks.

Shortbread Cookies

This category includes cookies such as Chocolate-Dipped Pecan Logs, Very Short Shortbread, and Noah Bedoahs. Their doughs contain no liquid, so they can be beaten without worry.

Oven Temperature: I like to bake these cookies at a low temperature (250° to 300°F) for a long time to ensure crunchiness throughout. As a rule of thumb, the bigger the cookie, the lower the oven temperature.

Pan Preparation: Line cookie sheets with parchment or place the batter directly on the cookie sheets. Because of the cookies' high butter content and the absence of liquid, the sheets do not need greasing.

Shaping: These cookies can be molded by hand or dropped from a spoon onto the cookie sheets.

Testing for Doneness: The cookies should be lightly golden and baked throughout, so I test for doneness by cutting one in half to insure that there is no doughy strip.

Cooling and Eating: These cookies taste best when they're well cooled or even the next day when the flavors have settled.

Storing: Stored in an airtight container in or out of the refrigerator, these cookies last for weeks. If they do get soggy, you can crisp them again by warming them in a preheated 275°F oven for 10 minutes.

Rolled Cookies

Rolled cookies, such as Ruby Jems, are made from a stiff dough that has been chilled before it is rolled out and cut. You can mix the dough in a food processor, with an electric mixer, or by hand.

Oven Temperature: This varies between 350° and 400°F depending on the recipe.

Pan Preparation: Line cookie sheets with parchment or grease them lightly with butter or oil. Use an ungreased sheet for cookies that contain a lot of butter.

Shaping: Chill the dough in slabs and then roll it out ⅛ to ¼ inch thick; the thickness will vary with the recipe. Use cookie cutters to make special shapes or the top of a glass dipped in flour for round cookies. I usually don't like to reroll the scraps left when the cookies have been cut out because the dough gets tough with overworking, so I cut the cookies as close together as possible. I use a pancake spatula to lift the cut-out cookies onto the cookie sheets.

Testing for Doneness: Rolled cookies are ready when they have just begun to turn golden around the edges.

Cooling: These cookies cool best directly on the cookie sheet. They're delicate and may break if

you try to move them while they're hot.

Eating: Let rolled cookies cool before you eat them to allow the floury taste to settle down.

Storing: Use your trusty airtight plastic container for storing these cookies in the freezer or refrigerator. The dough also stores well for 4 to 5 days in the refrigerator, or it can be frozen.

Filled Pastry Cookies

Pastry cookies, which include such delicacies as Rugalah and Maya's Pocketbooks, are made from a rich dough filled with fruit, jam, nuts, cheese, or whatever and rolled into distinctive shapes.

Oven Temperature: Use a hot oven, 375° to 400°F. The dough must be chilled before baking, then cooked quickly so that the considerable amount of butter doesn't melt out of the dough and these pastries keep their shape.

Pan Preparation: Line cookie sheets with parchment or grease them lightly with butter or oil.

Shaping: This varies depending on the cookie.

Testing for Doneness: The dough should be lightly golden in color.

Cooling: Remove pastries with filling from the cookie sheet immediately; use a pancake spatula to place them on a plate or cooling rack. If they sit on the sheet, their filling may harden and stick to the pan or parchment.

Eating: The texture of some pastry cookies is better on the second day (Rugalah is an example). Crisp pastries, such as Maya's Pocketbooks, taste best the day they're made.

Storing: Store pastry cookies in an airtight plastic container. You can freeze or refrigerate them with no problem. The dough, too, can be stored for 4 to 5 days in the fridge and can be frozen for up to several weeks.

Serving

*W*hatever the taste or shape of cookie, I encourage you to think creatively when it comes to serving them because, contrary to conventional wisdom, cookies can provide an elegant closing to a dinner party as well as a casual snack after school. Even hearty cookies like Soho Globs or Chocolate Chips or Oatmeal Raisin work well as a dessert if you make them small and dainty, and most cookies complement sorbet or ice cream perfectly as a garnish.

In fact, the well-dressed cookie can go anywhere. Cover a platter with a doily and build a cookie mosaic using a variety of sizes, shapes, and colors or go for an Ali Baba's cave effect and pile them high on a plate in an embarrassment of riches.

Or maybe forget about entertaining altogether and whip up a batch of your favorite cookies the next time you crave a little something sweet and need to summon up those days of childhood.

Chocolate Chip Cookies

7here is little doubt that the chocolate chip or Toll House cookie is America's favorite; so much so that it may qualify as one of the basic food groups. This adaptation is crisp around the edges and chewy in the middle. To achieve that consistency, it's crucial that you take the cookies out of the oven when the centers are light colored and puffy and the edges are golden. The slightly underdone centers will drop when they cool and become chewy. With these cookies, I always figure on ending up with fewer than the stated recipe yield because everyone who wanders into the kitchen can't seem to resist sticking a fingerful of the dough into their mouths. But then, neither can I.

INGREDIENTS

2 cups plus 1 tablespoon all-purpose flour
1 teaspoon baking soda
3/4 teaspoon salt
1 cup (2 sticks) unsalted butter at room temperature
1 cup plus 1 tablespoon (lightly packed) light brown sugar
1/2 cup plus 2 tablespoons granulated sugar
1 teaspoon vanilla extract
2 large eggs, at room temperature
1 1/2 cups semisweet chocolate chips

1. Preheat the oven to 375°F. Line several cookie sheets with parchment paper or grease them lightly with butter or vegetable oil.

2. Sift the flour, baking soda, and salt together into a small bowl and set aside.

3. Using an electric mixer on medium speed, cream the butter, both sugars, and the vanilla together in a medium-size bowl until light and fluffy, 1½ to 2 minutes. Stop the mixer twice to scrape the bowl with a rubber spatula.

4. Add the eggs and beat on medium speed until they are blended, about 30 seconds. Scrape the bowl.

5. Add the dry ingredients and mix on low speed for 15 seconds. Scrape the bowl.

6. Add the chocolate chips and blend until they are mixed in, 5 to 8 seconds.

7. Drop the dough by generously rounded tablespoonfuls (the equivalent of 3 level teaspoons) 2 inches apart onto the prepared cookie sheets.

8. Bake the cookies until the edges are dark golden and the center is light and slightly puffed up, 11 to 12 minutes. Remove the cookies from the oven and allow them to cool on the sheets. These are best eaten the same day they are baked.

Makes 24 large cookies

Note: This dough also works beautifully when it's refrigerated a minimum of 4 hours; it tends to produce a thicker, chewier cookie that is crisp around the   edges.

Coconut Chocolate- Chip Cookies

*7*asting like a sweet shortbread, this cookie packs an extra punch of coconut and chocolate chips.

INGREDIENTS

2¼ cups all-purpose flour
½ teaspoon baking soda
1 cup (2 sticks) unsalted butter, at
    room temperature
¾ cup sugar
1 teaspoon vanilla extract
1 large egg, at room temperature
1½ cups shredded coconut
1 cup semisweet chocolate chips

1. Preheat the oven to 325°F. Line several cookie sheets with parchment paper or grease them lightly with butter or vegetable oil.

2. Sift the flour and baking soda together into a small bowl and set aside.

3. Using an electric mixer on medium speed, cream the butter, sugar, and vanilla together in a medium-size mixing bowl until light and fluffy, about 1½ minutes. Stop the mixer twice to scrape the bowl with a rubber spatula.

4. Add the egg and mix at medium speed until it is incorporated, about 15 seconds. Scrape the bowl.

5. Add the dry ingredients on low speed and mix until blended, 20 to 25 seconds.

6. Add the coconut and chocolate chips and blend until they are mixed in, about 10 seconds.

7. Drop the dough by heaping tablespoonfuls about 2 inches apart onto the prepared cookie sheets, then flatten them out with your fingers to about 2 inches in diameter.

8. Bake the cookies until they are crunchy to the touch and golden around the edges, 20 to 25 minutes. Allow them to cool on the cookie sheets.

Makes 36 cookies

Orange Pecan Chocolate-Chip Cookies

*O*ranges and chocolate are such an ideal match to me that I wonder why I don't come across tons of desserts combining them. Here the taste of orange is strong and the cookie is crunchy, so together they make a tangy variation on a classic chocolate-chip cookie theme.

INGREDIENTS

2 cups all-purpose flour
1 tablespoon baking powder
½ teaspoon salt
10 tablespoons (1¼ sticks) unsalted butter, at room temperature
½ cup granulated sugar
1 cup (lightly packed) light brown sugar
1 tablespoon grated orange zest
1 teaspoon vanilla extract
2 large eggs, at room temperature
1½ cups semisweet chocolate chips
1½ cups chopped pecans

1. Preheat the oven to 350°F. Line several cookie sheets with parchment paper or lightly grease them with butter or vegetable oil.

2. Sift the flour, baking powder, and salt together into a small bowl and set aside.

3. Using an electric mixer on medium-high speed, cream the butter, both sugars, the orange zest, and vanilla together in a medium-size mixing bowl until light and fluffy, about 1½ minutes. Stop the mixer twice to scrape the bowl with a rubber spatula.

4. Add the eggs one at a time and beat on medium speed after each addition until the egg is incorporated, about 10 seconds. Scrape the bowl with a rubber spatula after each addition.

5. Add the dry ingredients and mix on low speed until almost blended. Scrape the bowl.

6. Add the chocolate chips and nuts and mix until blended, 5 to 8 seconds.

7. Drop the dough by slightly rounded tablespoonfuls about 2 inches apart onto the prepared cookie sheets. Flatten them with the palm of your hand.

8. Bake the cookies until they are golden in color, 15 to 16 minutes. Allow them to cool on the sheets. They will get crunchier as they sit.

Makes 48 cookies

Soho Globs

*T*he first time I was introduced to a glob at the Soho Charcuterie (a popular nouvelle American restaurant in the 1980s) in New York, I was outraged at the price. Two dollars indeed, I fumed until I bit into one and immediately went back for two more. Globs are the ideal combination of a bittersweet chocolate flavor and a chewy consistency, all studded with pecans and chocolate chips—kind of cookiedom's answer to the brownie. And then there's the name. No wonder I became a believer.

INGREDIENTS

5 ounces semisweet chocolate
3 ounces unsweetened chocolate
6 tablespoons (¾ stick) unsalted
    butter, at room temperature
⅓ cup all-purpose flour
1 teaspoon baking powder
¼ teaspoon salt
2 large eggs, at room
    temperature
2 teaspoons vanilla extract
1 tablespoon instant espresso
    powder
¾ cup sugar
¾ cup semisweet chocolate
    chips
⅓ cup chopped pecans
⅓ cup chopped walnuts

1. Preheat the oven to 325°F. Line several cookie sheets with parchment paper or grease them lightly with butter or vegetable oil.

2. Melt the 8 ounces semisweet and unsweetened chocolate and the butter in the top of a double boiler placed over simmering water. Allow it to cool slightly.

3. Sift the flour, baking powder, and salt together into a small bowl and set aside.

4. Using an electric mixer on medium speed, beat the eggs, vanilla, and espresso powder in a medium-size mixing bowl until they are mixed together, about 10 seconds.

5. Add the sugar to the egg mixture and blend it all until thick, about 1 minute. Scrape the bowl.

6. Add the melted chocolate and blend 1 minute more. Scrape the bowl.

7. Add the flour mixture on low speed and mix until blended, 10 seconds. Fold in the chocolate chips and nuts by hand or with the mixer on low speed.

8. Drop the dough by generously rounded tablespoonfuls about 2 inches apart onto the prepared cookie sheets.

9. Bake the cookies until they rise slightly and form a thin crust, about 13 minutes. Immediately remove the cookies from the cookie sheets and place them on a rack to cool.

Makes 20 cookies

Big Jakes

A dark moist cookie studded with white chocolate that causes my son Jake's face to light up with joy and coats his entire lower face with chocolate.

I N G R E D I E N T S

1 recipe Soho Globs omitting the chocolate chips and nuts (recipe precedes)
³⁄₄ cup white chocolate chips or chopped white chocolate

Prepare the recipe as directed substituting the white chocolate for the chips and nuts.

Makes 20 cookies

Peanut Butter Cookies

H ere is Rosie's version of the classic peanut butter cookie. On the first day, they're chewy in the center and crunchy around the edge, but if there are any left over for day two, you'll find that they'll get crisper throughout.

I N G R E D I E N T S

1½ cups plus 2 tablespoons all-purpose flour
½ teaspoon baking soda
¼ teaspoon salt
8 tablespoons (1 stick) unsalted butter, at room temperature
½ cup plus 2 tablespoons peanut butter, creamy or crunchy
½ cup plus 1 teaspoon granulated sugar
½ cup plus 1 teaspoon (lightly packed) light brown sugar
½ teaspoon vanilla extract
1 large egg, at room temperature

1. Sift the flour, baking soda, and salt into a small bowl and set aside.

2. Using an electric mixer on medium speed, cream the butter, peanut butter, both sugars, and the vanilla together in a medium-size mixing bowl until light and fluffy, about 1½ minutes. Stop the mixer twice to scrape the bowl with a rubber spatula.

3. Add the egg and beat on medium speed until blended, about 1 minute. Scrape the bowl.

4. Add the dry ingredients to the peanut butter mixture and mix on low speed until blended, about 15 seconds. Scrape the bowl and mix several seconds more.

5. Place the dough in a small covered bowl and refrigerate it for several hours or overnight.

6. Fifteen minutes before baking, preheat the oven to 350°F. Line several cookie sheets with parchment paper or grease them lightly with butter or vegetable oil.

7. Measure out heaping tablespoonfuls of the dough and roll them into balls with your hands. Place the balls 2 inches apart on the prepared cookie sheets. Bake the cookies until they are dark gold around the edges and slightly puffy and light in the center, about 15 minutes. Allow the cookies to cool on the cookie sheets.

Makes 18 large cookies

Sunken Kisses

*I*n my household, baking these little peanut butter cookies is an occasion because I put my kids in charge of unwrapping the Hershey's Chocolate Kisses and placing one carefully in the middle of each cookie. You've never seen such concentration. By unanimous decision, though, the making doesn't hold a candle to the eating.

INGREDIENTS

1¾ cups all-purpose flour
1 teaspoon baking soda
¼ teaspoon salt
8 tablespoons (1 stick) unsalted butter, at room temperature
¾ cup (lightly packed) light brown sugar
¾ cup granulated sugar
½ cup peanut butter, smooth or crunchy
1 teaspoon vanilla extract
1 large egg, at room temperature
48 Hershey's Chocolate Kisses, removed from their wrappers

1. Preheat the oven to 375°F. Line 2 cookie sheets with parchment paper or grease them lightly with butter or vegetable oil.

2. Sift the flour, baking soda, and salt together into a small bowl and set aside.

3. Using an electric mixer on medium speed, cream the butter, brown sugar, ¼ cup of the granulated sugar, the peanut butter, and vanilla in a medium-size mixing bowl until light and fluffy, 2 to 3 minutes. Stop the mixer twice to scrape the bowl with a rubber spatula.

4. Add the egg and blend on medium speed until it is almost incorporated, about 10 seconds. Scrape the bowl.

5. Add the dry ingredients on low speed and blend 15 seconds. Stop the mixer to scrape the bowl and paddle, then blend until the dough is smooth, about 5 seconds more.

6. Measure out 48 rounded teaspoonfuls of the dough and roll them into balls with your hands.

7. Dip one side of each ball in the remaining ½ cup granulated sugar (optional) and place them 2 inches apart and sugar side up on the prepared cookie sheets.

8. Bake the cookies until they are light gold, 8 to 10 minutes. Remove the sheets from the oven. Immediately top each cookie with a Chocolate Kiss, wide side down, and press it firmly in the center of the cookie to imbed the kiss.

9. Carefully remove the cookies from the sheets and place them on a plate or cooling rack.

Makes 48 cookies

Ginger-snappers

I don't know if the "snap" in gingersnaps refers to the crispness of the cookie or the bite of the ginger, but I do know that Nabisco gingersnaps were a staple in our household when I was growing up. My mother loved to eat two or three at bedtime, dunking them into a glass of milk until they became soft, and giving me a bite of her treat. These ginger cookies don't snap when you break them—they're soft and chewy—but their ginger taste is distinctive.

INGREDIENTS

2½ cups all-purpose flour
2 teaspoons baking soda
½ teaspoon salt
2 teaspoons ground cinnamon
1 tablespoon plus 2 teaspoons ground ginger
12 tablespoons (1½ sticks) unsalted butter, at room temperature
1 cup (firmly packed) dark brown sugar
1 large egg, at room temperature
¼ cup unsulphured molasses
1 tablespoon grated lemon zest
¼ cup granulated sugar

1. Preheat the oven to 350°F. Line several cookie sheets with parchment paper or lightly grease them with butter or vegetable oil.

2. Sift the flour, baking soda, salt, cinnamon, and ginger together into a small bowl and set aside.

3. Using an electric mixer on medium-high speed, cream the butter and brown sugar in a medium-size mixing bowl until light and fluffy, 2 minutes. Stop the mixer twice to scrape the bowl with a rubber spatula.

4. Add the egg and beat on medium speed until blended, about 10 seconds. Scrape the bowl with the spatula.

5. Add the molasses and lemon zest and beat until blended, 10 seconds.

6. Fold in half the dry ingredients by hand using several broad strokes of the spatula, then fold in the remaining half. Mix on low speed until blended, about 20 seconds.

7. Measure out rounded tablespoonfuls of the dough and roll them into balls with your hands.

8. Roll the balls in the granulated sugar and place them 2 inches apart on the prepared cookie sheets.

9. Bake the cookies just until the edges are lightly golden and the center is puffy, about 12 minutes. Do not overbake them or they will become hard. Remove the cookies carefully from the sheets with a pancake spatula. Place them on a rack to cool.

Makes 26 cookies

Oatmeal Lace Cookies

*T*his cookie is very sweet like those caramels orthodontists outlawed because they stuck in your braces but which you snuck anyway because who could resist. Delicate and crisp, they're particularly good as an accent to ice cream.

I N G R E D I E N T S

2 tablespoons all-purpose flour
1 cup rolled oats
1 teaspoon ground cinnamon
8 tablespoons (1 stick) butter,
*   cut into 8 pieces*
¾ cup (lightly packed) light brown
*   sugar*
2 tablespoons water
1 large egg, at room temperature
1 teaspoon vanilla extract
¼ cup finely chopped walnuts

1. Preheat the oven to 350°F. Line several cookie sheets with parchment paper or lightly grease them with butter or vegetable oil. Have ready a large bowl of ice water.

2. Combine the flour, oats, and cinnamon in a small bowl and set aside.

3. Place the butter, brown sugar, and 2 tablespoons water in a medium-size saucepan; heat over low heat until the butter is melted, about 2 minutes. Increase the heat to medium-high and allow the mixture to come to a full boil. Boil for 1 minute.

4. Place the saucepan slightly into the bowl of ice water and whisk constantly for about 3 minutes to cool the mixture.

5. Transfer the mixture to a medium-size bowl, stir in the egg and vanilla rapidly with a whisk, then stir in the flour mixture and the nuts with a wooden spoon.

6. Place the mixing bowl slightly into the bowl filled with ice water and allow the dough to thicken slightly (don't stir), about 4 minutes.

7. Drop the dough by level teaspoonfuls about 2 inches apart onto the prepared cookie sheets.

8. Bake until the cookies are golden with darker edges, 10 to 12 minutes. Allow the cookies to cool on the sheets for 30 to 40 minutes, then remove them carefully with a spatula. Eat them that day or store them in an airtight container. These cookies are best eaten the day they're baked because they tend to lose their crispness.

*Makes
24 cookies*

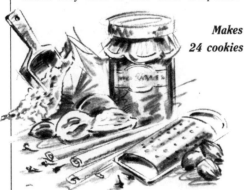

Crispy Orange-Oatmeal Wafers

*D*elicate and crispy, this cookie is particularly nice as a garnish for ice cream.

INGREDIENTS

*¾ cup all-purpose flour
½ teaspoon baking soda
½ teaspoon salt
8 tablespoons (1 stick) butter,
    at room temperature
½ cup granulated sugar
½ cup (lightly packed) light brown
    sugar
½ teaspoon vanilla extract
1 tablespoon grated orange zest
1 large egg, at room
    temperature
1½ cups rolled oats*

1. Preheat the oven to 400°F. Line several cookie sheets with parchment paper or lightly grease them with butter or vegetable oil.

2. Sift the flour, baking soda, and salt together into a small bowl and set aside.

3. Using an electric mixer on medium speed, cream the butter, both sugars, the vanilla, and orange zest together in a medium-size bowl until light and fluffy, about 1½ minutes. Stop the mixer twice to scrape the bowl with a rubber spatula.

4. Add the egg and mix on medium-low speed to incorporate it, about 20 seconds.

5. Add the dry ingredients and mix on medium-low speed for 10 seconds. Scrape the bowl, then mix until blended, about 5 seconds more. Scrape the bowl.

6. Add the oats and mix for several seconds on low speed to blend them in.

7. Drop the dough by rounded teaspoonfuls about 2 inches apart onto the prepared cookie sheets.

8. Bake the cookies until crisp and lightly golden with darker golden edges, about 8 minutes. Allow the cookies to cool on the sheets.

Makes 50 cookies

Chocolate Meringue Drops

I'm a sucker for these elegantly simple and not-so-little treats. This recipe produces a meringue that's crusty outside, chewy inside, and sweet every inch of the way.

INGREDIENTS

4 large egg whites, at room temperature
⅛ teaspoon salt
1¼ cups sugar
1 teaspoon vanilla extract
½ cup semisweet chocolate chips

1. Preheat the oven to 300°F. Lightly grease several cookie sheets with butter. Sprinkle flour over the sheets and shake to distribute the flour. Then turn the sheets upside down over the sink to knock off any excess flour.

2. Using an electric mixer on medium-low speed, beat the egg whites with the salt in a medium-size mixing bowl until frothy, about 40 seconds. Gradually add the sugar, then raise the mixer speed to high and add the vanilla. Beat the mixture for 50 seconds, stop to scrape the bowl with a rubber spatula, then continue beating until the mixture forms very stiff peaks, 60 to 75 seconds longer. Then gently fold in the chocolate chips with the rubber spatula.

3. Drop the mixture by slightly rounded teaspoonfuls about 1 inch apart onto the prepared cookie sheets.

4. Bake the cookies until they turn a very light beige, 25 to 30 minutes. Cool the cookies on the cookie sheets.

Makes 75 cookies

Chocolate Macaroons

*T*he recipe for these cookies comes from the archives of Leah Winograd, erstwhile caterer of bar mitzvahs, baker extraordinaire and mother of my partner Eliot. Bored with the usual Passover fare, she substitutes these for the occasion, though I like to make them year-round. They have a thin outer crust and a chewy inside.

INGREDIENTS

4 ounces semisweet chocolate
2 ounces unsweetened chocolate
2 large egg whites
½ cup sugar
1 teaspoon vanilla extract
2 cups shredded coconut

1. Preheat the oven to 375°F. Line a cookie sheet with parchment paper, or grease it lightly with butter or vegetable oil.

2. Melt both chocolates in the top of a double boiler placed over simmering water, then cool the chocolate to tepid.

3. Beat the egg whites in a medium-size mixing bowl with an electric mixer on medium-high speed until frothy, about 30 seconds.

4. Gradually add the sugar and continue beating until the mixture is the consistency of marshmallow fluff, about 30 seconds more. Blend in the vanilla, then fold in the melted chocolate, then the coconut.

5. Drop rounded tablespoonfuls of the dough about 1½ inches apart onto the prepared cookie sheet.

6. Bake the cookies until a light crust forms on the outside, about 13 minutes. Cool on the cookie sheet or remove the cookies to a cooling rack.

Makes 12 cookies

Hermits

*T*here's lots of disagreement about the attributes of a good hermit—the cookie, that is. I'm a strong advocate of something dark, spicy, and chewy, which is what you'll find in this recipe. Although these cookies are basically made from a drop cookie batter, I make them in freeform strips, then cut them after baking. It is important to store these cookies in an airtight container to preserve their chewiness.

INGREDIENTS

COOKIES
2 cups plus 1 tablespoon all-purpose flour
2 teaspoons baking soda
¼ teaspoon salt
1¾ teaspoons ground cinnamon
2 teaspoons ground ginger
1¾ teaspoons ground cloves
9 tablespoons (1 stick plus 1 tablespoon) unsalted butter, at room temperature
1 cup (lightly packed) light brown sugar
1 large egg, at room temperature
¼ cup unsulphured molasses
¾ cup raisins

GLAZE
1½ cups plus 3 tablespoons confectioner's sugar
2 tablespoons plus 2½ teaspoons milk
½ teaspoon grated lemon or orange zest

1. Preheat the oven to 375°F. Line a cookie sheet with parchment paper or leave it ungreased.

2. Sift the flour, baking soda, salt, cinnamon, ginger, and cloves together into a small bowl and set aside.

3. Using an electric mixer on medium speed, cream the butter and sugar together in a medium-size mixing bowl until light and fluffy, about 1½ minutes. Stop the mixer twice to scrape the bowl with a rubber spatula.

4. Add the egg and mix on medium speed until blended, 20 to 30 seconds. Scrape the bowl.

5. Add the molasses and mix until blended.

6. Add the dry ingredients and the raisins and mix on medium speed until the dough comes together, about 1 minute.

7. Divide the dough in half. Shape each half into a log 1½ inches in diameter by 12 inches long. Arrange the logs on the prepared cookie sheet, leaving at least 3 to 4 inches between them.

8. Bake the logs until they are golden but still very soft to the touch and puffy in the center, 17 to 18 minutes. (The dough cracks during baking and it will still seem slightly raw on the inside even when the logs are done.) The logs flatten out and lengthen as they bake.

9. Cool the logs on the sheet. Cut into 2-inch-wide slices when cool. Each log makes 7 cookies.

10. Prepare the glaze: Place all the ingredients in a small bowl and stir them vigorously with a whisk until blended.

11. Drizzle the glaze over the strips or use a pastry brush to paint the surface of the strips with the glaze. Allow the glaze to harden before eating or storing the cookies.

Makes 14 cookies

Nutballs

*B*y tradition, these cookies are a staple at Mexican weddings, and I like to serve them around the winter holidays, which goes to show, I guess, that they melt in your mouth in any climate and on any occasion.

I N G R E D I E N T S

---

8 tablespoons (1 stick) unsalted butter, at room temperature
2 tablespoons granulated sugar
1 teaspoon vanilla extract
1 cup all-purpose flour, sifted
1 cup walnuts, finely chopped
1 cup confectioner's sugar, sifted

1. Preheat the oven to 300°F. Line 2 cookie sheets with parchment paper or leave them ungreased.

2. Using an electric mixer on medium speed, cream the butter, granulated sugar, and vanilla until light and fluffy, 1½ to 2 minutes. Stop the mixer once or twice to scrape the bowl with a rubber spatula.

3. Add the flour and mix on low speed until it is blended in, about 45 seconds. Scrape the bowl once or twice during mixing.

4. Add the nuts and mix until well blended, about 10 seconds.

5. Measure out generously rounded teaspoonfuls of dough and roll them into balls with your hands. Place these balls about 2 inches apart on the prepared cookie sheets.

6. Bake the cookies until they just begin to turn golden, about 30 minutes. To test for doneness, remove one cookie from the sheet and cut it in half. There should be no doughy strip in the center.

7. Roll the cookies in the confectioner's sugar while they are still hot, then cool on the cookie sheets. Serve them when they have cooled.

Makes 35 cookies

Mandelbrot

*I*t wasn't until I went to college that I began to learn about some of the delicacies of my Jewish heritage, and mandelbrot was one of them. At that time, my roommate Michelle Menzies introduced me to this zwieback-like cookie that her grandmother had taught her to make. It's more or less the Jewish counterpart to Italian anise biscuits, but without the anise and with a generous helping of nuts.

INGREDIENTS

3 cups all-purpose flour
2 teaspoons baking powder
¾ teaspoon salt
½ cup quick-cooking oatmeal
1 cup (2 sticks) unsalted butter,
    at room temperature
1¼ cups sugar
2 teaspoons vanilla extract
1 tablespoon fresh lemon juice
3 large eggs, at room temperature
1 cup almonds, walnuts, or pecans,
    finely chopped
1 tablespoon ground cinnamon

1. Preheat the oven to 350°F. Line 2 cookie sheets with parchment paper or lightly grease them with butter or vegetable oil.

2. Sift the flour, baking powder, and salt together in a medium-size bowl; stir in the oatmeal and set aside.

3. Using an electric mixer on medium-high speed, cream the butter, 1 cup of the sugar, the vanilla, and lemon juice together in a medium-size mixing bowl until light and fluffy, 2 to 2½ minutes. Stop the machine twice during the mixing to scrape the bowl with a rubber spatula.

4. Add the eggs one at a time on medium speed, mixing until each egg is partially incorporated, about 5 sec-

onds. Scrape the bowl after each addition. After the last egg has been added, beat the mixture on high speed for several seconds.

5. Mix in half the dry ingredients by hand with the rubber spatula, then blend with the electric mixer on low speed for several seconds. Add the remaining dry ingredients and mix on low speed until the dough is smooth, about 5 seconds. Add the nuts with a few more turns of the mixer.

6. Divide the dough into quarters. Using floured hands, lay one-quarter of the dough lengthwise on a prepared cookie sheet, molding it into a cylindrical strip 8½ inches in length by 2 inches in diameter. Place it a couple of inches from the edge of the pan. Form a second strip on that sheet 3 inches from the first strip, then place 2 more strips on the other cookie sheet in the same fashion.

7. Mix the remaining ¼ cup sugar with the cinnamon. Sprinkle the cinnamon sugar generously over each strip.

8. Bake the dough strips until firm to the touch and lightly golden, about 20 to 25 minutes.

9. Remove the sheets from the oven, but leave the oven on. Cut each strip into ¾-inch-thick slices and arrange all the slices on the sheets about ½ inch apart. Bake until crisp and golden, about 15 minutes. Cool the cookies on the sheets.

Makes 48 cookies

Lemon Cake Cookies

---

*7*hese cookies took so many tries to perfect that they almost got named Those Damn Lemon Cookies. I knew exactly what I wanted — something halfway between a sponge cake and a pound cake with a distinctive flavor — but there were times when I thought I'd have better luck finding it by advertising in the personals. Patience brought success, and here is a soft, moist cookie, wearing a most fetching lemon glaze.

INGREDIENTS

COOKIES
2½ cups plus 1 tablespoon cake flour (see Note)
¾ teaspoon baking powder
¾ teaspoon baking soda
½ teaspoon salt
9 tablespoons (1 stick plus 1 tablespoon) butter, at room temperature
1 cup plus 2 tablespoons sugar
1 tablespoon grated lemon zest
2 large egg yolks, at room temperature
1 whole large egg, at room temperature
1¼ cups sour cream, at room temperature

GLAZE
6 tablespoons (¾ stick) unsalted butter
1½ cups confectioner's sugar
3 tablespoons fresh lemon juice

1. Preheat the oven to 375°F. Line several cookie sheets with parchment paper or lightly grease them with butter or vegetable oil.

2. Sift the flour, baking powder, baking soda, and salt together into a small bowl and set aside.

3. Using an electric mixer on medium speed, cream the butter, sugar, and lemon zest in a medium-size bowl until light and fluffy, about 2 minutes. Scrape the bowl.

4. Add the egg yolks and mix on medium speed until blended, about 10 seconds. Scrape the bowl, then add the whole egg and mix until blended, 10 seconds more.

5. Add the sour cream and mix on medium-low speed until blended, about 8 seconds.

6. Fold in the dry ingredients by hand, then turn the mixer on low speed for 5 seconds. Scrape the bowl with the rubber spatula and mix on low until the batter is smooth and velvety, 10 seconds. Give the batter a stir or two with the spatula.

7. Drop the batter by large rounded tablespoonfuls about 2 inches apart onto the prepared cookie sheets.

8. Bake until the cookies puff up, are firm to the touch, and just begin to turn golden, about 12 minutes. Remove the cookies from the sheets with a spatula and place them on a cooling rack. Allow them to cool completely.

9. Meanwhile prepare the glaze: Melt the butter in a small pan over low heat. Place the sugar in a medium-size bowl. Add the butter and lemon juice to the sugar and beat vigorously with a whisk until the mixture is smooth and creamy.

10. Once the cookies have cooled, dip the entire rounded top of each into the glaze. Place the cookies on the cookie sheets and allow them to sit until the glaze hardens, several hours. (If it is a humid day, refrigerate them in order to speed the process.)

Makes 36 cookies

Note: Although cake flour gives these cookies a superior texture, you may substitute 2 cups plus 3 tablespoons all-purpose flour for it.

Butter-Glazed Nutmeg Mounds

*T*hese are soft, cakelike cookies, flavored with nutmeg and topped with an old-fashioned buttery glaze. I like them even better several hours after they're made when the flavors come into their own and the consistency is softer and moister. Stored in an airtight container, they last a while— assuming you can resist raiding the cookie jar for that long.

INGREDIENTS

COOKIES
2¾ cups cake flour (see Note)
¾ teaspoon baking soda
¾ teaspoon baking powder
1 tablespoon plus 1 teaspoon ground nutmeg
½ teaspoon salt
9 tablespoons (1 stick plus 1 tablespoon) unsalted butter, at room temperature
1½ cups (lightly packed) light brown sugar
2 teaspoons vanilla extract
2 large egg yolks, at room temperature
1 whole large egg, at room temperature
1 cup sour cream, at room temperature

GLAZE
6 tablespoons (¾ stick) unsalted butter
1½ cups confectioner's sugar
1 teaspoon vanilla extract
3 tablespoons hot water

1. Preheat the oven to 375°F. Line several cookie sheets with parchment paper or lightly grease them with vegetable oil or butter.

2. Sift the flour, baking soda, baking powder, nutmeg, and salt together into a small bowl and set aside.

3. Using an electric mixer on medium-high speed, cream the butter, brown sugar, and vanilla together in a medium-size bowl until light and fluffy, about 2 minutes. Stop the mixer twice to scrape the bowl with a rubber spatula. Scrape the bowl a third time before going on to the next step.

4. Add the egg yolks and blend on medium speed for about 10 seconds. Scrape the bowl then add the whole egg and mix until blended, about 10 seconds. Scrape the bowl again.

5. Add the sour cream and mix on medium-low speed until well blended, about 10 seconds. Scrape the bowl.

6. Fold in the dry ingredients by hand, then turn the mixer on low speed and mix about 5 seconds. Scrape the bowl with the spatula and mix on low until the batter is smooth and velvety, 10 seconds. Give the batter a stir or two with the spatula.

7. Drop the batter by heaping table-spoonfuls about 2 inches apart onto the prepared cookie sheets.

8. Bake the cookies until they are just golden in color and firm to the touch, but not crusty, about 12 minutes. Using a metal spatula, carefully lift the cookies from the sheet and place them on a rack to cool.

9. While the cookies are cooling, prepare the glaze: Melt the butter in a small frying pan over medium-low heat until golden in color, 3 minutes.

10. Place the confectioner's sugar in a small bowl, add the butter, vanilla,

and hot water, and beat vigorously with a whisk until the mixture is smooth and creamy.

11. When the cookies have cooled, dip the rounded top of each into the glaze. Place the cookies on the cookie sheets and allow them to sit until the glaze hardens, several hours. (If it is a humid day, refrigerate them in order to speed the process.)

Makes 36 cookies

Note: Although cake flour gives these cookies a superior texture, you may substitute 2½ cups all-purpose flour for it.

Maya Pies

I confess that before my anti-preservative days, I was a fan of Devil Dogs and I recall with fondness their velvety texture and the contrast of those chocolate buns with the sweet cream filling. Even when I gave up eating chemicals, I didn't want to give up Devil Dogs completely, so I came up with a version, named after my daughter Maya, made from wholesome ingredients, which I like to think is just as good as our childhood memories. Their texture improves on the second day, so store them in an airtight container overnight.

INGREDIENTS

COOKIES
4 ounces unsweetened chocolate
14 tablespoons all-purpose flour
6 tablespoons cake flour
1 teaspoon baking powder
½ teaspoon baking soda
10 tablespoons (1¼ sticks) unsalted butter, at room temperature
½ teaspoon vegetable oil
1 cup granulated sugar
3 large eggs, at room temperature
½ cup plus 1 tablespoon milk, at room temperature
3 tablespoons sour cream, at room temperature

FILLING
½ cup milk
1½ tablespoons all-purpose flour
1¾ cups confectioner's sugar
12 tablespoons (1½ sticks) unsalted butter, at room temperature
½ teaspoon vanilla extract

1. Preheat the oven to 375°F and line 2 cookie sheets with cooking parchment or grease them lightly with butter or vegetable oil.

2. Melt the chocolate in the top of a double boiler placed over simmering water. Set it aside.

3. Sift both flours, the baking powder, and baking soda together into a small bowl and set aside.

4. Using an electric mixer on medium-high speed, cream the butter, oil, and granulated sugar together in a medium-size mixing bowl until light and fluffy, about 2 minutes. Stop the mixer once or twice to scrape the bowl with a rubber spatula.

5. Add the eggs one at a time and blend on medium speed for 10 seconds after each addition, scraping the bowl with the rubber spatula each time.

6. Add the milk and sour cream and beat on medium speed until blended, about 5 seconds, then on high speed for 3 seconds more. The mixture will not appear smooth.

7. Fold in the chocolate with the spatula until the batter is uniform in color.

8. Fold the dry ingredients in by hand with 6 or 7 broad strokes of the spatula, then mix on low speed until the batter is velvety, about 10 seconds, stopping once to scrape the bowl with the rubber spatula. Finish mixing by hand.

9. Drop the batter by rounded tablespoonfuls 2 inches apart onto the prepared cookie sheets. Bake the cookies until they have risen, spring back to the touch, and a tester inserted in the center of a cookie comes out dry, about 10 minutes.

10. Carefully lift the cookies from the sheets with a metal spatula and place them on a cooling rack.

11. While the cookies are cooling prepare the filling: Mix the milk and flour in a medium-size saucepan over low heat. Cook, stirring constantly, until a paste is formed, 2 to 3 minutes. Transfer the paste to a mixing bowl and allow it to cool for about 20 minutes in the refrigerator.

12. Add the confectioner's sugar, butter, and vanilla to the cooled paste, then beat it with the paddle attachment of an electric mixer on medium speed for 1 minute, then on high speed until light and fluffy, 3 to 4 minutes more.

13. When the cookies are completely cool, turn half the cookies upside down, spread each with a rounded tablespoon of filling, and top them with the remaining cookies. Store the cookies in an airtight container and eat them the next day. They will continue to soften overnight.

Makes 13 double cookies

Pecan Crunchies

*7*hese crunchy, melt-in-your-mouth cookies are perfect for any occasion, and an all-time favorite at Rosie's.

INGREDIENTS

2 cups all-purpose flour
3/4 teaspoon salt
1 cup pecan pieces
1 cup plus 2 tablespoons (2¼ sticks) unsalted butter, at room temperature
⅓ cup (lightly packed) light brown sugar
¾ cup plus 3 tablespoons granulated sugar

1. Sift the flour and salt together into a small bowl and set aside.

2. Grind the pecans in a food processor until they are finely chopped but not powdery, about 30 seconds. Set them aside.

3. Using an electric mixer on medium speed, cream the butter, brown sugar, and ¼ cup plus 3 tablespoons of the granulated sugar in a medium-size mixing bowl until the ingredients are light and fluffy, about 2 minutes. Scrape the bowl with a rubber spatula.

4. Add the dry ingredients and the pecans and beat on medium-low speed for 20 seconds. Scrape the bowl, then beat until the flour and nuts are completely incorporated, about 15 seconds.

5. Spread a 2-foot length of waxed paper on a work surface. With floured fingers, shape the dough into a rough log about 18 to 20 inches in length along the length of one side of the paper. Roll the log in the waxed paper and twist the ends like a hard candy wrapper. Refrigerate the dough for 2 hours. You can cut the log in half in order to fit it in the refrigerator.

6. Remove the log from the refrigerator and, with the dough still in the waxed paper, gently roll it back and forth on the work surface to round the log.

7. Place the log back in the refrigerator for several more hours.

8. Preheat the oven to 300°F. Line 2 cookie sheets with parchment or leave them ungreased.

9. Place the log on the counter, unwrap it, and cut the log into ⅓-inch-thick slices.

10. Dip one side of each cookie in the remaining ½ cup granulated sugar and place it sugar side up an inch apart on the cookie sheets.

11. Bake the cookies until they are firm to the touch and slightly golden, about 25 minutes. Be careful not to underbake these cookies, which alters the texture significantly. To test for doneness, remove one cookie from the sheet and cut it in half. There should be no doughy strip in the center. Cool on the cookie sheets.

Makes 48 cookies

Black and Whites

*7*his is a crunchy cookie with alternating strips of vanilla and chocolate doughs. They are wonderful with tea, coffee, or milk and last forever if stored in an airtight container.

INGREDIENTS

½ cup semisweet chocolate chips
2 ounces unsweetened chocolate
1¼ cups sifted all-purpose flour
¾ teaspoon baking powder
1 cup (2 sticks) unsalted butter, at room temperature
1 cup sugar
1½ teaspoons vanilla extract
1 large egg, at room temperature

1. Line a 9 × 5 × 3-inch loaf pan with waxed paper that overhangs the long sides.

2. Melt both chocolates in a double boiler placed over simmering water. Allow the chocolate to cool.

3. Sift the flour and baking powder together into a small bowl and set aside.

4. Using an electric mixer on medium speed, cream the butter, sugar, and vanilla in a medium-size mixing bowl until light and fluffy, about 2 minutes. Stop the mixer once or twice to scrape the bowl with a rubber spatula.

5. Add the egg to the butter mixture and mix on high speed for several seconds. Scrape the bowl and mix the ingredients on medium speed until they are blended, 5 to 8 seconds.

6. Add the dry ingredients and blend on medium speed until incorporated, 5 to 8 seconds.

7. Take one-third of the dough (a scant cup) and place it in a small bowl.

8. Add the melted chocolate to the remaining two-thirds of the dough and mix until the dough is uniform in color, about 5 seconds.

9. Press half the chocolate dough (a generous cup) over the bottom of the loaf pan. Smooth the surface of the dough as much as possible.

10. Press the vanilla dough over the chocolate dough. Smooth the surface as much as possible.

11. Cover the vanilla dough with the remaining chocolate dough and cover the top with a piece of waxed paper.

Refrigerate the dough overnight.

12. The next day preheat the oven to 375°F. Line several cookie sheets with parchment paper, or lightly grease them with butter or vegetable oil.

13. Lift the chilled dough out of the pan using the overhanging pieces of waxed paper. Remove the waxed paper and cut the dough lengthwise in half into two 9 × 2½-inch strips.

14. Cut each strip crosswise into slices ¼ inch thick. Place the slices 1 inch apart on the prepared cookie sheets.

15. Bake the cookies until the vanilla strips are lightly golden, 12 to 15 minutes. They must be watched very carefully during the last 5 minutes of baking so that they don't burn.

16. Lift the paper from the sheets and place it on a counter or remove the individual cookies with a spatula and allow them to cool on a rack.

Makes 72 cookies

Butterscotch-Cinnamon Icebox Cookies

*T*he brown sugar combined with the butter gives these cookies their distinctive flavor, and the walnuts give them their crunch.

INGREDIENTS

2 cups all-purpose flour
¾ teaspoon salt
1 cup (2 sticks) unsalted butter, at room temperature
½ cup plus 3 tablespoons (lightly packed) dark brown sugar
2 teaspoons vanilla extract
2½ teaspoons ground cinnamon
½ cup chopped pecans, walnuts, or almonds
2 tablespoons granulated sugar

1. Sift the flour and salt together into a small bowl and set aside.

2. Using an electric mixer on medium speed, cream the butter, brown sugar, vanilla, and 1½ teaspoons of the cinnamon together in a medium-size mixing bowl until light and fluffy, 2½ to 3 minutes. Stop the mixer once or twice to scrape the bowl with a rubber spatula.

3. Add the dry ingredients and mix on low speed until the mixture is fluffy again, about 45 seconds. Scrape the bowl.

4. Add the nuts and mix on low speed just until they are incorporated, several seconds.

5. Place a 2-foot length of waxed paper on a work surface. Shape the dough into a rough log 18 to 20 inches long along the length of one side of the paper. Roll the dough up in the waxed paper and twist the ends like a hard candy wrapper. Refrigerate the dough for 2 hours.

6. Remove the log from the refrigerator. Using your hands, roll the wrapped dough gently back and forth on the work surface to smooth out the cylinder. Refrigerate for 4 to 6 hours or overnight.

7. Fifteen minutes before baking, preheat the oven to 275°F. Line several cookie sheets with parchment paper, or leave them ungreased.

8. Remove the log from the refrigerator, unroll it, and cut cookie slices that are a generous ⅓ inch thick.

9. Mix the granulated sugar with the remaining 1 teaspoon cinnamon. Dip one side of each cookie in the cinnamon sugar and place the cookies sugar side up an inch apart on the prepared cookie sheets.

10. Bake the cookies until they are

golden, about 40 minutes. To test for doneness, remove one cookie from the oven and cut it in half. There should be no doughy strip in the center. Cool the cookies on the sheets.

Makes 50 to 60 cookies

Very Short Shortbread Cookies
(for people of all heights)

I treasure this recipe, which was introduced into my parents' home by my Swedish nanny, Inga. I loved to watch her rub the butter and flour together with a skill that seemed so innate I doubted I would ever master it. To my pleasure, it turned out to be an easy and quick process, so even though you can use a food processor for this recipe, I like to make it by hand in honor of Inga (who was, by the way, very tall).

INGREDIENTS

2½ cups all-purpose flour
½ cup sugar
½ teaspoon salt
1 cup (2 sticks) unsalted butter, slightly cool

1. Preheat the oven to 300°F. Line several cookie sheets with parchment paper or leave them ungreased.

2. Sift the flour, sugar, and salt together in a large bowl.

3. Cut the butter into about 32 pieces and distribute them throughout the flour mixture. Rub the pieces into the mixture with your fingers and continue to work the mixture with your hands until all the ingredients hold together and form a dough, 4 to 5 minutes.

4. Measure out generously rounded teaspoonfuls of the dough and roll them into balls with your hands. Place the balls 1½ inches apart on the prepared cookie sheets. Use the prongs of a fork to flatten the cookies to ¼ inch thick by making crisscross indentations on the top.

5. Bake the cookies until they are lightly golden in the center and a bit darker around the edges, 30 to 35 minutes. Cool the cookies on the sheets, then store them in an airtight container.

Makes 48 cookies

Noah Bedoahs

*O*ne of my favorites, these are mounds of shortbread with chocolate chips and walnuts. They bake low and long to achieve a wonderfully crunchy texture.

INGREDIENTS

1³⁄₄ cups plus 2 tablespoons all-purpose flour
¹⁄₂ teaspoon baking powder
¹⁄₄ teaspoon salt
1 cup (2 sticks) unsalted butter, at room temperature
¹⁄₂ cup sugar
³⁄₄ cup semisweet chocolate chips
¹⁄₂ cup chopped walnuts or pecans

1. Preheat the oven to 275°F. Line 2 cookie sheets with parchment paper or leave them ungreased.

2. Sift the flour, baking powder, and salt together into a small bowl and set aside.

3. Using an electric mixer on medium speed, cream the butter and sugar together in a medium-size mixing bowl until light and fluffy, about 1½ minutes. Stop the mixer to scrape the bowl several times with a rubber spatula.

4. Add the dry ingredients on low speed and continue to blend for 10 seconds. Increase the speed to medium-high and beat until fluffy, 2 to 2½ minutes. Scrape the bowl.

5. Add the chocolate chips and nuts with several turns of the mixer, then complete the mixing by hand with a wooden spoon.

6. Measure out generously rounded tablespoonfuls of dough and roll them into balls with your hands.

7. Place the balls 1½ inches apart on the cookie sheets, and press them down lightly to form a flat bottom.

8. Bake the cookies until they are crunchy and golden, about 1 hour. To test for doneness, remove one cookie from the sheet and cut it in half. There should be no doughy strip in the center. Allow the cookies to cool on a rack.

Makes 15 cookies

Chocolate-Dipped Pecan Logs

*T*his shortbread cookie is chock-full of nuts and then dipped in bittersweet chocolate.

INGREDIENTS

**1 cup (2 sticks) unsalted butter,
   at room temperature
¹/₂ cup plus 2 tablespoons sugar
2 teaspoons vanilla extract
2¹/₂ cups all-purpose flour
¹/₂ teaspoon salt
¹/₂ cup coarsely chopped pecans
6 ounces bittersweet chocolate**

1. Preheat the oven to 325°F. Line 2 cookie sheets with parchment paper or leave them ungreased.

2. Using an electric mixer on medium speed, cream the butter, sugar, and vanilla in a medium-size mixing bowl until light and fluffy, about 1½ minutes. Stop the mixer once or twice to scrape the bowl with a rubber spatula.

3. Add the flour and salt and blend on medium speed about 1 minute. Scrape the bowl and add the nuts with several more turns of the mixer.

4. Measure out slightly rounded tablespoonfuls of dough and shape them into little logs 2½ inches long. Place the logs a minimum of 1½ inches apart on the prepared cookie sheets. Flatten them slightly with your palm so that they are about 1½ inches wide.

5. Bake the cookies until they are lightly golden, about 30 to 35 minutes. Cool on the cookie sheets.

6. When the cookies have cooled, melt the chocolate in the top of a double boiler placed over simmering water.

7. Pour the melted chocolate into a small deep bowl and dip half of each cookie into the chocolate, using the rim of the bowl to scrape any excess chocolate off the bottom of the cookie.

8. As they are dipped, place the cookies on a large sheet of waxed paper and allow them to set until the chocolate hardens, several hours. If it is a humid day, refrigerate them in order to speed the process.

Makes 36 cookies

Rosie's Butter Cookies

*T*his butter cookie with its dollop of jam in the middle echoes something in nearly everyone's past: a grandmother or aunt who served them when you visited, a neighborhood bakery that sold them by the pound, or a roommate's relative who sent them during exam week, bless all their hearts. With this classic recipe, you can carry on the tradition. Do not devour these cookies when they're hot (hard as it may be to resist) because the jam can burn the roof of your mouth.

INGREDIENTS

2¹⁄₄ cups all-purpose flour
¹⁄₄ teaspoon baking powder
¹⁄₄ teaspoon salt
1 cup (2 sticks) unsalted butter,
*   at room temperature*
¹⁄₂ cup sugar
¹⁄₂ cup raspberry preserves with seeds

1. Sift the flour, baking powder, and salt together into a small bowl and set aside.

2. Using an electric mixer on medium-high speed, cream the butter and sugar together in a medium-size mixing bowl until light and fluffy, about 2 minutes. Stop the mixer twice to scrape the bowl with a rubber spatula.

3. Add the dry ingredients and mix on low speed for several seconds. Scrape the bowl, then turn the mixer to high speed and beat until the batter is light and fluffy, about 1 minute.

4. Refrigerate the batter in plastic wrap or a covered container for 3 hours.

5. Fifteen minutes before baking, preheat the oven to 275°F. Line 2 cookie sheets with parchment paper or leave them ungreased.

6. Measure out rounded teaspoonfuls of dough and roll them into balls with your hands.

7. Place the balls about 1½ inches apart on the prepared cookie sheets. Then make a firm indentation in the center of each cookie with your thumb or index finger.

8. Bake the cookies until lightly golden, 25 to 30 minutes. Remove the sheet from the oven and increase the heat to 325°F.

9. Place ½ teaspoon jam in the center of each cookie and return the sheet to the oven.

10. Bake the cookies just until the jam melts and spreads, about 10 minutes. Allow the cookies to cool on the sheets before eating.

Makes 48 cookies

Ruby Gems

---

*T*hese were among my favorite cookies when I was a kid because the jam center seemed like a special reward. And then there was that yummy mustache of confectioner's sugar that I could lick off when I was done.

I N G R E D I E N T S

**1 large egg yolk, at room
  temperature**
1 teaspoon vanilla extract
3 cups all-purpose flour
⅔ cup granulated sugar
¼ teaspoon salt
**1 cup plus 1 tablespoon (2 sticks
  plus 1 tablespoon) unsalted
  butter, very cold, cut into
  about 16 pieces**
Apricot or raspberry preserves
1 cup confectioner's sugar

1. Using a fork, stir the egg yolk and vanilla together in a small cup.

2. Process the flour, granulated sugar, and salt in a food processor for about 10 seconds.

3. Add the butter and process the mixture until it resembles coarse meal, 20 to 30 seconds.

4. With the machine running, add the yolk mixture through the feed tube and process for 5 seconds. Scrape the bowl, then process until the liquid is evenly absorbed, about 10 seconds.

5. Remove the dough and place it on a work surface. Work the dough with your hands just until you can form it into a mass. Divide the dough in half and shape it into 2 thick disks. Wrap each disk in plastic wrap. Refrigerate the dough several hours or overnight.

6. When you're ready to prepare the cookies, preheat the oven to 350°F. Lightly grease several cookie sheets with vegetable oil or butter. Remove the dough from the refrigerator and allow it to soften slightly.

7. Place each piece of dough between 2 new pieces of plastic wrap or waxed paper and roll it out ⅛ inch thick (see page 165 for rolling technique).

8. Remove the top piece of plastic wrap and, using a 2-inch round cookie cutter, cut out approximately 22 circles from each half. Make small holes in the center of half the circles with a smooth bottle cap or a small cookie cutter. Place the circles about ¾ inch apart on the prepared cookie sheets. Gather up the dough scraps and reroll the dough to make as many more cookies as possible.

9. Bake the cookies until the edges just begin to turn golden, about 15 minutes. Remove them from the oven and cool on the sheets.

10. Place ½ teaspoon preserves in the center of each cookie without a hole. Sprinkle confectioner's sugar over the ones with holes and place them on top of the jammed cookies so that the jam forms a perfect little glob in the middle.

Makes at least 22 cookies

Rugalah

I first tasted rugalah at Ebinger's Bakery in Queens when I was 10 years old and became an instant convert, so much so that the memory lingered for years after Ebinger's closed. Much later, I came up with my own recipe for this Russian tea pastry. I use the same rich cream cheese dough filled with preserves and nuts that I remember from my Ebinger's days, and I've yet to meet anyone who doesn't end up feeling the same way I do about it. These pastries look lovely piled high in a natural basket lined with a crocheted doily. The dough is very moist and difficult to work with, so put on your patience cap and work very slowly and methodically.

I N G R E D I E N T S

DOUGH
1 cup all-purpose flour
½ teaspoon salt
8 tablespoons (1 stick) unsalted butter,
     at room temperature
9 ounces cream cheese,
     at room temperature

FILLING
¾ cup apricot preserves
2 tablespoons sugar
1 teaspoon ground cinnamon
¼ cup chopped pecans
     or walnuts
½ cup golden raisins

GLAZE
1 large egg

1. Sift the flour and salt into a small bowl and set aside.

2. Using an electric mixer on medium speed, cream the butter and cream cheese together in a medium-size mixing bowl until light and fluffy, 1½ to 2 minutes. Stop the mixer once or twice to scrape the bowl with a rubber spatula.

3. Add the dry ingredients and mix until blended, about 20 seconds, stopping the mixer once to scrape the bowl.

4. Shape the dough into 2 equal thick rectangles, wrap each in plastic wrap, and freeze them for 2 hours.

5. Remove 1 dough rectangle from the freezer and roll it out between 2 pieces of plastic wrap into a rectangle about 9 × 8 inches (see page 165 for rolling technique). It may be necessary to refrigerate the dough for 30 minutes during the rolling process, because it will become a bit sticky. Once rolled, refrigerate the dough for 30 minutes. While it is resting, remove the second rectangle from the freezer and roll it out the same way you did the first.

6. To fill the dough, unwrap one rectangle and place it on plastic wrap on your work surface. Spread half the preserves evenly over the rectangle, leaving uncovered a ½-inch strip along the length of one side.

7. Mix the cinnamon and sugar together. Sprinkle half the cinnamon sugar, nuts, and raisins over the preserves.

8. Loosen the edge of the dough that is covered with jam with a knife or spatula and roll it toward the uncovered edge like a jelly roll, peeling off the plastic wrap as you roll. The seam should be on the underside. Wrap the roll in plastic and refrigerate it. Repeat the process with the other dough rectangle. Keep the filled rolls refrigerated for 2 hours.

9. Fifteen minutes before baking, preheat the oven to 375°F. Line 2 cookie sheets with parchment paper or lightly grease them with butter or vegetable oil.

10. For the glaze, lightly beat the egg with a fork. Use a pastry brush to apply the glaze to the outside of the roll. Using a thin, sharp knife, carefully cut the rolls into pieces about 1¼ inches long.

11. Place the rugalah about 1 inch apart on the prepared cookie sheets.

12. Bake the rugalah until golden, about 25 minutes. (Some of the jam will ooze out and start to darken.) Use a spatula to remove the rugalah from the pan immediately and place them on a rack to cool. When they are cool, place them in an airtight container for a day before serving so that the taste and consistency have a chance to settle.

Makes 30 pieces

Maya's Pocketbooks

*W*hen I was young, our cook, Martha, always had a little dough left over when she made her fabulous fruit pies. She'd give it to me to make what I called pocketbooks, which I filled with jam, baked, and got to eat way before the pie was done. These miniature turnovers are the latter day version of my early creations.

INGREDIENTS

2½ cups all-purpose flour, sifted
3 tablespoons sugar
¾ teaspoon salt
1 cup (2 sticks) cold unsalted butter, cut into 16 pieces
3 large egg yolks
2 tablespoons ice water
About 1 cup fruit preserves (the thicker the better)

1. Place the flour, sugar, and salt in a food processor and process for about 6 seconds.

2. Add the butter to the flour mixture and process until all the ingredients are blended, 10 to 15 seconds.

3. Whisk the egg yolks and ice water

together. While the machine is running, pour the yolks through the feed tube, and pulse 15 times, then process until the dough comes together, 5 seconds more.

4. Remove the dough from the machine and knead it with 6 or 7 turns. Shape the dough into 2 thick disks, wrap each in plastic, and refrigerate at least 1 hour.

5. Preheat the oven to 400°F. Line several cookie sheets with parchment paper or lightly grease them with butter or vegetable oil.

6. Roll out each piece of dough between 2 pieces of plastic wrap or waxed paper ⅛ inch thick (see page 165 for rolling technique). Using a

2¾-inch round cookie cutter, cut out 20 round cookies from each piece. (On a humid day, it may be necessary to refrigerate the rolled-out dough for 15 minutes before cutting.)

7. Place 1 level teaspoon of fruit preserves on half of one side of each circle and fold the other side over. Seal the seams by pinching the edges together. Make a fork prick in the center of each pocketbook. Place the pocketbooks about 1 inch apart on the prepared cookie sheets.

8. Bake the pocketbooks until they are golden, about 12 minutes. Cool on a rack before serving.

Makes 40 pocketbooks

CHAPTER FOUR

Harvard Squares

ot so long ago I read that somebody who pays attention to such things found that Americans ate over two billion brownies in one year, which comes to about nine per person. Right there I began to get suspicious. I mean, only nine?

After the brownie counters finished, the market researchers had their say and announced that men eat more brownies than women, particularly in the 13-to-34 and 45-to-54 age groups. (Females peak in brownie consumption between the ages of two and five, probably because at that age, they haven't yet been taught to worry about which part of their body will be wearing the calories.) The researchers went on to determine that southerners prefer homemade brownies, while northerners eat ready-made ones, and everyone eats more brownies on Fridays and Sundays than the rest of the week. Brownies are a hot item these days, they concluded, because they're "the ultimate comfort food, like mashed potatoes."

Now I could have saved all these people a lot of trouble, since I've known since early childhood that brownies are one of life's basic necessities. Moreover, I kept on consuming them well past the age of five, and my innocence wasn't shattered until I went away to college and had to wean myself from my mother's brownies. In desperation, I tried a Duncan Hines extra-fudgy mix, adding more chocolate and butter to make sure it was robust enough, and, to no one's surprise but my own, it was not what I had in mind.

Unwilling to go through life without a really good brownie to my name, I said good-bye to mixes and shortcuts and began experimenting with variations on my mother's recipe. I spent many hours — particularly around exam time — searching for something appropriate to my maturing taste buds: something deeply chocolate, sufficiently chewy and sweet enough to give me that brownie rush, but not anything gloppy or so saccharine that it made my teeth itch afterwards. In short, I was on a quest for the essential brownie. Many fiascoes later, I came up with the version I use to this day, the brownie that in many ways defines Rosie's.

The Bar Scene

It might have been possible to stop at brownies when Rosie's first opened, but I had a hankering for other kinds of bars and squares and figured other people would too. So early on, I added Congo Bars, Boom Booms, Honeypots, and later Walnut Dream Bars, Dagwoods, and Lemon Cream Cheese Squares.

In 1976 Rosie's and its brownies got a boost from an American original named C. P. Luongo, who strolled into my store one day to announce that he was writing a book called *America's Best*—restaurants, hotels, trains, ice cream, you know the sort of compendium. I remember being impressed that he had figured out how to make a living from such an enjoyable pastime, and I liked him even better when he proclaimed our brownies the best in the country. Other awards followed: so many Best of Boston citations from *Boston Magazine* that they put us in their Hall of Fame, a vote from *Chocolatier* magazine for our brownie as one of their all-time best, requests from *Gourmet* for recipes.

Then we got our strangest vote of confidence when a teacher friend who was carrying a book bag full of her students' final papers and a batch of Chocolate Orgasms (Rosie's luscious fudge-frosted brownies) was robbed on her way home. Two days later, the bag was returned to her with everything intact except the Chocolate Orgasms which were nowhere to be found.

To what do I attribute this , tiny piece of immortality? I think it's true that brownies and their counterparts are an accessible indulgence and a comfort food, though that label sounds more like Cream of Wheat to me. They remind us of childhood, allow us to be self-indulgent in reasonable proportions, and are easy to make, highly portable, and more American than apple pie. Most important, they taste good.

Still, I balk at the suggestion that brownies and other pastry bars are only for kids. When I serve them as dessert at grown-up dinner parties, I receive only praise. I come across them for sale at fancy food shops from coast to coast. And if my customers are any indication, it's not just southern men of a certain age eating them on Sundays.

Belly Up to the Bar

*W*hen it comes to baking bars and squares, the only rule that applies is that they're relatively easy and quick to make—something you *can* whip up without planning and keep around for a snack. Beyond that, each recipe works differently to produce a distinctive taste and texture, though they fall into three basic categories.

Brownielike Bars

These include Chocolate Orgasms and Dagwoods, bars that contain many of the same ingredients as cakes but are proportionately different. As a rule, they contain less flour and no liquid, depending on eggs for moisture instead.

Preparing the Pan: Grease a baking pan lightly with butter or vegetable oil. If you want to remove a batch uncut from the pan, line the bottom with baking parchment.

Baking: The oven is usually set to 350°F but some recipes call for 375°F. Bake on the center rack of the oven.

Unlike cakes, you can vary the baking time of these bars slightly to produce different textures and still get good results. As the bars bake, a crust forms over the surface, so if you want chewy bars, you have to catch them when the crust is still paper thin. When the center is almost level with the sides, insert a cake tester in the middle and if it comes out dry or with moist crumbs, but no syrupy batter, remove the pan from the oven. The center will drop as it cools, and the texture will be chewy. For airier and cakier bars, allow the batter to bake longer — until the center has risen slightly and formed a slightly thicker crust. Keep in mind that this principle doesn't apply to baking cakes, even when you bake them in a flat pan like bars.

Cutting: You can cut these bars warm or cool using a thin, sharp knife. If the bars are completely cool, try dipping the knife in hot water before each cut to make it easier.

Storing: Stored in an airtight container, these bars will stay moist without refrigeration for about three days, but the chewier the bar, the longer its shelf life. When refrigerated, the bars will last for a week or two, and they freeze very well.

Shortbread Bars

Shortbread bars, such as Lemon Cream Cheese Squares, Dutch Butter Bars, Honeypots, or Walnut Dream Bars, are made either from a simple shortbread batter or by adding a topping to a prebaked shortbread base.

Preparing the Pan: It's not absolutely necessary to grease the pans because shortbread contains enough butter to keep it from sticking, but I like to be on the safe side and do it anyway.

Spreading the Batter in the Pan: If the batter is extremely fluffy or sticky, I find it helps to dip my fingertips in flour before gently spreading the shortbread over the bottom of the pan.

Glazing the Base: When the recipe calls for a liquid topping, I glaze the base before baking it. Pour an egg white directly on the top of the batter, tilt the pan from side to side to make sure the surface is covered, then spill the excess egg white into the sink. As the base bakes, the egg white hardens and forms a thin crust to keep the base from absorbing the liquid.

Baking: I've found that the shortbread that is golden in color is the most flavorful, so I bake the base of these bars at 350°F until it turns light gold. I then chill it before adding the topping to make sure the base stays crunchy.

Cutting: These cut best when they've cooled some. Sugary bars with gooey centers, such as Walnut Dream Bars or Pecan Bars, should be cut as soon as they cool; if you wait too long, the top caramelizes and is hard to cut. Use a cleaver or sturdy knife.

Shortbread bars with soft toppings, such as Whitecaps and Tart Lemon Squares, can be cut later, but it's best to use a thin knife that has been dipped in hot water and wiped dry before each cut. The heat melts the topping just enough for the knife to glide through.

Bars made of one layer of shortbread, such as Dutch Butter Bars, should be cut when they're still hot, so the dough doesn't crack. Bars with a bottom and top crust, such as Jam Sandwiches and Linzer Bars, can be cut after they've cooled, but need a knife run around the sides of the pan while they're still hot so that the jam filling doesn't stick to the pan.

Storing: Keep bars with soft toppings in airtight containers in the refrigerator or freezer. All other shortbread bars can be stored at room temperature or in the fridge for several days.

Crummy Bars

My one entry in this category is Apple Crumb Bars. These bars consist of two layers of crumbs with a filling in between. They tend to be more fragile than other bars, so if they're to be eaten by hand, I serve them cold because they're sturdier that way.

Preparing the Pan: Grease the pan lightly with butter or vegetable oil.

Baking: The temperature varies from 350°F to 425°F, depending on the recipe.

Cutting: These bars are cut best with a thin knife when they've cooled, but run a knife around the edge of the pan while they're still hot to prevent the filling from sticking.

Storing: Keep these bars in an airtight container in the refrigerator. They'll last for a week and can be frozen as well. Unfrosted bars that get soggy can be rebaked briefly in a cool oven (300°F) to restore their crispness.

Serving

The spirit of bars comes a lot from how you cut them up and serve them. In hearty squares, they make a good afternoon or TV-watching snack, and when cut into dainty finger food, they turn into an elegant dessert suitable for any party. For the latter, I cut each bar into three or four pieces, depending on its richness, and arrange the pieces symmetrically on a small, doily-covered platter. If you're serving more than one kind of bar, use the differences in color, texture, and shape to create a pattern. I've found that people love bite-size pieces because that allows them to sample and enjoy without having to face up to just how much they've consumed.

I have to confess that bars are my favorite kind of dessert to make, although, saying that, I feel like the parent who hastens to protest that she loves all her children equally. Still there's something so dependable about a good brownie. Newsletters and conventions for chocolate lovers may come and go, but I believe that fudge brownies are here to stay. I take great comfort in knowing that when everything else in life is a mess, I can still bake a batch of Congo Bars in half an hour.

Rosie's Award-Winning Brownies

*G*rowing up, there was nothing I craved more than a good brownie. It took me years to come up with my own version—fudgy, but not too sweet. Countless all-nighters slaving over a hot mixing bowl and all those inches on my thighs proved to be worth it, though, when it was named Best Brownie in America.

INGREDIENTS

4 ounces unsweetened chocolate
8 tablespoons (1 stick) unsalted butter, at room temperature
1¼ cups plus 1 tablespoon sugar
½ teaspoon vanilla extract
3 large eggs, at room temperature
¾ cup all-purpose flour
½ cup plus 2 tablespoons chopped walnuts

1. Preheat the oven to 325°F. Lightly grease an 8-inch square pan with butter or vegetable oil.

2. Melt the chocolate and butter in the top of a double boiler placed over simmering water. Cool the mixture for 5 minutes.

3. Place the sugar in a medium-size mixing bowl and pour in the chocolate mixture. Using an electric mixer on medium speed, mix until blended, about 25 seconds. Scrape the bowl with a rubber spatula.

4. Add the vanilla. With the mixer on medium-low speed, add the eggs one at a time, blending after each addition until the yolk is broken and dispersed, about 10 seconds. Scrape the bowl after the last egg and blend until velvety, about 15 more seconds.

5. Add the flour on low speed and mix for 20 seconds; finish the mixing by hand, being certain to mix in any flour at the bottom of the bowl. Stir in ½ cup of the nuts.

6. Spread the batter evenly in the prepared pan and sprinkle the remaining 2 tablespoons of nuts over the top.

7. Bake the brownies on the center oven rack until a thin crust forms on top and a tester inserted in the center comes out with a moist crumb, about 35 minutes. (The center of the brownies should never quite rise to the height of the edges.)

8. Remove the pan from the oven and place it on a rack to cool for 1 hour before cutting the brownies. Serve the next day (it takes a day for the flavor to set) and don't forget the tall glass of milk.

Makes 9 to 12 brownies

Chocolate Orgasms

*O*kay, Daddy, now you can admit you were wrong — this is a great name. After all, it has become Rosie's most famous dessert. Although people of all ages come to my store and eat big versions of this bar, when I make them at home, I like to cut them into small squares, top each one with a whole walnut or raspberry, and arrange them on a paper lace doily. They are also wonderful served in a small bowl with vanilla, chocolate chip, coffee, or mint ice cream.

I N G R E D I E N T S

1 recipe Rosie's Award-Winning Brownies (nuts are optional; page 135)
1½ ounces unsweetened chocolate
¼ cup evaporated milk
⅓ cup sugar

1. Prepare the brownies and allow them to cool completely. Don't cut them yet.

2. To prepare the frosting, melt the chocolate in the top of a double boiler placed over simmering water.

3. Pour the evaporated milk into an electric blender and add the sugar and the melted chocolate. Blend the frosting on medium-low speed until it thickens, about 50 seconds (the sound of the machine will change when this process occurs).

4. Using a frosting spatula, spread the frosting evenly over the surface of the cooled brownies and allow them to sit for 1 hour before cutting.

Makes 36 small brownies

Boom Booms

I won't tell you what these were named after — those of us who were around for Rosie's beginnings will guard that secret — but I will tell you that they are a wonderful combination of a dark fudge brownie marbled with a sweet cream cheese mixture. They are beautiful to look at as well.

I N G R E D I E N T S

1 recipe Rosie's Award-Winning Brownies, batter without nuts (page 135)
8 ounces cream cheese, chilled
1½ teaspoons all-purpose flour
5 tablespoons sugar
1 large egg, at room temperature
¼ teaspoon vanilla extract

1. Preheat the oven to 300°F. Lightly grease an 8-inch square pan with butter or vegetable oil.

2. Prepare the brownie batter, omitting the nuts, and set aside.

3. For the cream cheese filling, place all the remaining ingredients in a food processor and process until blended, about 45 seconds. Set aside.

4. Spread about two-thirds of the brownie batter in the prepared pan. Spread the cream cheese filling over the brownie batter. Using a spoon, scoop the remaining brownie batter over the filling in nine equal mounds arranged in rows of threes so that there is some space between them.

5. Run a chopstick or the handle of a wooden spoon back and forth the length of the pan, making parallel lines about 1½ inches apart, then do the same thing in the other direction as if making a grid. This will marbleize the two mixtures. Shake the pan gently back and forth to level the batter.

6. Bake the bars on the center oven rack until a tester inserted in the center comes out clean or with some moist crumbs, about 50 minutes. Allow the brownies to cool for 1 hour before cutting.

Makes 9 to 12 brownies

Mint Brownies

*T*he flavor of mint and chocolate combine beautifully in this bar without losing their integrity.

INGREDIENTS

1 recipe Rosie's Award-Winning Brownies without nuts or Extra Extra Fudgy Brownies without nuts (page 135 or 138)

MINT BUTTERCREAM
1 cup confectioner's sugar
4 tablespoons (½ stick) unsalted butter, at room temperature
2 teaspoons peppermint extract

GLAZE
4 ounces bittersweet chocolate
2 teaspoons light corn syrup

1. Prepare the desired brownies and allow them to cool completely (you can place the pan in the refrigerator or freezer to speed up the process).

2. To prepare the buttercream, using an electric mixer on high speed, cream the sugar, butter, and extract until white and fluffy, 2 to 2½ minutes.

3. Spread the buttercream evenly over the cooled brownie cake and freeze for 1 hour.

4. After the hour is up, melt the chocolate for the glaze in the top of a double boiler placed over simmering water. Remove the pan from the water and stir the corn syrup into the melted chocolate.

5. Allow the glaze to cool to the point where it is no longer hot but is still loose and spreadable. Using a frosting spatula, spread the glaze over the buttercream. Immediately place the pan in the refrigerator and allow the chocolate to harden for about 30 minutes.

6. Cut the brownies with a thin, sharp knife that has been dipped in hot water and dried before each cut.

Makes 16 brownies

Extra Extra Fudgy Brownies

A brownie made for fudge fanatics. These are the ones to make if you're chocolate level is about a quart low.

INGREDIENTS

1½ ounces semisweet chocolate
2½ ounces unsweetened chocolate
8 tablespoons (1 stick) unsalted butter
1 cup plus 2 tablespoons sugar
3 large eggs
7 tablespoons all-purpose flour
½ cup plus 2 tablespoons chopped walnuts

1. Preheat the oven to 325°F. Lightly grease an 8-inch square pan with butter or vegetable oil.

2. Melt both chocolates and the butter in the top of a double boiler placed over simmering water. Cool the mixture for 5 minutes.

3. Place the sugar in a medium-size mixing bowl and pour in the chocolate mixture. Using an electric mixer on medium speed, mix until blended, about 25 seconds. Scrape the bowl with a rubber spatula.

4. With the mixer on medium-low speed, add the eggs one at a time, blending after each addition until the yolk is broken and dispersed, about 10 seconds. Scrape the bowl after the last egg and blend until velvety, about 15 seconds more.

5. Add the flour on low speed and mix for 20 seconds; finish the mixing by hand, being certain to mix in any flour at the bottom of the bowl. Stir in ½ cup of the nuts.

6. Spread the batter evenly in the prepared pan and sprinkle the remaining 2 tablespoons nuts over the top.

7. Bake the brownies on the center oven rack until a tester inserted in the center comes out with a moist crumb, about 25 minutes. Allow the brownies to cool for 1 hour before cutting.

Makes 9 to 12 brownies

D D's

*T*hese brownies ought to be served with a D D alert because they are decidedly a Deadly Dessert. They're dark, dense, delicious and *de rigueur* for chocolate lovers. The recipe requires a strong upper arm for folding in the egg whites, but other than that, it's a cinch.

I N G R E D I E N T S

---

12 ounces semisweet chocolate
4 ounces unsweetened chocolate
1 cup (2 sticks) unsalted butter
9 large eggs, separated, at room
 temperature
1 cup plus 2 tablespoons sugar
Strawberry or raspberry jam for
 serving (optional)
1/2 recipe Whipped Cream (page 86) for
 serving (optional)

1. Melt both chocolates and the butter in the top of a double boiler placed over simmering water. Allow the mixture to cool until it is only slightly warm.

2. Preheat the oven to 325°F. Lightly grease a 13 × 9-inch pan with butter or vegetable oil.

3. Using an electric mixer on medium speed, beat the egg yolks and 3/4 cup plus 2 tablespoons sugar in a medium-size mixing bowl until thick and pale, about 2 minutes. Stop the mixer once or twice to scrape the bowl with a rubber spatula.

4. With the mixer on medium-low speed, add the chocolate mixture and mix until the batter is uniform in color, about 10 seconds. Scrape the bowl, then mix for several seconds more.

5. In another mixing bowl, whip the egg whites on medium-high speed until frothy, about 30 seconds. Gradually add the remaining 1/4 cup sugar and continue beating the whites to soft peaks, 45 seconds more.

6. Stir one-third of the whites into the batter to loosen it, then fold the remaining whites into the mixture carefully by hand, using a rubber spatula. Pour the batter evenly into the prepared pan.

7. Bake the brownies on the center oven rack until the top has risen and set and a tester inserted in the center comes out clean, about 40 minutes.

8. Place the pan on a rack to cool for 1 hour before cutting. Cut the brownies into bars and serve them as they are or spread a thin layer of strawberry or raspberry jam over the surface of the bars and cover that with a layer of whipped cream.

Makes 12 to 16 brownies

Chunky Chocolate Bars

7he name really says it all because what makes these bars unusual is their texture. They're something like what a Cadbury's fruit-and-nut bar would be if it could be a brownie: mouthfuls of chocolate with raisins and walnuts in every bite. Although they taste good as soon as they've cooled, they hold together better and crumble less if you wait a day to eat them. Give it a try.

INGREDIENTS

3 ounces unsweetened chocolate
8 tablespoons (1 stick) unsalted butter, at room temperature
1 cup sugar
1 teaspoon vanilla extract
2 large eggs, at room temperature
½ cup all-purpose flour
½ cup chopped walnuts
¼ cup chopped dates
½ cup raisins

1. Melt the chocolate in the top of a double boiler over simmering water. Cool slightly.

2. Preheat the oven to 350°F. Lightly grease an 8-inch square pan with butter or vegetable oil.

3. Using an electric mixer on medium speed, cream the butter, sugar, and vanilla in a medium-size mixing bowl until light and fluffy, 2 to 3 minutes. Stop the mixer to scrape the bowl twice with a rubber spatula.

4. Add the chocolate and mix on medium speed until blended, about 8 seconds. Scrape the bowl.

5. Add the eggs and blend the mixture on high speed for 3 seconds. Scrape the bowl, then mix on medium speed until the eggs are blended in, about 15 seconds. The batter will not be smooth.

6. On low speed, add the flour and mix until it is almost incorporated. Scrape the bowl. Add the nuts, dates, and raisins and mix until blended, about 5 seconds. Spread the batter evenly in the prepared pan.

7. Bake the bars on the center oven rack until a tester inserted in the center comes out clean, about 35 minutes. Place the pan on a rack to cool completely before cutting.

Makes 12 to 16 bars

White Chocolate Brownies

*B*uttery and chewy, this bar is an uncommon alternative to its counterpart, the fudge brownie.

INGREDIENTS

8 tablespoons (1 stick) unsalted butter
4 ounces white chocolate
2 large eggs, at room temperature
1/2 teaspoon salt
1 cup sugar
1 teaspoon vanilla extract
1 cup all-purpose flour

1. Preheat the oven to 325°F. Lightly grease an 11 × 7-inch baking pan with butter or vegetable oil.

2. Melt the butter in the top of a double boiler placed over simmering water. When the butter has melted, add the chocolate and melt.

3. Using an electric mixer on medium-high speed, beat the eggs and salt in a medium-size mixing bowl until frothy, about 30 seconds. Gradually add the sugar and continue beating until the eggs are thick and pale, about 1½ minutes. Scrape the bowl with a rubber spatula.

4. Add the chocolate mixture and the vanilla and mix on medium-low speed until blended, about 5 seconds. Scrape the bowl.

5. Mix in the flour on low speed until blended, scraping the bowl with the rubber spatula once during blending. Pour the batter evenly into the prepared pan.

6. Bake the brownies on the center oven rack until a tester inserted in the center comes out clean, about 40 minutes. Allow the brownies to cool on a rack for 1 hour before cutting.

Makes 12 brownies

Dagwoods

*I*n my humble opinion, it's texture and thickness that makes this the perfect butterscotch brownie. The recipe came from my mother-in-law, Barbara, who insisted that you had to mix it by hand with a wooden spoon. Old-fashioned superstition, I scoffed, pulling out my KitchenAid and setting to work. Barbara was right, of course. You can make these brownies with a machine, but they come out differently and not nearly as good. So, chastised, I now make them by hand, and I've found that it's just as quick and easy.

1¼ cups all-purpose flour
*1½ cups (lightly packed) light brown
    sugar*
1½ teaspoon baking powder
⅛ teaspoon salt
2 large eggs, at room temperature
*10 tablespoons (about 9½ tablespoons
    cold) melted unsalted butter*
2 teaspoons vanilla extract
½ cup chopped walnuts

1. Preheat the oven to 350°F. Lightly grease an 8-inch square pan with butter or vegetable oil.

2. Blend the flour, sugar, baking powder, and salt in a medium-size bowl with a wooden spoon.

3. In another medium-size bowl, beat the eggs with a whisk until blended. Whisk in the melted butter and the vanilla.

4. Make a well in the center of the dry ingredients and pour the wet ingredients into the well. Using the wooden spoon, stir until the mixture is blended.

5. Add the nuts with a few broad strokes. Spread the batter evenly in the prepared pan.

6. Bake the bars on the center oven rack until golden and a tester inserted in the center comes out clean or with moist crumbs, 35 to 40 minutes. Place the pan on a rack to cool for 1 hour before cutting.

Makes 9 to 12 bars

Congo Bars

*T*he Congo Bar is a chewy butterscotch brownie full of chocolate chips and nuts. I have no idea where the name came from, but regardless of its roots, this was one of Rosie's first products and it remains a perennial favorite.

1⅓ cups all-purpose flour
1½ teaspoons baking soda
½ teaspoon salt
*9 tablespoons (1 stick plus
    1 tablespoon) unsalted butter,
    at room temperature*
*1¾ cups (lightly packed) light brown
    sugar*
1¼ teaspoons vanilla extract
2 large eggs, at room temperature
1 cup semisweet chocolate chips
½ cup chopped walnuts

1. Preheat the oven to 350°F. Lightly grease a 13 × 9-inch baking pan with butter or vegetable oil.

2. Blend the flour, baking soda, and salt in a small bowl with a wooden spoon. Set aside.

3. Using an electric mixer on medium speed, cream the butter, sugar, and vanilla in a medium-size bowl until light and fluffy, about 2 minutes. Stop the mixer once or twice to scrape the bowl with a rubber spatula.

4. Add the eggs and mix on high speed for 3 seconds, then on medium speed until blended, about 5 more seconds.

5. Add the flour mixture and mix on low speed until almost blended, 8 to 10 seconds. Stop the mixer once to scrape the bowl.

6. Add the chocolate chips and nuts and mix on low speed for 5 seconds. Finish the mixing by hand with a wooden spoon. Spread the batter evenly in the prepared pan.

7. Bake the bars on the center oven rack until the top has formed a rich golden crust and dropped below the level of the darker golden outer edges, 30 minutes. These bars cannot be tested by inserting a tester because they remain very gooey inside. Cool for 30 minutes in the pan placed on a rack before cutting. They are best eaten the first day. Leftovers must be stored in an airtight container in the refrigerator.

Makes 12 bars

Jayne Mansfields

My heroes have always been actresses. The other little girls were panting over Rock Hudson and Ricky Nelson while I was hanging pictures of Marilyn Monroe and Jayne Mansfield all over my walls. These are for you Jayne — blond, cakey, sweet, with an occasional chocolate chip.

I N G R E D I E N T S

1¹/₂ cups plus 2 tablespoons cake flour
¹/₄ teaspoon baking powder
¹/₈ teaspoon baking soda
¹/₂ teaspoon salt
12 tablespoons (1¹/₂ sticks) unsalted butter, at room temperature
1¹/₂ cups (lightly packed) light brown sugar
2 teaspoons vanilla extract
3 large eggs, at room temperature
³/₄ cup semisweet chocolate chips

1. Preheat the oven to 350°F. Lightly grease an 11 × 7-inch baking pan with butter.

2. Sift the flour, baking powder, baking soda, and salt together into a small bowl and set aside.

3. Using an electric mixer on medium speed, cream the butter, sugar, and vanilla in a medium-size mixing bowl until light and fluffy, about 1½ minutes. Scrape the bowl with a rubber spatula.

4. Add the eggs one at a time and beat on medium speed after each addition until partially blended, 5 seconds. Scrape the bowl, then beat until the batter is blended, 20 seconds more.

5. With the mixer on low, add the dry ingredients and beat until almost blended, about 15 seconds. Scrape the bowl.

6. Add the chips and mix on low speed until they are blended in, about 5 seconds. Stir the batter several times with a rubber spatula. Spread the batter evenly in the prepared pan.

7. Bake the bars on the center oven rack until the top has risen and set, and is golden in color, 26 to 28 minutes. (The top won't spring back when touched; a depression remains.) Allow the bars to cool for 1 hour on a rack before cutting.

Makes 12 bars

Peanut-Butter Chocolate-Chip Bars

*Y*ou start with a blond brownie, add peanut butter and a generous helping of chocolate chips, and, if my son and his neighborhood cohorts are any indication, you've got the perfect treat. (My older acquaintances are fond of them too.) The precise flour measurements are a must.

INGREDIENTS

- 1⅓ cups plus 1 tablespoon plus 1 teaspoon all-purpose flour
- 2 teaspoons baking powder
- ⅛ teaspoon baking soda
- ¼ teaspoon salt
- 8 tablespoons (1 stick) unsalted butter, at room temperature
- ½ cup commercial smooth peanut butter
- ½ cup granulated sugar
- ½ cup plus 2 tablespoons (lightly packed) light brown sugar
- 1 teaspoon vanilla extract
- 2 large eggs, at room temperature
- 1 cup semisweet chocolate chips

1. Preheat the oven to 350°F. Lightly grease an 11 × 7-inch baking pan with butter or vegetable oil.

2. Sift the flour, baking powder, baking soda, and salt together into a medium-size mixing bowl and set aside.

3. Using an electric mixer on medium-high speed, cream the butter, peanut butter, both sugars, and the vanilla until light and fluffy, about 1½ minutes. Stop the mixer to scrape the bowl with a rubber spatula.

4. Add the eggs one at a time and beat on medium speed until partially blended after each addition, about 10 seconds. After the last addition, beat until blended, about 30 seconds, stopping the mixer twice to scrape the bowl.

5. Add the dry ingredients to the batter and mix with a spatula until the flour is absorbed. Then mix on low speed until blended, 7 to 10 seconds. Scrape the bowl, especially the bottom.

6. Add the chocolate chips and blend for several seconds. Scrape the bowl. Spread the batter evenly in the prepared pan.

7. Bake the bars on the center oven rack until the edges are deep golden and the center is lightly golden and slightly puffy, 25 to 30 minutes. The center will drop when the bars are taken out of the oven, creating a chewy texture. Cut the bars into squares after they have cooled a bit on the rack.

Makes 12 bars

Orange Birthday Cake Bars

*T*his pound-cake-like bar doesn't really fit into any of the categories in this chapter. But it is an easy-to-handle and not overly sweet bar. It's great for 1- to 2-year-old birthday parties as well as a delicious treat for grown-ups.

INGREDIENTS

CAKE
2¼ cups cake flour
1 teaspoon baking soda
½ teaspoon salt
1 cup (2 sticks) unsalted butter, at room temperature
3 ounces cream cheese, at room temperature
1¾ cups granulated sugar
2 teaspoons vanilla extract
1 tablespoon grated orange zest
4 large eggs, at room temperature

GLAZE
1 cup sifted confectioner's sugar
4 tablespoons (½ stick) unsalted butter, melted
3 tablespoons fresh orange juice
1 teaspoon fresh lemon juice
Pinch of salt

1. Preheat the oven to 350°F. Lightly grease a 15 × 10-inch jelly-roll pan with butter or vegetable oil.

2. For the cake, sift the flour, baking soda, and salt together in a small bowl and set aside.

3. Using an electric mixer on medium-high speed, cream the butter, cream cheese, granulated sugar, vanilla, and orange zest together in a medium-size mixing bowl until light and fluffy, about 2 minutes. Stop the mixer once or twice to scrape the bowl with a rubber spatula.

4. Add the eggs one at a time and beat on medium-low speed until each yolk is partially blended, 10 seconds. Scrape the bowl after each addition.

5. Fold in half the dry ingredients with the rubber spatula until partially incorporated, then turn the mixer to low and blend for several seconds. Repeat with the remaining dry ingredients, blending for 10 seconds with the electric mixer. Finish the mixing by hand with a few broad strokes of the spatula. Spread the batter evenly in the prepared pan.

6. Bake until the cake is lightly golden, springs back to the touch, and a tester inserted in the center comes out clean, 20 to 25 minutes. Allow the cake to cool completely on a rack while preparing the glaze.

7. Place all the ingredients for the glaze in a small bowl and stir vigorously with a whisk until blended.

8. Pour the glaze over the cake and spread it evenly with a frosting spatula. Allow the glaze to harden, 3 to 4 hours before serving.

Makes 24 bars

Brownie Shortbread

I've added a layer of brownie to the top of a crunchy shortbread for those days when you can't decide which you prefer.

INGREDIENTS

BASE
1 cup all-purpose flour
¼ cup sugar
8 tablespoons (1 stick) unsalted butter, at room temperature, cut into 8 pieces

TOPPING
3 ounces unsweetened chocolate
8 tablespoons (1 stick) unsalted butter
2 large eggs, at room temperature
¾ cup sugar
½ teaspoon baking powder

1. Preheat the oven to 350°F. Lightly grease an 11 × 7-inch baking pan with butter.

2. For the base, process the flour and sugar in a food processor about 15 seconds. Add the butter and process until the dough comes together, 20 to 30 seconds.

3. Pat the dough gently over the bottom of the prepared pan. Bake on the center oven rack until it is lightly golden, about 20 minutes. Place the base in the refrigerator for 15 minutes to cool completely. Keep the oven on.

4. Meanwhile prepare the topping: Melt the chocolate and butter in the top of a double boiler over simmering water. Cool slightly.

5. Beat the eggs, sugar, and baking powder together in a medium-size bowl with a whisk. Add the chocolate mixture and stir vigorously with the whisk until the batter is blended.

Spread the chocolate mixture evenly over the base.

6. Bake the bars until the top rises and forms a very thin crust, about 20 minutes. The center will drop as it cools. (A tester inserted in the middle may come out with a fudgy, crumbly batter on it, but it should not be liquidy.) Cool completely on a rack. Cut the shortbread with a thin knife.

Makes 12 bars

Honeypots

*T*hese sweet, crunchy, buttery bars were part of my original Babycakes repertoire. My good friend Karen McCarthy was my partner then, and we rewarded ourselves for spending endless hours over hot stoves and not-so-hot accounts with a Honeypot apiece at the end of the day. It was usually too late for anyone else to be around, which is a good thing because we'd close our eyes and moan loudly from sheer pleasure.

INGREDIENTS

BASE
1 cup all-purpose flour
1/2 cup confectioner's sugar
8 tablespoons (1 stick) unsalted butter, at room temperature, cut into 8 pieces
1 egg white for glazing

TOPPING
6 tablespoons (3/4 stick) unsalted butter
1/2 cup (lightly packed) light brown sugar
1/2 cup honey
1 1/4 cups chopped walnuts
1/4 cup heavy (whipping) cream
1 teaspoon vanilla extract

1. Preheat the oven to 350°F. Lightly grease an 8-inch square pan with butter.

2. For the base, process the flour and confectioner's sugar in a food processor for 20 seconds. Add the butter and process until the dough comes together, 20 to 30 seconds.

3. Pat the dough gently over the bottom of the prepared pan and glaze it with the egg white: Pour the egg white on the dough and tip the pan from side to side so that the white spreads over the surface. Pour off the excess.

4. Bake the base on the center oven rack until golden, about 25 minutes. Place the base in the refrigerator for 15 minutes to cool completely. Keep the oven on.

5. Meanwhile prepare the topping: Combine the butter, brown sugar, and honey in a medium-size saucepan. Heat, stirring the mixture with a wooden spoon, over medium-low heat until it begins to boil. Boil without stirring for 5 minutes.

6. While the mixture is boiling, put the nuts in a medium-size bowl; add the cream and the vanilla and stir to combine.

7. Add the boiled honey mixture to the nuts mixture and stir the ingredients together. Pour the topping evenly over the cooled base.

8. Bake the bars on the center oven rack until the entire surface is bubbling, about 25 minutes.

9. Place the pan on a cooling rack and cool for 1 hour. Then run a sharp knife around the sides of the pan and let cool completely. Cut into bars with a cleaver or very strong knife.

Makes 16 bars

Cherry Cheesecake Bars

A luscious layer of cheesecake studded with cherries or berries atop a crunchy shortbread crust.

INGREDIENTS

BASE
1 cup all-purpose flour
3 tablespoons confectioner's sugar
7 tablespoons unsalted butter,
*   at room temperature, cut into*
*   7 pieces*
1/2 teaspoon vanilla extract
1 egg white for glazing

TOPPING
1/2 cup drained canned pitted sour
*   cherries or fresh blueberries*
8 ounces cream cheese,
*   at room temperature*
1 cup sour cream, at room temperature
7 tablespoons granulated sugar
2 large egg yolks
1 teaspoon vanilla extract
2 teaspoons all-purpose flour

1. Preheat the oven to 350°F. Lightly grease an 8-inch square baking pan with butter.

2. For the base, process the flour and confectioner's sugar in a food processor for several seconds. Add the butter and vanilla and process until the dough comes together, 20 to 30 seconds.

3. Pat the dough gently over the bottom of the prepared pan and about 1½ inches up the sides. Glaze it with the egg white: Pour the egg white on the dough and tip the pan from side to side so that the white spreads over the surface. Pour off the excess.

4. Bake the base on the center oven rack until lightly golden, about 30 minutes. Place the base in the refrigerator for 15 minutes to cool completely. Keep the oven on.

5. Meanwhile prepare the topping: Wrap the cherries in paper towels to absorb any liquid.

6. Place the remaining topping ingredients in a food processor and process until blended, about 15 seconds.

7. Pour the topping evenly over the base, then arrange the cherries or blueberries evenly on the topping.

8. Bake the bars on the center oven rack until set, about 1 hour. Allow them to cool completely, then refrigerate overnight.

9. The next day cut the bars with a sharp knife that is dipped in hot water and wiped dry before each cut. Allow the bars to warm to room temperature before serving.

Makes 12 bars

Lemon Cream Cheese Squares

I think of these squares as portable cheesecake for, like the best of that genre, they're rich and tart. Of course, from the baker's viewpoint, they're much easier than making cheesecake, especially with their shortbread crust and relatively short baking time.

INGREDIENTS

BASE
1 cup all-purpose flour
¼ cup confectioner's sugar
8 tablespoons (1 stick) unsalted butter, at room temperature, cut into 8 pieces
1 egg white for glazing

TOPPING
10 ounces cream cheese, at room temperature
½ cup plus 1 tablespoon granulated sugar
2 teaspoons grated lemon zest
¼ cup plus 1 tablespoon sour cream, at room temperature
6 tablespoons fresh lemon juice
2 large eggs, at room temperature
1 teaspoon vanilla extract

1. Preheat the oven to 350°F. Lightly grease an 8-inch square baking pan with butter.

2. For the base, process the flour and confectioner's sugar in a food processor for several seconds. Add the butter and process until the dough comes together, 20 to 30 seconds.

3. Pat the dough gently over the bottom of the prepared pan and about 1 inch up the sides. Glaze it with the egg white: Pour the egg white on the dough and tip the pan from side to side so that the white spreads over the surface. Pour off the excess.

4. Bake the base on the center oven rack until golden, about 25 minutes. Place the base in the refrigerator for 15 minutes to cool completely. Keep the oven on.

5. Meanwhile prepare the topping: Using an electric mixer on medium-high speed, cream the cream cheese, granulated sugar, and lemon zest together in a medium-size bowl until light and fluffy, 2 to 3 minutes. Stop the mixer once or twice to scrape the bowl with a rubber spatula.

6. Add the sour cream and lemon juice and beat the mixture on medium-high speed until smooth, about 1 minute. Scrape the bowl.

7. Add the eggs and vanilla and beat on medium-high speed until smooth and creamy, about 10 seconds. Spread the topping evenly over the base.

8. Bake the bars on the center oven rack until the top is slightly golden and a tester inserted in the center comes out dry, about 1 hour. If the topping bubbles up during baking, prick the bubbles with a toothpick or a thin knife.

9. Allow the bars to cool completely on a rack. Cut them with the point of a thin sharp knife that is dipped in hot water and wiped dry before each cut.

Makes 12 to 16 bars

Pecan Bars

*I*f you like pecan pie, you'll love this portable version: a crunchy, buttery crust with a gooey nut topping.

I N G R E D I E N T S

BASE
1¼ cups all-purpose flour
½ cup plus 2 tablespoons confectioner's sugar
10 tablespoons (1¼ sticks) unsalted butter, at room temperature, cut into 10 pieces
1 egg white for glazing

TOPPING
½ cup (lightly packed) light brown
  sugar
½ cup granulated sugar
10 tablespoons dark corn syrup
2 large eggs, at room temperature
¼ teaspoon vanilla extract
Pinch of salt
3 tablespoons unsalted butter, melted
1½ cups chopped pecans

1. Preheat the oven to 350°F. Lightly grease a 9-inch square pan with butter or vegetable oil.

2. For the base, process the flour and confectioner's sugar in a food processor for several seconds. Add the butter and process until the dough comes together, 20 to 30 seconds.

3. Pat the dough gently over the bottom of the prepared pan and push it ½ inch up the sides with your thumb. Glaze it with the egg white: Pour the egg white on the dough and tip the pan from side to side to spread the white over the surface. Pour off the excess.

4. Bake the base on the center oven rack until lightly golden, about 30 minutes. Place the base in the refrigerator for 15 minutes to cool completely. Keep the oven on.

5. Meanwhile prepare the topping: Gently whisk together both sugars, the corn syrup, eggs, vanilla, and salt in a medium-size bowl until blended.

6. Stir in the melted butter, then the nuts. Pour the topping evenly over the base.

7. Bake the bars until the topping is set and forms a crust, about 50 minutes.

8. Allow the bars to cool for 15 minutes on a rack, then run a sharp knife around the sides of the pan. Cool the bars completely and cut into squares. A cleaver or very firm knife works best.

Makes 16 bars

Walnut Dream Bars

*T*his is a bar that refuses to compromise. It's sweet, chewy, full of butter, nuts, and coconut, and it rapidly attained cult status among Rosie's customers. Be forewarned, though: a small bite goes a long way. These bars can be stored forever in an airtight container in your fridge.

INGREDIENTS

BASE
1 cup all-purpose flour
½ cup plus 1 tablespoon (lightly
    packed) light brown sugar
8 tablespoons (1 stick) unsalted
    butter, at room temperature,
    cut into 8 pieces

TOPPING
1 cup (lightly packed) light brown
    sugar
¼ cup plus 3 tablespoons dark
    corn syrup
2 teaspoons vanilla extract
2 tablespoons unsalted butter, melted
1½ tablespoons all-purpose flour
2 large eggs, at room temperature
1 cup coarsely chopped walnuts
½ cup shredded coconut

1. Preheat the oven to 350°F. Lightly grease an 11 × 7-inch baking pan with butter or vegetable oil.

2. For the base, process the flour and sugar in a food processor for several seconds. Add the butter and process until the dough comes together, 20 to 30 seconds.

3. Pat the dough gently over the bottom of the prepared pan.

4. Bake the base on the center oven rack until golden around the edges, 10 to 12 minutes. Place the base in the refrigerator for 15 minutes to cool completely. Keep the oven on.

5. Meanwhile prepare the topping: Using a hand-held whisk, beat the sugar, corn syrup, vanilla, butter,

flour, and eggs in a medium-size bowl until blended.

6. Stir in the walnuts and coconut with a rubber spatula. Spread the topping evenly over the base.

7. Bake the bars on the center oven rack until the top is golden and set, about 25 minutes. Allow them to cool completely before cutting.

Makes 16 bars

Tart Lemon Squares

I wanted to devise a lemon square recipe, so I decided to research the topic. And where else do you go for research but the library? All those lemon squares with degrees didn't add up to much, though. They were too sweet, and I was looking for something tart enough to make my lips pucker, so I had to come up with a recipe of my own. To contrast with the lemon topping, I added a sweet and crunchy shortbread base. I usually serve these squares with fresh or thawed frozen raspberries to add color and a dollop of whipped cream to cut the lemon. Of course, they're great just the way they are.

INGREDIENTS

BASE
1 cup all-purpose flour
¼ cup confectioner's sugar
8 tablespoons (1 stick) unsalted butter, at room temperature, cut into 8 pieces
1 egg white for glazing

TOPPING
2 large eggs, at room temperature
1 cup granulated sugar
2 tablespoons all-purpose flour
1½ tablespoons grated lemon zest
½ teaspoon baking soda
3 tablespoons fresh lemon juice
Confectioner's sugar for sprinkling

1. Preheat the oven to 350°F. Lightly grease an 8-inch square baking pan with butter.

2. For the base, process the flour and confectioner's sugar in a food processor for several seconds. Add the butter and process until the dough comes together, 20 to 30 seconds.

3. Press the dough gently and evenly over the bottom of the prepared pan. Glaze it with the egg white: Pour the egg white on the dough and tip the pan from side to side so that the white spreads over the surface. Pour out the excess.

4. Bake the base on the center oven rack until lightly golden, about 25 minutes. Place the base in the refrigerator for 15 minutes to cool completely. Keep the oven on.

5. Meanwhile prepare the topping: Gently whisk the eggs in a medium-size bowl until lightly mixed. Add the remaining topping ingredients and continue to whisk gently until they are blended.

6. Pour the topping evenly over the base. Bake the bars until the top is set and golden, about 25 minutes. Allow the lemon squares to cool completely.

7. Sprinkle the surface with confectioner's sugar and cut into squares with a sharp knife that is dipped in hot water and wiped dry before each cut. If you plan to keep the bars for longer than a day, put them in an airtight container and refrigerate or freeze them to preserve the crispness of the base.

Makes 9 to 12 bars

Rhubarb Bars

*7*his is one of my all-time favorite desserts; it's fruity, tart, sweet, crunchy, and buttery all in one dessert, and that's pretty exciting.

INGREDIENTS

BASE
1 cup all-purpose flour
5 tablespoons confectioner's sugar
8 tablespoons (1 stick) unsalted butter,
    at room temperature, cut into
    8 pieces
1 egg white for glazing

TOPPING
1 large egg, at room temperature
$^3/_4$ cup granulated sugar
$2^1/_2$ tablespoons all-purpose flour
$^1/_4$ teaspoon salt
3 cups sliced ($^1/_4$ inch thick) rhubarb

1. Preheat the oven to 350°F. Lightly grease an 8-inch square baking pan with butter.

2. Process the flour and confectioner's sugar in a food processor for several seconds. Add the butter and process until the dough comes together, 20 to 30 seconds.

3. Pat the dough gently over the bottom of the prepared pan. Glaze it with the egg white: Pour the egg white over the dough and tip the pan from side to side so that the white spreads over the surface. Pour out the excess.

4. Bake the base on the center oven rack until golden, about 25 minutes. Place the base in the refrigerator for 15 minutes to cool completely. Keep the oven on.

5. Meanwhile prepare the topping: In a large bowl stir the egg, granulated sugar, flour, and salt together with a

whisk. Add the rhubarb and toss.

6. Spread the rhubarb mixture evenly over the base.

7. Bake the bars on the center oven rack until set and lightly golden, about 50 minutes. Cool completely before cutting.

Makes 9 to 12 bars

Whitecaps

*T*hese bars look to me like whitecaps on a stormy sea, which is how they got their name. Nothing stormy about their taste, though: They're a sweet, buttery shortbread topped with jam and meringue. Lemon juice added to the jam enhances the contrast of flavors.

INGREDIENTS

BASE
$1^1/_2$ cups all-purpose flour
$^3/_4$ cup confectioner's sugar
12 tablespoons ($1^1/_2$ sticks) unsalted
    butter, at room temperature,
    cut into 12 pieces

TOPPING
4 large egg whites, at room
    temperature
$^1/_2$ cup plus 1 teaspoon granulated
    sugar
$^3/_4$ cup raspberry or apricot preserves
2 teaspoons fresh lemon juice
Generous $^1/_2$ cup shredded coconut

1. Preheat the oven to 350°F. Lightly grease a 13×9-inch baking pan with butter or vegetable oil.

2. For the base, process the flour and confectioner's sugar in a food processor for several seconds. Add the butter and process until the dough comes together, 20 to 30 seconds.

3. Pat the dough gently over the bottom of the prepared pan.

4. Bake on the center oven rack until golden in color, 25 to 30 minutes. Place the base in the refrigerator for 15 minutes to cool completely. Keep the oven on.

5. Meanwhile prepare the topping: Beat the egg whites in a medium-size mixing bowl with an electric mixer on medium-high speed until frothy, about 50 seconds. Gradually add the granulated sugar and continue beating until the whites resemble Marshmallow Fluff, about 30 seconds.

6. Remove the base from the freezer. Stir the preserves and lemon juice together and spread the mixture evenly over the surface.

7. Using a frosting spatula, spread the egg whites over the jam and make small peaks on the surface to form the whitecaps. Sprinkle the coconut over these whitecaps.

8. Bake the bars on the center oven rack until the peaks and coconut are golden, 15 to 20 minutes. Rotate the pan after 10 minutes.

9. Remove the pan from the oven and allow it to cool for 1 hour. Cut the bars with the tip of a sharp knife that is dipped in hot water and wiped dry before each cut.

Makes 24 bars

Jam Sandwiches

*N*o, these won't do in your child's lunchbox along with a handful of carrot sticks, but they are a great after-school treat. They consist of two delicate, buttery bars sandwiched together with raspberry or apricot preserves, kind of a high-class Pop Tart.

I N G R E D I E N T S

1¼ cups all-purpose flour
¼ cup plus 1 tablespoon granulated sugar
10 tablespoons (1¼ sticks) unsalted butter, chilled, cut into 8 to 10 pieces
1 egg white for glazing
½ cup raspberry, strawberry, or apricot preserves
Confectioner's sugar for sprinkling

1. Preheat the oven to 350°F. Have ready an 8-inch square baking pan.

2. Process the flour and granulated sugar in a food processor for 10 seconds. Add the butter and process until the dough comes together, 20 seconds.

3. Divide the dough in half. Cover one half with plastic and place it in the refrigerator. Pat the other half of the dough gently over the bottom of the prepared pan. Glaze it with egg white: Pour the egg white on the dough and tip the pan from side to side so that the white spreads over the surface. Pour off the excess.

4. Bake the base on the center oven rack until golden brown, 15 to 20 minutes. When the base is baked, place it in the refrigerator for 15 minutes to cool completely. Keep the oven on.

5. Spread the preserves evenly over the base.

6. Roll out the remaining half of the dough between two pieces of plastic wrap to an 8-inch square. Peel the top piece of plastic from the dough and flip the dough over the jam. Press the dough gently into the sides of the pan to seal the edges. Gently peel the remaining piece of plastic from the dough and remove any excess dough that has climbed up the sides of the pan. Prick the top crust in four or five places with the tip of a sharp knife.

7. Bake the bars on the center oven rack until the top turns golden, 30 to 35 minutes.

8. Remove the pan from the oven and place it on a cooling rack to cool completely. Cut the bars and store them in an airtight container. Serve them the next day when the flavor has settled. I like to sprinkle confectioner's sugar over the top.

Makes 16 bars

Linzer Bars

*7*hese bars boast the same unbeatable combination of spice-and-nut base and raspberry jam as a Linzertorte, but they're much quicker and easier to make. They can be just as elegantly served cut into small pieces and sprinkled with confectioner's sugar.

INGREDIENTS

DOUGH
11 tablespoons (1 stick plus 3 tablespoons) unsalted butter, at room temperature
2 cups confectioner's sugar, sifted
1 teaspoon ground cinnamon
Grated zest of 1 small lemon
1 whole large egg, at room temperature
1 large egg white, at room temperature
1⅓ cups all-purpose flour
1 cup ground almonds

FILLING
¾ cup raspberry preserves

TOPPING
1 egg white for glazing
3 tablespoons crushed, slivered, or
*   chopped almonds*

1. For the dough, using an electric mixer on low speed, cream the butter, sugar, cinnamon, and lemon zest together in a medium-size mixing bowl until just mixed. Scrape the bowl with a rubber spatula, then mix on medium speed until smooth, 2 to 3 minutes more. Stop the mixer once or twice to scrape the bowl.

2. Add the egg and egg white and mix on medium speed until incorporated, about 10 seconds. Scrape the bowl.

3. Blend in the flour and almonds with the mixer on low speed until they are incorporated, 5 to 8 seconds.

4. Divide the dough in half. Wrap each piece in plastic wrap and refrigerate it for at least 4 hours.

5. Fifteen minutes before you're ready to prepare the bars, preheat the oven to 350°F. Lightly grease a 9-inch square baking pan with butter or vegetable oil.

6. Gently press half the dough over the bottom of the prepared pan. Bake on the center oven rack until lightly golden but not hard, about 25 minutes. Place the base in the refrigerator for 15 minutes to cool completely. Keep the oven on.

7. Meanwhile prepare the top: Place the second half of the dough between two pieces of plastic wrap and, with your fingers and the palms of your hands, flatten it into a square slightly larger than the pan or roll it out with a rolling pin.

8. When the base is cool, spread the preserves evenly over it, leaving a ¼-inch border on all sides.

9. Peel the top piece of plastic from the remaining dough and flip the dough over the jam. Press the dough into the sides of the pan to seal the edges. Gently peel the remaining piece of plastic from the dough and remove any excess dough that has climbed up the sides of the pan.

10. For the topping, glaze the top of the dough with the egg white: Pour the egg white on the dough and tip the pan from side to side so that the white spreads over the surfaces. Pour off the excess. Sprinkle the almonds over the top.

11. Bake the bars on the center oven rack until the top is golden and firm, about 40 minutes.

12. Put the pan on a rack and cool for 10 minutes. Run a frosting spatula or knife around the sides of the pan. The bars cut best when completely cool.

Makes 16 to 20 bars

Dutch Butter Bars

*W*hen I decided that my kids were old enough to begin collecting taste memories, these bars were among the first treats I offered them. They seemed like a good transitional food since they taste like rich zwieback: not too much sugar but nice and buttery. That makes them appropriate for adults, too, at all hours of the day and night, when they want just a little sweet but a lot of flavor.

I N G R E D I E N T S

1¼ cups plus 2 tablespoons all-purpose flour
Pinch of salt
1 cup (2 sticks) unsalted butter, at room temperature
¾ cup plus 2 teaspoons sugar
2 teaspoons vanilla extract
1 large egg, lightly beaten with a fork, at room temperature
¼ teaspoon ground cinnamon
1 egg white for glazing

1. Preheat the oven to 350°F. Have ready an 8-inch square baking pan.

2. Sift the flour and salt together into a medium-size mixing bowl and set aside.

3. Using an electric mixer on medium speed, cream the butter, ¾ cup of the sugar, and the vanilla in a medium-size mixing bowl until light and fluffy, about 2 minutes. Stop the mixer once or twice to scrape the bowl with a rubber spatula.

4. Add the egg and beat on medium speed until the egg is incorporated, about 10 seconds. Scrape the bowl.

5. Add the dry ingredients on medium-low speed and mix for 10 seconds. Scrape the bowl and mix until the flour is incorporated, about 5 more seconds. Pat the dough evenly over the bottom of the pan.

6. Mix the remaining sugar with the cinnamon. Glaze the dough with the egg white: Pour the egg white on the dough and tip the pan from side to side so that the white spreads over the surface. Pour off the excess. Sprinkle the cinnamon sugar over the top.

7. Bake the bars on the center oven rack until firm to the touch and golden in color, about 30 minutes. Remove the pan from the oven.

8. Reduce the oven heat to 250°F. Have ready a cookie sheet.

9. Cut the bars into 4-inch squares with the tip of a sharp knife. Allow the bars to sit for 15 minutes.

10. Remove the bars from the pan with a pancake spatula and place them an inch apart on the cookie sheet.

11. Bake the bars until they are crisp and golden around the edges, about 1 hour.

12. Cool the bars completely on a rack, then store them in an airtight container. Their flavor improves with time.

Makes 16 bars

Apple Crumb Bars

*W*ith a tart apple filling wedged between two layers of a crumb mixture, these bars can be served warm with whipped cream or vanilla ice cream, or cooled and simply eaten out of hand.

I N G R E D I E N T S

FILLING
3½ *cups peeled, sliced (⅜ inch thick) apples (3 to 4 medium, preferably McIntosh)*
7 *tablespoons apple cider or juice, or as needed*
2 *tablespoons fresh lemon juice*
¾ *teaspoon ground cinnamon*
¼ *teaspoon salt*
2 *teaspoons cornstarch*

CRUMB LAYERS
½ *cup plus 2 tablespoons all-purpose flour*
¼ *cup (lightly packed) light brown sugar*
2 *tablespoons granulated sugar*
¾ *cup quick-cooking oatmeal*
⅛ *teaspoon salt*
5 *tablespoons unsalted butter, chilled, cut into 5 pieces*

1. In a small saucepan, simmer the apples, 3 tablespoons of the cider, the lemon juice, cinnamon, and salt over medium heat just until the apples lose their crispness, 3 to 4 minutes. (The time will vary depending on the type of apple and the season.)

2. Drain any juice (this, too, will vary depending on the type of apple) into a measuring cup and add enough of the remaining cider to measure ¼ cup. Transfer the apples to a small bowl.

3. Dissolve the cornstarch in the cider, then pour this mixture into the small saucepan. Cook, stirring constantly, over medium-low heat until thickened, 2 to 3 minutes. Pour this mixture over the apples and toss to coat. Refrigerate while you prepare the crumb layers.

4. Preheat the oven to 425°F. Lightly grease an 8-inch square baking pan with butter.

5. Place the flour, both sugars, the

oatmeal, and salt in a food processor and pulse briefly 5 times.

6. Add the butter and pulse 8 to 10 times until it is incorporated evenly. Pat half the crumb mixture firmly over the bottom of the prepared pan.

7. When the apple mixture has cooled, cut the apple slices into ½-inch pieces. Spread the apple mixture carefully over the base and sprinkle the remaining crumbs over the top.

8. Bake the bars on the center oven rack until the crumbs are golden and the apple mixture is bubbling along the sides of the pan, about 25 minutes.

9. Cool the bars completely on a rack, then place them in the refrigerator to chill before cutting. Store the bars in an airtight container in the refrigerator.

Makes 9 to 12 bars

CHAPTER FIVE

Cutie

Pies

Plus Tarts and Baked Fruit Desserts

Rifling through the archives of useless information I keep, I came across a bunch of clippings and quotes about pies, and all I could think was that pies couldn't have been made to symbolize more if Hallmark cards and Madison Avenue had collaborated in the cause.

To wit, from a 1950 Betty Crocker cookbook: "Pies had become distinctively American, as glamorous and exciting as this thrilling new nation!" Next, the whimsy of Donald Robert Perry Marquis: "I love you as New Englanders love pie." (He's the guy who created Archy and Mehitabel, and I figure anyone who can make a cockroach lovable deserves attention.) Finally, there's the Norman Rockwell drawing of an aproned grandmother taking a steaming pie from the oven to bestow upon her family.

Talk about conditioning! I mean the poor woman who didn't dedicate her life to creating the perfect pie for those she loved would be condemned as a crummy mother and a questionable American.

Normally I'd assume that Madison Avenue was responsible for the packaging, but, blessedly, pies have been around longer than advertising. The first women arriving in America from Europe hollowed out pumpkins and squashes, filled them with milk, and baked them as a treat. When summer brought fruits and progress brought a little extra time, these women added crusts. Later, frontier women baked as many as twenty-one pies each week, which doesn't even leave a day off for good behavior. So much for progress.

But then pie making has traditionally been a test of a woman's mettle. My friend Martha swears that her Hungarian-born grandmother wasn't officially betrothed until she could make strudel pastry delicate enough to see through.

Much as I like to think that we've come a long way, pie baking still seems to be a womanly activity, and I'm not sure I object to that. Pies reflect the pleasures of pampering yourself and the people you're baking for, making them a kind of currency of generosity. On top of that, they can be sophisticated and elegant, which, to my mind, makes them something women can be proud to claim.

I think of the fifties as the golden age of pie, as well as diners, movie detectives, and truck stops. I have fond memories of a Horn and Hardart Automat in

New York with its slices of pie tucked neatly behind rows of glass windows. It looked like a wall of post office boxes, only Automat windows seldom disappointed when you slipped your nickel in the slot, opened the door, and reached inside.

I first tasted coconut cream pie at an Automat, but before that we made pies from the beach plums and blackberries growing in the dunes at Fire Island, and afterwards (in the sixties, I confess), I fell in thrall to Crucheon's Fudge Pie in Berkeley.

To that list of favorites, I'd now add tarts. Though close relatives to pies, they haven't played a big part in the American dessert scene until recently when we became smitten with anything European. But since nothing marks our country so much as its ability to absorb, tarts are now on their way to being as American as Michael Jackson.

Four and Twenty Blackbirds

*A*ll of which leads to my main point: You can put nearly anything in a pie or tart. I think that's one of the reasons they're tied to the seasons more than other desserts. Some pie ingredients are good only at certain times of the year, and our bodies and palates seem to have atavistic cravings for different tastes, textures, and densities depending on the weather. So we eat dried fruit, nut, or chocolate pies with solid winter meals; rhubarb, strawberry, or chiffon pies when spring brings the first fruits; berry, peach, or cream pies as light summer treats; and all the largess of the harvest—apple and pumpkin pies—in the fall.

Fear of Flaking

*M*artha with the Hungarian grandmother and strudel dowry likes to say she's going to write an Anxiety Cookbook that chronicles all the things that can go wrong with a recipe. None of those soothing or rah-rah cookbooks for her; she doesn't trust them. Frankly, I don't think she'll ever get around to it (the prospect makes her too anxious), but if she does I intend to contribute a chapter about the affliction that keeps perfectly capable cooks from approaching the simplest pie. I call it "crustophobia," and I'm convinced that one day someone will discover an obscure monograph of Freud's entitled something like "Flake and Taboo" or "Civilization and Its Dishcontents."

I'm an expert on this because I'm a former sufferer, having spent years trying to make the entirely beautiful pie crust. Then, dear reader, I made two discoveries that changed my pie-baking career: First, I began using a food processor, and secondly, I came to understand that there's no such thing as an ugly pie crust—imperfections are what gives pies distinction. At that point, I relaxed, and pie crust became, well, as easy as pie.

The End-of-Anxiety Pie Crusts

*T*he recipes in this book use the following four kinds of crusts, which are reliable and easy to prepare when you follow my step-by-step methods:

1. **Basic Pie Crust** made with flour, butter, water, and sometimes sugar.

2. **Basic Pastry Crust** or **Pâte Sucrée** made with flour, butter, eggs, sugar, and sometimes water or milk.

3. **Basic Shortbread Crust** made with flour, butter, and sugar only (no liquid or eggs).

4. **Crumb Crust** (the easiest) made with butter, crushed cookies, and sometimes nuts, grated chocolate, coconut, etc.

Basic Pie and Pastry Crusts

These crusts can be mixed in a food processor or by hand. I find the machine method reliable and easy, so I've put it first. But some people believe that when you make a crust by hand, you get a greater feel for the texture of the dough, so you may prefer that technique. For both methods, make sure that your butter is cold when you start.

Mixing with a Food Processor

1. Place the dry ingredients (such as flour, salt, and sugar) in a food processor and process for 20 seconds.

2. Mix all liquid ingredients (such as water and egg) together in a cup and add an ice cube to chill them.

3. Cut the butter into 8 pieces per stick and distribute them evenly on top of the dry ingredients. Then process for 15 to 20 seconds or until the mixture resembles coarse meal.

4. Remove the ice cube from the liquid and add the liquid in a steady stream to the butter mixture while the food processor is running. Process just until it is distributed throughout the dough and the dough holds together. To test, pinch a piece the size of a marble between your thumb and forefinger; if it doesn't stick together, add more liquid.

Mixing by Hand

1. Sift the dry ingredients into a large mixing bowl or place them directly in the bowl and stir them around with a whisk.

2. Mix all liquid ingredients together in a cup and add an ice cube.

3. Cut the butter into 8 pieces per stick and distribute them evenly over the dry ingredients. Use both thumbs and forefingers to rub the butter into the flour mixture or cut it in with a pastry cutter. Continue until the mixture resembles coarse meal.

4. Remove the ice cube from the liquid and sprinkle the liquid over the dry ingredients while tossing them with a fork to distribute the moisture. When the dough can be gathered into a ball, it should be worked no longer.

Rolling the Dough

1. When the dough is the right consistency, gather it into a mass

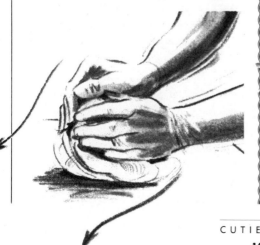

with your hands and place it on a lightly floured surface. Knead it several times with the heel of your palm so that it holds together.

2. Form the dough into a chubby disk (if the recipe requires a top crust also, make two disks). Wrap each disk in plastic and chill it for 1 hour. Doughs that contain sugar, such as Pie Crust 2, often can be rolled out right away.

3. When the dough is chilled, place it between two large (18 to 20 inches long) pieces of plastic wrap or waxed paper, and roll it out with a rolling pin. (It may be necessary to overlap pieces of plastic wrap or waxed paper to make them large enough.) Roll evenly, always beginning each roll at the center. Roll the pin outward, each time in a different direction. Lift the rolling pin after each roll. Don't roll the pin back and forth.

4. After you've rolled once in each direction, peel the top piece of plastic off the dough, then place it back. Flip the dough over and do the same thing on the second side. This keeps the dough from sticking to the wrap, giving it more room to expand.

5. Continue to roll the dough out, peeling off the plastic and putting it back again until it is ⅛ inch thick and at least 2 inches larger than your pie pan. Don't expect a perfect circle or beautiful edges. They're neither likely nor necessary.

6. Remove the top piece of plastic. Fold the crust in half, with the plastic on the inside, and lay the straight folded edge along the center of the pan. Unfold the crust to cover the pan, but leave the plastic wrap on.

Alternatively, lay the crust over your arm, plastic side against your skin. Gently lower the crust into the plate, using your hand as a guide.

7. Press the crust gently into the pan and smooth it with your fingers, taking special care at the corners of the pan and the flutes if the pan has them. Do not stretch the dough by hand because stretched dough shrinks

Problems with Pie Dough

— ❖ —

The pie crust recipes in this book are quite elastic and there really shouldn't be any problems with them if you follow the directions carefully. But if for some reason the dough cracks when being rolled, lift up the plastic wrap and pinch the dough together with your fingers, or cut off a little strip from another section and place it over the crack. Place the plastic wrap over the dough and roll right over the crack.

If you should pull up a chunk of dough when you remove the plastic wrap, leaving a hole, scrape the dough off the wrap, place it on the hole, and use your fingers to pinch it back in place. Then cover the dough with a fresh piece of plastic wrap and roll over the hole. This can happen when the dough gets too warm, so it's best to then slide your dough onto a plate or platter and refrigerate it for 15 to 20 minutes before proceeding.

during baking. When the crust is patted into place, peel off the remaining piece of plastic.

8. If you are making a single-crust pie, trim the excess dough and rough edges evenly with scissors and finish the edge decoratively. For a two-crust pie, trim the bottom crust so that it just overlaps the edge of the pan by about ¼ inch; you can make a finished edge when you cover the pie with the top crust (see Decorative Edges on page 170).

9. If you've put the crust in a tart pan, roll a rolling pin across the top of the pan to cut off any excess dough. You can press some of the extra into the sides of the tart shell to make them thicker and stronger.

10. Refrigerate all pie and tart shells for at least 30 minutes if they are to be prebaked.

Upper Crusts

Roll out the top crust in the same way you roll out the bottom one, between two pieces of plastic wrap or waxed paper until it is ⅛ inch thick and 2 inches larger than your pie pan. Peel off the top piece of plastic and flip the dough onto the pie filling. Peel off the second piece of plastic. Trim the edge of the dough ¾ inch larger than the bottom crust and tuck the edge of the top crust under the edge of the bottom crust all around. Make several little slits in the top crust with the point of a sharp knife so that steam can escape while the pie bakes.

To Prebake a Pie Crust

If you have two pie pans of the same size, I suggest the following simple method. It is a good technique for savory crusts, such as Basic Pie Crust 1, which contains no sugar, because it prevents the dough from shrinking, leaving you with a nice tall crust.

1. Lightly grease a pie pan with butter. Carefully fit a pie crust into the pan, then refrigerate it for at least 30 minutes.

2. Once chilled, cover the crust with a piece of baking parchment and stack the second pan into the first.

3. Flip both pans and bake the crust upside down between the two pans in a preheated 400°F oven for about 15 minutes.

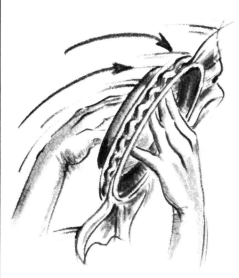

4. Remove the top pan and continue baking until the bottom of the crust is golden (about 5 minutes more). Take it out of the oven and replace the top pan.

5. Turn the whole thing right-side-up so that what was the top pan contains the crust, and carefully remove the pan that is now on top as well as the parchment.

6. If you're going to fill this crust and bake it again, cut this baking time to about 15 minutes total (12 minutes in the double pan, then 3 minutes in the single). Remove the crust when it is very lightly golden.

A Baking Alternative or Baking a Pie Crust That Contains Sugar

1. Fit a pie crust into a pan and refrigerate it for at least 30 minutes.

2. Remove the crust from the refrigerator and prick the bottom and sides in several places with a fork.

3. Line the crust with baking parchment or aluminum foil that has been greased on the underside. Fill it with rice, beans, or pie weights (little metal bean-shaped weights available at kitchen stores).

4. Bake the crust in a preheated 400°F oven until the edge is golden and the sides seem firm enough to support themselves, about 15 minutes.

5. Remove the weights and parchment very carefully so as not to disturb the crust, and continue to bake it until it is golden brown on the inside bottom, about 5 minutes. If it puffs during baking, prick it with a fork to let the steam escape. Crusts that will be baked a second time need only 2 to 3 minutes more baking time once the weights have been removed.

6. Allow the crust to cool completely before filling. If you bake the crust again after it is filled, cover the rim with aluminum foil before you put it in the oven to keep it from burning.

Basic Shortbread Crust

Since this is an eggless crust, you don't have to worry about overbeating. That means you can make it in a food processor or with an electric mixer without anxiety.

Using an Electric Mixer

1. Have the butter at room temperature.

2. Cream the butter and sugar (and vanilla) with the mixer at medium to medium-high speed until light and fluffy, 1½ minutes.

3. Add the dry ingredients with the mixer at low speed, then beat at medium speed until the dough becomes light and fluffy again. This time varies a lot depending

on the proportions of ingredients but is usually about 2 minutes.

4. Gather the dough into a ball with your hands.

5. Dip your fingertips in flour so that the dough doesn't stick to them and pat the dough gently into a pie plate. Glaze with egg white (page 133) if the base will be covered with a wet filling after prebaking.

6. Prebake the crust at 300°F without using pie weights until it is a rich golden color, 40 to 45 minutes. Shortbread rises more than flaky dough and it needs to cook slowly to create a crunchy texture and a buttery flavor.

7. Allow the crust to cool before adding the filling.

Using a Food Processor

1. Place the dry ingredients in a food processor and process for 20 seconds.

2. Add the butter (cold or at room temperature) and process until the dough comes together (1½ to 2 minutes for cold butter, 30 to 40 seconds for butter at room temperature). Then follow steps 4 through 7, preceding.

Crumb Crusts

1. Put the crumbs, sugar, grated chocolate, nuts, or whatever the recipe calls for in a medium-size bowl and stir them together with a wooden spoon.

2. Melt the butter and pour it into the bowl with the crumbs. Toss the mixture with two forks or your fingers until the butter is fully distributed.

3. Pat the crumbs firmly over the bottom and up the sides of a pie pan to form a crust.

4. Bake it in a preheated 375°F oven until it is crisp and golden, about 10 minutes.

5. Allow the crust to cool completely before filling it so that it stays crunchy, and avoid pouring hot fillings into crumb crusts because they penetrate the crust easily and make it soggy.

Decorative Edges for Pies and Tarts

A pretty edge is a must for a well-turned-out pie or tart. As with anything to do with pastry, once you get it, it's as easy as — well, you know.

Forked Edge

Fold the overlapping dough under the crust at the rim of the pan to make a thick edge. Press the back of a fork into it all around, making a pattern with the tines. Dip the fork in flour before you use it and dip it again whenever it begins to stick.

Fluted Edge

Fold the overlapping dough under the crust at the rim of the pan to make a thick edge. Make flutes (tiny waves around the edge of the crust) with a gentle pinching motion: with the thumb and index finger of one hand, push the outer edge of the crust inward while, at the same time, the index finger of the other hand pushes the inner edge of the crust outward between the other two fingers. For a fancier version, dip a fork in flour and press with its back instead of your index finger.

Rope Edge

Fold the overlapping edge of the crust under the rim of the pan to make a thick edge. Pinch a small piece of the dough between your thumb and the first knuckle of your index finger, angling your hand slightly. Repeat this pinching motion around the edge of the crust, putting your index finger in the depression your thumb has just made.

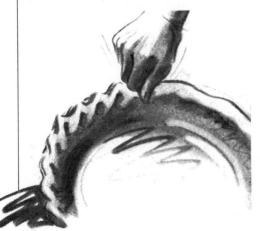

Lattice Top

1. Roll out dough to about 9 inches wide and 2 inches longer than the diameter of your pie. The dough should never be thicker than ⅛ inch. With a sharp knife, cut about 10 strips ¾ inch wide.

2. Lay half of the strips across the top of the pie or tart, spacing them equally and parallel to each other.

3. To weave the lattice, start at the outer edge and fold every other strip halfway back on itself. Lay one of the remaining strips across those on the pie that aren't folded back. Unfold the others over the new strip, and fold back the ones that haven't originally been folded back. Add a second strip parallel to the first and continue weaving until half the pie is done. Repeat this process on the other side of the pie.

4. Brush the underside of the strips with milk at the point where they meet the bottom crust and press down gently with your finger to make sure they adhere.

Fruit Fillings

*C*onquering crust is half the battle, but like books and their covers, what you put inside a pie matters too. I'm a longtime fan of fresh fruit pies and tarts and classic desserts like brown bettys. Each fruit has its own characteristics, though, so you'll need to take a few variables into consideration when you're shopping and baking.

I've found that because most fruit is naturally sweet, it's unnecessary to add a lot of sugar. Then, too, tart fruit provides a contrast to a sweet crumb topping or pastry crust. Lemon juice, lemon zest, and cinnamon work well to enhance a fruit's flavor, and I sometimes mix orange and lemon juice for the liquid to pour over the fruit. But in all pies and tarts, it's important to let the taste of the fruit come through, so whatever I add, I add it sparingly.

Apples

The best apple for baking is a firm apple because it holds its shape as it cooks. In the fall when apples are at their best, I recommend McIntosh, Cortlands, and Granny Smiths; you can put any combination of these together in a pie. After apple season, though, most of the Cortlands and McIntoshes you find have been stored and become soft, so I suggest baking with Granny Smith for the rest of the year. Keep in mind that Granny Smiths are tart apples and may require more sugar than the Cortlands.

I add apple cider or orange juice as well as lemon juice to the apples because, as the liquid boils, it cooks the apples more evenly. The kind of apple you use dictates how much liquid you need. Obviously, the crisper the apple, the more liquid required. For instance, if a pie made exclusively with Granny Smiths requires ¼ cup liquid, one made with juicier apples might need only a tablespoon or two or none at all. The recipes in this chapter specify how much liquid to add, but you may need to experiment to find the right amount for the apples available to you. Keep in mind that soft apples and too much liquid will make your pie a mushy one.

Peaches, Pears, Plums, Nectarines, and Other Soft Fruits

Soft fruits appear in the stores at various stages of ripeness, so various, in fact, that it's hard to make any generalizations about them. When they're very ripe, they need no additional juice, other than fresh lemon juice for flavor, but with less ripe fruit, you can add any juice to the filling to get the proper consistency.

For the times when you can't find soft fruit that's ripe, rather than turn to the frozen food section for a Mrs. Smith's pie, try peeling and slicing a pie's worth (6 to 8 cups) of the too-hard fruit into ½-inch slices and simmering them with ½ cup of orange or apple juice in a covered saucepan. Toss the slices occasionally just until they lose their hardness, 3 to 5 minutes, then use the fruit and the juice as the recipe requires.

Thickening

I thicken my fruit fillings with cornstarch to produce a transparent and slightly viscous juice. The juicier the fruit, the more cornstarch you need, but too little is always better than too much. As a rule of thumb, use 1½ tablespoons cornstarch for every 6 cups fruit.

Fruit for Tarts

— ❖ —

Fruit fillings for tarts need to be firmer than fruit fillings for pies because you remove the tarts from their pans for serving. To ensure that the tart will hold together, I often cook the filling a little with a thickener before I pour it into the crust so that the liquid doesn't make the crust soggy.

Baking Temperatures for Fruit Pies

*P*reheat the oven to 450°F 20 minutes before you put your pie in. Bake the pie in the center of the oven for 15 minutes at this temperature. Reduce the heat to 350°F and bake it for 45 to 60 minutes (if the top crust is getting too dark, cover it loosely with a piece of aluminum foil while it bakes) until the fruit starts to bubble. You'll be able to tell when this bubbling happens with any kind of top because the juice will ooze out of the crumb topping or through the slits of a top crust. I put a baking sheet on the bottom rack of the oven or directly under the pie to catch drips, which also works as a test for doneness: When the drips look thick, the pie is done or close to it. Let your pies cool on a rack and serve them when they are still warm.

Mousse-, Custard-, and Chiffon- Filled Pies

*W*ith the exception of the Vanilla Custard Tart, these fillings are always placed in fully baked pie or tart shells. For a discussion of the techniques involved, refer to the instructions in The Old Smoothies chapter.

Storing

*Y*ou can keep any leftover fruit pie overnight under a glass dome or covered with plastic wrap. Chiffon, mousse, custard, and cream pies must all be stored in the refrigerator, but it's best to take them out of the fridge an hour before you serve them so that the flavor isn't blunted.

To keep leftover pieces of these delicate pies looking fresh, "bubble" them with plastic wrap by inserting toothpicks around the edge of the pie and a few in the center, then lowering a generous piece of plastic wrap over the toothpicks and tucking it carefully under the edge of the pie dish. This bubble keeps the pie from drying out or changing color and its top from getting mushed.

Basic Pie Crust 1

A classic recipe, flaky and buttery. Remember, pastry, especially one made from butter, is easier to prepare if the kitchen is cool rather than warm.

INGREDIENTS

SINGLE CRUST FOR A 9-INCH PIE
   (standard or deep dish)
1½ cups all-purpose flour
¼ teaspoon salt
9 tablespoons (1 stick plus 1 tablespoon) unsalted butter, chilled,
   cut into 9 pieces
3 tablespoons ice water

DOUBLE CRUST
2¼ cups all-purpose flour
½ teaspoon salt
13½ tablespoons (1 stick plus 5½
   tablespoons) unsalted butter,
   chilled, cut into 14 pieces
4½ tablespoons ice water

1. Process the flour and salt in a food processor for 20 seconds. (Or whisk them together by hand in a large mixing bowl.)

2. Distribute the butter evenly over the flour and process until the mixture resembles coarse meal, 15 to 20 seconds. (Or rub the butter into the flour with your fingertips or cut it in with a pastry blender.)

3. With the food processor running, pour the ice water in a steady stream through the feed tube and process just until the dough comes together. (Or sprinkle the water over the mixture while tossing with a fork.)

4. Knead the dough for several turns on a lightly floured surface to bring it together.

5. Shape the dough into a thick disk (or 2 disks for a double crust), wrap in plastic, and refrigerate at least 1 hour.

6. To roll out the dough, place the chilled dough between 2 pieces of plastic wrap or waxed paper and roll it out to a circle 2 inches bigger than the size of the pie pan (see page 165 for rolling directions).

7. Fit the dough into a 9-inch pie plate and trim the edges (see page 170 for decorative edges). Keep the crust in the refrigerator until ready to fill. If prebaking the crust, refrigerate it for at least 30 minutes before baking. (See page 167 for baking directions.)

Makes one or two 9- or 10-inch crusts

Basic Pie Crust 2

*T*his crust is slightly sweeter than Basic Pie Crust 1 and has a texture that is somewhat more crunchy than flaky.

INGREDIENTS

SINGLE CRUST FOR A 9-INCH PIE
(standard or deep dish)
1½ cups all-purpose flour
2 tablespoons sugar
12 tablespoons (1½ sticks) unsalted
*   butter, chilled, cut into 12 pieces*
2 tablespoons ice water

DOUBLE CRUST
2¼ cups all-purpose flour
3 tablespoons sugar
1 cup plus 2 tablespoons (2¼ sticks)
*   unsalted butter, chilled, cut into*
*   18 pieces*
3 tablespoons ice water

1. Process the flour and sugar in a food processor for 20 seconds. (Or whisk them together by hand in a large mixing bowl.)

2. Distribute the butter evenly over the flour and process until the mixture resembles coarse meal, 15 to 20 seconds. (Or rub the butter into the flour with your fingertips or cut it in with a pastry blender.)

3. With the food processor running, pour the ice water in a steady stream through the feed tube and process just until the dough comes together. (Or sprinkle the water over the mixture while tossing with a fork.)

4. Knead the dough for several turns on a lightly floured surface to bring it together.

5. Shape the dough into a thick disk (or 2 disks for a double crust), wrap in plastic, and refrigerate at least 1 hour.

6. To roll out the dough, place the chilled dough between 2 pieces of plastic wrap or waxed paper and roll it out to a circle 2 inches bigger than the size of the pie pan (see page 165 for rolling directions).

7. Fit the dough into a 9-inch pie plate and trim the edges (see page 170 for decorative edges). Keep the crust in the refrigerator until ready to fill. If prebaking the crust, refrigerate it for at least 30 minutes before baking. (See page 167 for prebaking directions.)

Makes one or two 9- or 10-inch crusts

Basic Tart Crust

*T*his is a sturdy and tasty crust that is dependable and easy to make.

INGREDIENTS

**SINGLE CRUST FOR
A 9- OR 10-INCH TART**
1 cup all-purpose flour
2½ tablespoons sugar
⅛ teaspoon salt
6 tablespoons (¾ stick) unsalted
    butter, chilled, cut into 6 pieces
1 tablespoon cold water
1 large egg yolk

DOUBLE CRUST
2 cups all-purpose flour
5 tablespoons sugar
¼ teaspoon salt
12 tablespoons (1½ sticks) unsalted
    butter, chilled, cut into 12 pieces
2 tablespoons cold water
2 large egg yolks

1. Process the flour, sugar, and salt in a food processor for 20 seconds. (Or whisk them together by hand in a large mixing bowl.)

2. Distribute the butter evenly over the flour and process until the mixture resembles coarse meal, 15 to 20 seconds. (Or rub the butter into the flour with your fingertips or cut it in with a pastry blender.)

3. Whisk together the cold water and egg yolk. With the food processor running, pour the egg mixture in a steady stream through the feed tube and process just until the dough comes together, 20 to 30 seconds. (Or sprinkle the egg mixture over the flour mixture while tossing with a fork.)

4. Knead the dough for several turns on a lightly floured surface to bring it together.

5. Shape the dough into a thick disk (or 2 disks for a double crust), wrap in plastic, and refrigerate or roll it out right away.

6. To roll out the dough, place the dough between 2 pieces of plastic wrap or waxed paper and roll it out to a circle 2 inches bigger than the size of the tart pan (see page 165 for rolling directions).

7. Fit the dough into a 9- or 10-inch tart pan and trim the edge by rolling over the top of the pan with a rolling pin. Keep the crust in the refrigerator until ready to fill. If prebaking the crust, refrigerate it for at least 30 minutes before baking. (See page 167 for prebaking directions.)

Makes one or two 9- or 10-inch crusts

Shortbread Tart Crust

A wonderfully crunchy crust with a buttery flavor. I use it for the Chocolate Berry Tart and The Meatless Mince Tart. It bakes at a lower temperature so that its texture is crisp throughout.

**SINGLE CRUST FOR A 9- OR
10-INCH TART**

*9¹/₂ tablespoons (1 stick plus
1¹/₂ tablespoons) unsalted butter,
at room temperature*

5 tablespoons confectioner's sugar

1 teaspoon vanilla extract

*1 cup plus 3 tablespoons all-purpose
flour*

DOUBLE CRUST

*1 cup (2 sticks) unsalted butter, at
room temperature*

¹/₂ cup confectioner's sugar

1¹/₂ teaspoons vanilla extract

2 cups all-purpose flour

1. Using an electric mixer on medium-high speed, cream the butter,
sugar, and vanilla in a medium-size
mixing bowl until light and fluffy,
about 1½ minutes. (For food processor
instructions, see page 164.)

2. Add the flour on low speed, then
increase the speed to medium and beat
until the mixture is light and fluffy
again, about 2 minutes.

3. Gather the dough into a ball. With
floured fingertips, press the dough
gently over the bottom and up the
sides of a 9- or 10-inch tart pan or
pie plate.

4. Preheat the oven to 300°F.

5. Place the pan on the center oven
rack and bake until a rich, golden
color, 40 to 45 minutes.

6. Allow the crust to cool completely
on a rack before filling.

Makes one or two 9- or 10-inch crusts

Cookie Crumb Crust

A crunchy butter crust that
takes on the flavor of the
cookie that it's made with. Plain
wafer cookies work best.

*1¹/₄ cups cookie crumbs from any plain
crunchy cookie, such as vanilla
wafers, chocolate wafers, or
graham crackers*

3 tablespoons sugar

*6 tablespoons (³/₄ stick) unsalted
butter, melted*

1. Stir the cookie crumbs and sugar
together in a small bowl. Add the
melted butter and toss with two forks
or your fingers until the butter is
evenly distributed.

2. Pat the crumbs firmly over the bottom and up the sides of a 9- or 10-inch pie plate.

3. Preheat the oven to 375°F.

4. Place the pie plate on the center oven rack and bake until the crust is crisp and golden, 8 minutes.

5. Allow the crust to cool completely on a rack before filling.

Makes one 9- or 10-inch crust

All-American Apple Pie

*T*he apple: wedding gift for the Greek gods, instrument of Sir Isaac Newton's enlightenment, proof of William Tell's loyalty, fertility symbol in medieval times, talisman against homesickness for the American colonists, raison d'être for Johnny Appleseed, one-time gift of choice for a favorite grade-school teacher, and last, but not least, an apple a day keeps the doctor away. It's stood for practically everything at one time or another, although, interestingly, not for Adam and Eve's newfound knowledge (the Bible doesn't identify the fruit they ate). If you'd like to play your part in posterity, try this version of the classic apple pie — not too sweet, but pleasantly spicy, and contained in a buttery crust.

INGREDIENTS

1 double-crust recipe Basic Pie Crust 1 or 2 (page 175 or 176), rolled out

6 to 8 Granny Smith apples, peeled, cored, and cut into ³⁄₈-inch-thick slices (8 cups)

³⁄₄ cup sugar

1 teaspoon ground cinnamon

¹⁄₂ teaspoon ground nutmeg

¹⁄₄ teaspoon salt

¹⁄₄ cup apple cider, apple juice, or orange juice

2 tablespoons fresh lemon juice

1¹⁄₂ tablespoons cornstarch

1 tablespoon unsalted butter

1 large egg mixed with 2 tablespoons water or milk for glazing

1. Place 1 crust in the pie plate. Refrigerate both the top and bottom crusts.

2. Preheat the oven to 450°F.

3. Place the apple slices in a large bowl with all the remaining ingredients except the butter and egg glaze. Toss them together with your hands to coat the apples evenly.

4. Scoop the apples into the bottom crust and dot the mixture with small pieces of the butter. Cover the apples with the top crust. Seal and trim the edge.

5. Make a pretty edge; cut 3 to 4 slits in the top crust; and using a pastry brush, brush the top with the egg glaze.

6. Bake the pie on the center oven rack for 15 minutes. Reduce the temperature to 350°F and continue baking until the top of the pie is golden and the filling is bubbling, about 1 hour 10 minutes longer. If the top crust is getting too dark, cover it with a piece of aluminum foil and continue to bake.

7. Remove the pie from the oven and cool it on a rack. Serve with vanilla ice cream.

Makes 8 to 12 servings

Sour Cream Apple Pie

I'm as much for apple pie as any mother or baseball fan, but I have to admit that this one gilds the lily just a bit. Because of its extra richness, it's important that you use tart, crisp apples. I like Granny Smith. I think of this as a harvest pie — with a little something extra on the top.

1 single-crust recipe Basic Pie Crust 1 or 2 (page 175 or 176), rolled out

APPLE FILLING
3 to 4 tart apples, peeled, cored, and cut into ¼-inch-thick slices (4 cups)
¼ cup (½ stick) unsalted butter, melted
½ cup (lightly packed) light brown sugar
2 tablespoons fresh lemon juice
1 teaspoon grated lemon zest
¼ cup golden raisins
1 tablespoon all-purpose flour

SOUR CREAM TOPPING
1¼ cups sour cream
2 large eggs
½ cup granulated sugar
1 teaspoon vanilla extract

SUGAR NUT TOPPING
¾ cup chopped pecans
2 tablespoons unsalted butter, melted
¼ cup (lightly packed) light brown sugar

1. Place the pie crust in the pie plate and refrigerate it until ready to use.

2. Preheat the oven to 375°F.

3. Toss the apples with the melted butter in a large bowl. Add the brown sugar, lemon juice, lemon zest, raisins, and flour; stir to coat the apple slices.

4. Scoop the apples into the crust.

5. Bake the pie on the center oven rack for 30 minutes.

6. Meanwhile whisk together in a medium-size bowl the sour cream, eggs, granulated sugar, and vanilla for the topping.

7. After the pie has baked for 30 minutes, pour the sour cream mixture over the apples. Continue baking until the topping is set, 30 to 35 minutes.

8. Meanwhile make the sugar nut topping by tossing the pecans, melted butter, and brown sugar in a small bowl with a wooden spoon.

9. Crumble the topping over the pie (it will not cover the whole surface) and continue baking until the topping bubbles, about 10 minutes. Don't worry if the sour cream topping rises up; it will fall when you take it out of the oven.

10. Remove the pie from the oven and cool it on a rack.

Makes 8 to 10 servings

Apple Tart

*H*ere is a basic, two-crust tart with simple flavors and little sugar beyond the natural sweetness of the fruit. For that reason, it's nice with a dusting of confectioner's sugar on top, and it works well as the ending to a heavy or light meal.

INGREDIENTS

1 double-crust recipe Basic Tart Crust (page 176), rolled out; top crust refrigerated, bottom crust lightly baked in 9-inch tart pan (page 167)
4 tablespoons (½ stick) unsalted butter
¼ cup granulated sugar
⅛ teaspoon salt
4 large apples, peeled, cored, and cut into ¼-inch-thick slices (4 generous cups)
1 large egg mixed with 2 tablespoons water or milk for glazing
Confectioner's sugar for sprinkling

1. Make the tart crust.

2. Preheat the oven to 425°F.

3. Heat the butter, granulated sugar, and salt in a medium-size skillet over medium heat until the mixture starts to caramelize, about 3 minutes. Add the apples and sauté them just until they have lost their crispness. This will vary considerably depending on the apples.

4. Spread the apples evenly in the baked tart shell. Paint the edge of the shell with a bit of egg glaze.

5. Remove the top crust from the refrigerator, peel off the top piece of plastic, and flip the dough over on top of the tart. Peel off the second piece of plastic wrap and use your index finger to press the dough onto the edge of the crust, allowing the excess to drop off.

6. Cut 3 or 4 slits in the top crust.

Bake the tart on the center oven rack until the top is golden, 30 to 35 minutes.

7. Remove the tart from the oven and allow it to cool. Sprinkle the tart with confectioner's sugar before serving.

Makes 8 to 10 servings

Apple-Cranberry Tart

*7*he union of apples and cranberries produces a tart filling which is set in a sturdy crust. Keep in mind that unless you want to end up with an applesauce tart, you need to use crisp apples, such as Granny Smith or Macouns. If you can't get hold of hard apples, adjust the recipe by simmering the filling for only 1 minute before putting it in the tart.

1. Make the tart crust and cool the baked shell.

2. Preheat the oven to 400°F.

3. Place the apples in a medium-size saucepan with the sugar, orange zest, and salt and toss to coat using a wooden spoon.

4. Dissolve the cornstarch in the orange juice and add it to the apples. Cover the pan and simmer the apples over medium-low heat just until they begin to lose their crispness, about 3 minutes. Stir them once after 1½ minutes.

5. Stir the cranberries into the apples, cover the pan, and bring the mixture to a simmer again. Cook just until the cranberries have softened slightly, about 2 minutes. Transfer the mixture to a bowl and refrigerate it while you prepare the topping.

6. For the topping, place the nuts, brown sugar, flour, oatmeal, and cinnamon in the food processor and process for 5 seconds. Or place all the ingredients except the butter in a large mixing bowl and toss them together with your hands or a large spoon.

7. If you used a food processor, transfer the mixture to a large mixing bowl. Add the melted butter and mix thoroughly with your hands or a large spoon.

8. Scoop the apple mixture into the tart shell and top with the nut crumb mixture.

9. Bake the tart on the center oven rack until the topping is a rich golden brown, 15 to 20 minutes. Drop a piece of aluminum foil lightly over the topping (do not mold or seal it) and continue baking the tart until the filling is bubbling, 25 to 30 minutes longer.

10. Remove the tart from the oven and allow it to cool for an hour or two before serving.

Makes 10 to 12 servings

Sour Cherry Tart

7he Boston Globe claims that George Washington would have named this the best cherry pie in town if it had been around when he slept here. Prepare to pucker along with George; those sour cherries mean business.

INGREDIENTS

1 double-crust recipe Basic Tart Crust (page 176)

1 cup cherry juice (from canned sour cherries if using, see below) or 1 cup fresh orange juice (if using fresh sour cherries)

1 tablespoon plus 1½ teaspoons cornstarch

½ cup plus 3 tablespoons (lightly packed) light brown sugar

1 teaspoon ground cinnamon

Scant ¼ teaspoon ground mace

1½ teaspoons grated orange zest

⅛ teaspoon salt

4 cups drained canned sour cherries (save the juice), or 4 cups pitted fresh sour cherries

2 tablespoons dry bread crumbs

1 large egg mixed with 2 tablespoons water or milk for glazing

1. Make the tart crust. Roll out the bottom crust in a circle and line a 9-inch tart pan with it. Roll out the top crust as for a lattice (see page 171). Refrigerate both the bottom and top crusts.

2. Preheat the oven to 400°F.

3. Combine ⅓ cup of the cherry or orange juice with the cornstarch in a small bowl and set aside.

4. Combine the remaining ⅔ cup juice, the sugar, cinnamon, mace, orange zest, and salt in a small saucepan and bring it to a boil over medium-low heat.

5. Pour the cornstarch mixture slowly into the boiling juice while stirring vigorously with a whisk. Reduce the heat to low and bring the mixture to a boil again. Boil until it thickens, about 5 minutes.

6. Pour this syrup over the cherries in a medium-size bowl and toss to coat.

7. Remove the pie plate from the refrigerator and distribute the bread crumbs evenly over the bottom of the tart crust. Pour in the cherry filling and spread it evenly.

8. Cut the top crust into lattice strips and arrange the strips over the filling (see page 171). Brush the lattice and outer edges of the tart with the egg glaze.

9. Place the tart pan on a cookie sheet (to catch any drippings) and bake on the lower oven rack until the crust is golden, about 45 minutes.

10. Remove the tart from the oven and cool it on a rack for 1 hour. Then push the bottom of the tart pan up

slightly to loosen it from the pan before the syrup has the chance to harden over the edges. Cool the tart for 4 to 5 more hours before serving. Serve with whipped cream or vanilla ice cream.

Makes 10 to 12 servings

Blueberry-Plum Crumb Pie

A sumptuous summer pie with a tart filling and a sweet (but not too sweet) crunchy topping. Vanilla ice cream is a must.

INGREDIENTS

1 single-crust recipe Basic Pie Crust 1 or 2 (page 175 or 176), fully baked (page 167)

CRUMB TOPPING
6 tablespoons (lightly packed) light brown sugar
¾ cup plus 2 tablespoons all-purpose flour
½ cup quick-cooking oatmeal
¼ teaspoon ground cinnamon
½ cup ground almonds or walnuts
8 tablespoons (1 stick) unsalted butter, melted

FILLING

3 cups fresh blueberries, rinsed, stemmed, and patted dry

7 to 8 red plums, not too ripe, pitted and cut into ¾-inch-thick slices (3 cups)

6 to 8 tablespoons granulated sugar

¼ teaspoon grated orange zest

1 tablespoon plus 1 teaspoon cornstarch

2 tablespoons fresh orange juice

1. Make the pie crust and cool the baked shell.

2. Preheat the oven to 400°F.

3. For the topping, mix the sugar, flour, oatmeal, cinnamon, and nuts in a medium-size bowl. Pour in the melted butter and stir with a wooden spoon until it is fully incorporated. Set aside.

4. For the filling, place the fruit, granulated sugar, and orange zest in a large mixing bowl.

5. Dissolve the cornstarch in the orange juice and pour it over the fruit. Toss the mixture with your hands or a large spoon.

6. Scoop the fruit into the pie shell. Use your hands to distribute the topping evenly over the fruit. Cover the edge of the crust with aluminum foil.

7. Place the pie on a cookie sheet on the center oven rack. Bake for 20 minutes. Reduce the heat to 350°F and continue baking until the pie juices are bubbling and begin to drip onto the cookie sheet, about 1 hour longer.

8. Remove the pie from the oven and carefully remove the foil. Cool the pie on a rack for several hours before serving.

Makes 8 to 12 servings

Peach Crumb Pie

*A*classic dessert that pays homage to one of the world's greatest fruits.

INGREDIENTS

1 single-crust recipe Basic Pie Crust 1 or 2 (page 175 or 176), fully baked (page 167)

TOPPING

1 cup plus 2 tablespoons all-purpose flour

½ cup plus 2 tablespoons (lightly packed) light brown sugar

1 teaspoon ground cinnamon

¼ teaspoon salt

10 tablespoons (1 stick plus 2 tablespoons) unsalted butter, chilled, cut into 10 pieces

FILLING

6 to 7 peaches, peeled, pitted, and cut into ¾-inch-thick slices (7 cups)

⅓ to ½ cup granulated sugar

½ teaspoon ground cinnamon

¼ teaspoon salt

1 tablespoon plus 1 teaspoon cornstarch

3 tablespoons fresh lemon juice

2 tablespoons fresh orange juice

1. Make the pie crust and cool the baked shell.

2. Preheat the oven to 400°F.

3. For the topping, place the flour, brown sugar, cinnamon, and salt in a food processor and process for several seconds to mix. Add the butter and pulse until the butter is completely mixed in and the topping forms large moist clumps. Set aside.

4. Place the peaches, granulated sugar, cinnamon, and salt in a large bowl.

5. Dissolve the cornstarch in the lemon and orange juices and pour it over the fruit. Toss the mixture with your hands or a large spoon. Scoop the fruit into the pie shell and set aside.

6. Use your hands to distribute the topping evenly over the fruit. Cover the edge of the crust with aluminum foil.

7. Place the pie on a cookie sheet on the center oven rack. Bake for 20 minutes. Reduce the heat to 350°F and continue baking until the pie juices are bubbling and begin to drip onto the cookie sheet, about 1 hour longer.

8. Remove the pie from the oven and carefully remove the foil. Cool the pie on a rack for several hours before serving.

Makes 8 to 12 servings

Nectarine Synergy

*7*his dessert made its debut at a farewell dinner party for the Hamiltons, our erstwhile neighbors from England. "So what do you think?" I asked. "Fabulous," someone said, then someone else mentioned "synergy," and we were so amused by the concept that the name stuck.

CRUST
1½ cups all-purpose flour
1 cup granulated sugar
½ teaspoon ground cinnamon
¼ teaspoon baking powder
8 tablespoons (1 stick) unsalted butter, at room temperature, cut into 8 pieces

TOPPING
¾ cup all-purpose flour
½ cup quick-cooking oatmeal
¾ of 1 slice white bread, cut in cubes
¾ cup (lightly packed) light brown sugar
8 tablespoons (1 stick) unsalted butter, chilled, cut into 8 pieces

FILLING
7 to 8 ripe nectarines, peeled, pitted, and cut into ½-inch-thick slices (8 cups)
6 tablespoons granulated sugar
2 tablespoons cornstarch
¾ teaspoon salt
1 teaspoon ground cinnamon
3 tablespoons fresh lemon juice

1. Preheat the oven to 400°F. Lightly grease a 9-inch square baking pan with butter or vegetable oil. Line a cookie sheet with aluminum foil.

2. For the crust, place the flour, granulated sugar, cinnamon, and baking powder in a food processor and process for 10 seconds. Add the butter and process until the mixture resembles coarse meal.

3. Gather the dough into a ball. With floured fingertips, press the dough gently over the bottom and 1½ inches up the sides of the prepared pan.

4. Place the pan on the center oven rack and bake the crust until it is golden in color, 12 to 15 minutes. Let it cool. Leave the oven on.

5. Place the prepared cookie sheet on the center oven rack.

6. While the crust cools, prepare the topping: Process the flour, oatmeal, bread, and brown sugar in a food processor for 30 seconds.

7. Add the butter; process until the mixture resembles coarse meal. Set aside.

8. For the filling, place all the filling ingredients in a large bowl and toss them together with your hands.

9. Scoop the fruit mixture into the crust and sprinkle the topping over it.

10. Reduce the oven temperature to 375°F and place the pan on the cookie sheet.

11. Bake until the top is light gold and crispy and the juices are bubbling, about 1½ hours.

12. Open the oven door, turn the temperature to broil, and allow the topping to broil for 2 to 3 minutes until it turns a deep gold. (If your broiler is separate, remove the Synergy from the oven and place it under the broiler.) You'll need to watch it so that it doesn't burn!

13. Allow the Synergy to cool a little on a rack. Serve it warm.

Makes 9 servings

Meatless Mince Tart for Christmas

*T*his tart has a real mince-meat taste even though it has no suet. Its buttery crust holds a sweet-tart mixture of dried fruit laced with brandy, and it tastes good warm or at room temperature topped with whipped cream. I like to serve it at on a large silver platter surrounded by greens and cranberries.

INGREDIENTS

CRUST

1½ cups all-purpose flour
6 tablespoons confectioner's sugar
12 tablespoons (1½ sticks) unsalted
    butter, chilled, cut into 16 pieces
2 teaspoons vanilla extract

FILLING

3 large apples (Granny Smiths
    preferably), peeled, cored, and
    cut into ½-inch cubes (4½ cups)
3 tablespoons fresh orange juice
1 tablespoon grated orange zest
½ cup (lightly packed) light brown
    sugar
½ cup raisins (golden or dark)
½ cup chopped dried apricots
¼ teaspoon salt
Slightly rounded ¼ teaspoon ground
    cinnamon
Slightly rounded ¼ teaspoon ground
    nutmeg
Slightly rounded ¼ teaspoon ground
    cloves
½ cup chopped walnuts or pecans
1½ teaspoons vanilla extract
2 tablespoons brandy

1 large egg mixed with 2 tablespoons
    water or milk for glazing

1. For the crust, process the flour and confectioner's sugar in a food processor for 20 seconds. Distribute the butter evenly over the flour mixture, add the vanilla, and process until the dough comes together, 1½ to 2 minutes.

2. Divide the dough in half. Wrap each piece in plastic wrap and chill for 1 hour.

3. Preheat the oven to 350°F.

4. Prepare the filling: Combine the apples, orange juice and zest, brown sugar, raisins, apricots, salt, and spices in a medium-size saucepan. Cover and simmer over low heat for 25 to 30 minutes.

5. Uncover the pan and simmer until the liquid evaporates. Stir the nuts, vanilla, and brandy into the apple mixture and let cool.

6. Remove one of the dough halves from the refrigerator and roll it out ¼ inch thick between two pieces of plastic wrap. Peel off the top piece of plastic, flip the dough into a 9-inch tart pan, and press it in lightly. Remove the remaining plastic and spread the filling evenly in the tart shell.

7. Roll out the top crust ¼ inch thick and slightly larger than the pan between two pieces of plastic wrap.

8. Brush the edge of the filled tart shell with a little of the glaze. Remove the top piece of plastic from the top crust and flip the crust over onto the filling. Remove the remaining plastic and use your index finger to press the top crust into the bottom crust, pinching off any excess dough.

9. Make several slits in the top crust with the tip of a sharp knife. Brush the top with the egg glaze.

10. Place the tart pan on a rack in the oven that is just below the center. Bake until the tart is a golden color, about 45 minutes.

11. Remove the tart from the oven and cool it completely on a rack.

Makes 12 to 16 servings

Lemon-Raisin Pie

I met my husband's parents for the first time at a Thanksgiving dinner at their home in Indianapolis, and I didn't expect much. I don't mean of them, of course, but of any Thanksgiving that differed from the traditions I had grown up with and considered the last word on holiday indulgence. But my mother-in-law, Barbara, managed to surprise, impress, and delight me by serving four or five desserts at one sitting. This pie was my favorite. It's sweet, tart, and crunchy all at once, and also deceptive because it's much richer than it appears. So server beware: Small wedges are advised.

1 single-crust recipe Basic Pie Crust 1 or 2 (page 175 or 176), lightly baked (page 167)
1¼ cups golden raisins
1 tablespoon grated lemon zest
½ cup fresh lemon juice
⅔ cup chopped walnuts
8 tablespoons (1 stick) unsalted butter, at room temperature
⅓ cup granulated sugar
⅓ cup (lightly packed) light brown sugar
¾ teaspoon ground cinnamon
¼ teaspoon salt
3 large eggs, at room temperature

1. Make the pie crust and cool the baked shell.

2. Preheat the oven to 350°F.

3. In a small bowl soak the raisins and lemon zest in the lemon juice for 10 minutes. Add the nuts.

4. Using an electric mixer on medium-high speed, cream the butter, both sugars, the cinnamon, and salt in a medium-size mixing bowl until light and fluffy, 2 to 3 minutes. Stop the mixer to scrape the bowl once or twice with a rubber spatula.

5. Add the eggs and beat on medium speed, stopping to scrape the sides of the bowl, until well mixed, about 8 seconds. The mixture will look curdled until it heats up in the baking.

6. Stir in the raisin mixture with a wooden spoon and pour the filling into the crust.

7. Bake the pie on the center oven rack until the top is set and light golden at the center and darker golden around the edges, 35 to 40 minutes. It will feel somewhat spongy to the touch.

8. Allow the pie to cool completely on a rack before serving.

Makes 8 to 12 servings

Pecan Pie

*T*ake a butter crust, fill it with pecans and syrupy caramel, make sure the flavor is sweet, and you've got a classic pie, unimpeded by any extraneous flavors.

INGREDIENTS

1 single-crust recipe Basic Pie Crust 1 or 2 (page 175 or 176), rolled out
1 cup sugar
1½ cups plus 2 tablespoons dark corn syrup
7 tablespoons unsalted butter, cut into large pieces
⅛ teaspoon salt
4 large eggs, lightly beaten with a fork, at room temperature
½ teaspoon vanilla extract
1½ cups pecan halves

1. Place the pie crust in the pie plate and refrigerate it until ready to use.

2. Preheat the oven to 350°F.

3. Heat the sugar and corn syrup in a small saucepan over low heat, stirring occasionally, until the sugar is dissolved, about 5 minutes. Transfer the mixture to a medium-size bowl.

4. Stir in the butter and the salt and allow the mixture to cool for 8 to 10 minutes, stirring occasionally.

5. Add the eggs and vanilla to the cooled sugar mixture while beating constantly with a whisk. Stir in the pecans. Pour the filling into the pie shell.

6. Bake the pie on the center oven rack until the top is fully risen, set, and crisp to the touch, 50 to 55 minutes. The surface will be covered with little cracks that will settle.

7. Remove the pie from the oven and cool it on a rack. Serve the following day with ice cream or whipped cream.

Makes 12 to 16 servings

Chocolate-Bourbon Pecan Pie

*F*udgy, delicious, and studded with pecans, this pie is a show-stopper.

INGREDIENTS

1 single-crust recipe Basic Pie Crust 1 or 2 (page 175 or 176), rolled out
4 ounces unsweetened chocolate
1 cup sugar
1 cup dark corn syrup
4 tablespoons (1/2 stick) unsalted butter, at room temperature
1/4 teaspoon salt
4 large eggs, at room temperature
1/4 cup bourbon
1 teaspoon vanilla extract
1 1/2 cups pecan halves

1. Place the pie crust in the pie plate and refrigerate it until ready to use.

2. Preheat the oven to 350°F.

3. Melt the chocolate in the top of a double boiler placed over simmering water. Set aside.

4. Heat the sugar and the corn syrup in a small saucepan over low heat, stirring occasionally, until the sugar is dissolved, about 5 minutes. Transfer the mixture to a medium-size bowl.

5. Stir in the butter and salt and allow the mixture to cool for 8 to 10 minutes, stirring occasionally.

6. Add the eggs and the bourbon to the cooled sugar mixture while beating constantly with a whisk.

7. Add the chocolate and vanilla and whisk vigorously until blended. Stir in the pecans. Pour the filling into the pie shell.

8. Bake the pie on the center oven rack until the top is risen, set, and crisp to the touch, 55 to 60 minutes. The surface will be covered with little cracks that will settle.

9. Remove the pie from the oven and cool it completely on a rack.

Makes 12 to 16 servings

Sweet-Potato Pecan Pie

*C*olumbus discovered the sweet potato along with America, and until about 1775, when the English talked about potatoes that was what they meant. Pecans are even more the province of our country, since they originally grew only in the American South. Even without such an impeccable pedigree, this would be the perfect southern dessert, although I'm a fan of it for those long northern winters.

INGREDIENTS

1 single-crust recipe Basic Pie Crust 1 or 2 (page 175 or 176), lightly baked in deep-dish pie plate (page 167)

FILLING
1¼ pounds sweet potatoes (about 2 large)
8 tablespoons (1 stick) unsalted butter, melted
¾ cup (lightly packed) dark brown sugar
2 large eggs, lightly beaten with a fork, at room temperature
1½ tablespoons fresh lemon juice
1 teaspoon grated lemon zest
¼ cup light cream or half-and-half
¼ teaspoon salt

TOPPING
¾ cup granulated sugar
¾ cup dark corn syrup
2 large eggs
1½ tablespoons unsalted butter, melted
2 teaspoons vanilla extract
Pinch of salt
Pinch of ground cinnamon
¾ cup pecan halves

1. Make the pie crust and cool the baked shell.

2. Preheat the oven to 450°F.

3. Bake the potatoes in the oven until they are soft, about 50 minutes. Reduce the oven temperature to 375°F.

4. Scoop the potatoes out of their skins into a medium-size bowl, add the remaining filling ingredients, and stir vigorously with a whisk until smooth and well blended. (This can also be done with an electric mixer on medium speed.) Set aside.

5. Put all the topping ingredients except the pecans in a medium-size bowl and stir them together with a wooden spoon. Then stir in the pecans.

6. Scoop the sweet potato filling into the pie shell, spread it evenly, and spread the topping over it. Cover the edge of the crust with aluminum foil.

7. Bake the pie on the center oven rack until the top rises and sets and is a rich golden color, about 1 hour.

8. Remove the pie from the oven and carefully remove the foil. Cool the pie on a rack and serve it while it is still warm.

Makes 8 to 12 servings

Deep-Dish Pumpkin Pie

*P*umpkins are one of the foods Americans can claim as all their own, since Europeans never laid eyes on them before the time of Columbus, and even after that they were pretty slow in figuring out what to do with this fleshy squash. Good old Yankee ingenuity came up with this ideal fall and winter dessert.

I N G R E D I E N T S

1 single-crust recipe Basic Pie Crust 1 or 2 (page 175 or 176), lightly baked in deep-dish pie plate (page 167)
1³/₄ cups (15-ounce can) pumpkin purée
¹/₂ cup plus 3 tablespoons (lightly packed) dark brown sugar
1¹/₂ teaspoons ground cinnamon
1 teaspoon ground nutmeg
¹/₂ teaspoon ground cloves
1¹/₂ teaspoons ground ginger
¹/₄ teaspoon salt
3 tablespoons molasses
1¹/₄ cups evaporated milk
3 large eggs
1 recipe Whipped Cream (page 86) for serving

1. Make the pie crust and cool the baked shell.

2. Preheat the oven to 375°F.

3. Place the pumpkin, brown sugar, spices, and salt in a large mixing bowl and blend with a whisk.

4. Add the molasses, milk, and the eggs; stir vigorously with the whisk until smooth.

5. Pour the filling into the pie shell. Cover the edge of the crust with aluminum foil.

6. Bake the pie on the center oven rack until the top is shiny and set and a tester inserted in the center comes out clean, about 1 hour.

7. Remove the pie from the oven and carefully remove the foil. Cool the pie on a rack. Serve the pie warm, cold, or at room temperature with a dollop of whipped cream.

Makes 10 to 12 servings

Florida Lime Pie

*T*his southern favorite used to take its name from a kind of lime found in the Florida Keys, which turns the color of your average lime inside out— that is, the green is on the inside and the yellow is outside. Key limes are almost impossible to get now, but do use fresh limes for a true flavor.

INGREDIENTS

*1 recipe Cookie Crumb Crust
    made with graham crackers
    (page 178), baked*

FILLING
*1 can (14 ounces) sweetened
    condensed milk*
*1/2 cup plus 2 tablespoons fresh lime
    juice (5 to 6 limes)*
2 large eggs
2 tablespoons grated lime zest
Dash of salt

TOPPING
8 ounces sour cream
1/4 cup sugar
1/8 teaspoon salt

Lime zest for garnish

1. Make the crumb crust and cool
the baked shell.

2. Preheat the oven to 350°F.

3. Place all the filling ingredients in
a medium-size mixing bowl and stir
them with a whisk until they are completely mixed. Pour the filling into the
pie shell.

4. Bake the pie on the center oven
rack until it begins to set, 10 minutes.
Remove the pie from the oven and
increase the heat to 425°F.

5. Whisk the topping ingredients
together in a small bowl and spread
the topping over the pie.

6. Bake the pie for 5 minutes more.
The topping will be loose when you

remove the pie, but it will set as it
cools. Cool on a rack, then chill the
pie for 6 hours before serving.

7. With a vegetable peeler or citrus
zester, shave strands of zest from a
whole lime around the edge of the pie
for garnish.

Makes 8 to 12 servings

Lemon Meringue Pie

*A*s American as Mom playing
baseball. I see Lemon
Meringue Pie as a creature of the
roadside diner, a special treat for
the weary truck driver or, better
yet, the handsome stranger who
pulls into town and wins the
heart of the good-natured waitress. Have you seen this movie
too?

INGREDIENTS

*1 single-crust recipe Basic Pie Crust 1
or 2 (page 175 or 176), fully
baked (page 167), or 1 recipe
Cookie Crumb Crust made with
graham crackers (page 178), baked*

FILLING
*6 tablespoons cornstarch
1½ cups water
¾ cup plus 2 tablespoons sugar
¾ cup fresh lemon juice
(about 3 lemons)
3 large egg yolks
3 tablespoons unsalted butter
1½ teaspoons grated lemon zest*

MERINGUE TOPPING
*5 large egg whites, at room temperature
½ cup sugar
½ teaspoon cream of tartar*

1. Make the pie crust and cool the baked shell.

2. Dissolve the cornstarch in the water in a medium-size saucepan. Add the sugar and cook the mixture over low heat, whisking constantly until it thickens, about 5 minutes.

3. Add the lemon juice and egg yolks and simmer, stirring occasionally, so the egg yolks cook, 3 minutes.

4. Strain the custard into a medium-size bowl and stir in the butter and lemon zest. Allow it to cool for 10 to 15 minutes, stirring occasionally with a wooden spoon.

5. Pour the custard into the pie crust. Place it in the refrigerator and allow it to set for 4 to 6 hours.

6. Preheat the oven to 350°F.

7. For the meringue, using an electric mixer on medium speed, beat the egg whites in a medium-size mixing bowl until frothy, about 50 seconds.

8. Gradually add the sugar and cream of tartar on medium speed. Increase the speed to medium-high and beat 15 seconds. Then increase the speed to high and beat until the meringue is shiny and holds stiff peaks, about 90 seconds more.

9. Use a rubber spatula to scoop and spread the meringue over the pie. Use the back of a metal spoon to make little peaks.

10. Cover the edge of the crust with aluminum foil. Bake the pie on the center oven rack until the tips and ridges are golden, about 15 minutes.

11. Remove the pie from the oven and carefully remove the foil. Allow the pie to cool on a rack for 1 hour, then refrigerate it for at least another hour before serving. Cut the pie with the tip of a thin sharp knife that has been dipped in hot water and wiped dry before each cut.

Makes 8 to 10 servings

Note: Water tends to form when meringue is baked on a water-based custard. If this occurs, after you have removed the first slice, tip the pan over the sink and pour off any excess liquid.

Banana Custard Pie

7his is a custard pie in the true sense of the word: It's richer than Croesus, smooth and creamy, layered with bananas, and topped with whipped cream.

INGREDIENTS

1 single-crust recipe Basic Pie Crust 1 or 2 (page 175 or 176), fully baked (page 167)

2¼ cups milk

½ cup sugar

¼ teaspoon salt

¼ cup cornstarch

3 large egg yolks

3 tablespoons unsalted butter, at room temperature, cut into 3 pieces

1 teaspoon vanilla extract

3 ripe bananas

2 tablespoons fresh lemon juice

1½ cups Whipped Cream (page 86) for topping

1. Make the pie crust and cool the baked shell.

2. Scald 2 cups of the milk with the sugar and salt in a heavy medium-size saucepan over low heat. Stir occasionally to dissolve the sugar.

3. Dissolve the cornstarch in the remaining ¼ cup milk in a small bowl. Whisk in the egg yolks.

4. Whisk the egg mixture into the scalded milk. Cook, whisking constantly, over low heat until it thickens and bubbles, about 3 minutes, then cook for 1 minute more. The custard should form loose mounds when dropped from a spoon back into the pan.

5. Remove the custard from the heat and stir in the butter and vanilla. Transfer the custard to a small bowl and cool for 15 minutes, gently stirring it several times to allow the steam to escape. Place a piece of plastic wrap directly on the surface of the custard and puncture the wrap in several places with the tip of a knife. Cool for 30 minutes in the refrigerator.

6. While the custard is cooling, cut the bananas into ¼-inch-thick slices and toss them with the lemon juice to prevent them from turning brown.

7. Spread half the custard in the pie shell with a spatula and cover it with a layer of bananas. Spread the remaining custard carefully over the bananas and arrange the remaining bananas on top. Spread the whipped cream over the bananas.

8. Chill the pie for at least 2 hours before serving.

Makes 8 to 12 servings

Coconut Custard Pie

I love anything with coconut in it, so this pie is one of my long-time favorites. It starts with a simple butter crust, which I fill with thick, coconut-rich pudding, then top with meringue.

I N G R E D I E N T S

1 single-crust recipe Basic Pie Crust 1 or 2 (page 175 or 176), fully baked (page 167)

FILLING
1½ cups heavy (whipping) cream
1¼ cups milk
¾ cup sugar
6 tablespoons cornstarch
2 large egg yolks
1 teaspoon vanilla extract
2 cups shredded coconut

MERINGUE TOPPING
5 large egg whites, at room temperature
½ cup sugar
½ teaspoon cream of tartar

1. Make the pie crust and cool the baked shell.

2. Scald the cream and ½ cup of the milk with the sugar in a heavy medium-size saucepan over low heat. Stir occasionally to dissolve the sugar.

3. Dissolve the cornstarch in the remaining ¾ cup milk. Whisk in the egg yolks.

4. Gradually add ½ cup of the hot cream mixture to the yolks while whisking vigorously. Whisk this mixture into the remaining scalded cream. Cook, whisking constantly, over low heat until it thickens, 5 to 6 minutes. Cook, continuing to whisk, 20 to 30 seconds more. The custard should form loose mounds when dropped from a spoon back into the pan.

5. Remove the custard from the heat and stir in the vanilla. Transfer the custard to a medium-size bowl and cool for 15 minutes, gently stirring it several times to allow the steam to escape.

6. Stir all but 3 tablespoons of the coconut into the custard. Place a piece of plastic wrap directly on the surface of the custard and puncture the wrap in several places with the tip of a knife. Cool for 1 hour at room temperature.

7. Preheat the oven to 350°F.

8. Scoop the custard into the pie shell and use a spatula to spread it evenly.

9. For the meringue, using an electric mixer on medium speed, beat the egg whites in a medium-size bowl until frothy, about 50 seconds.

10. Gradually add the sugar and cream of tartar on medium speed.

Increase the speed to medium-high and beat 15 seconds. Then increase the speed to high and beat until the meringue is shiny and holds stiff peaks, about 90 seconds more.

11. Use a rubber spatula to scoop and spread the meringue over the pie. Use the back of a metal spoon to make little peaks. Sprinkle the remaining coconut over the top.

12. Bake the pie on the center oven rack until the coconut and the meringue peaks are golden, about 15 minutes.

13. Cool for 15 minutes, then refrigerate the pie for 1 hour before serving.

Makes 8 to 10 servings

Vanilla Custard Tart

*U*nlike most custard tarts, this one is covered with a crust, combining the flavor of buttery dough and vanilla. It's delicious sprinkled with confectioner's sugar and served with sliced berries that have been tossed with sugar.

INGREDIENTS

1 double-crust recipe Basic Tart Crust (page 176), rolled out; top crust refrigerated, bottom crust lightly baked in 9-inch tart pan (page 167)

2 cups heavy (whipping) cream

2 cups milk

½ cup sugar

6 tablespoons cornstarch

8 large egg yolks

1 tablespoon vanilla extract

1 large egg mixed with 2 tablespoons water or milk for glazing

1. Make the tart crust and cool the baked shell.

2. Scald the cream and 1½ cups of the milk with the sugar in a heavy medium-size saucepan over low heat. Stir occasionally to dissolve the sugar.

3. Dissolve the cornstarch in the remaining ½ cup milk in a medium-size bowl. Vigorously whisk in the egg yolks.

4. Gradually add ½ cup of the hot cream mixture to the yolks while whisking vigorously. Whisk this mixture into the remaining scalded cream. Cook, whisking constantly, over low heat until it thickens, about 4 minutes, then cook for 1 minute more.

5. Remove the custard from the heat and stir in the vanilla. Transfer the custard to a ceramic bowl and cool for 15 minutes, gently stirring it several times to allow the steam to escape. Place a piece of plastic wrap directly on the surface of the custard and puncture the wrap in several places with the tip of a knife. Refrigerate for 15 minutes.

6. Preheat the oven to 350° F.

7. Scoop the custard into the tart shell and use a spatula to spread it evenly.

8. Brush the egg glaze along the edge of the shell. Lay the top crust over the custard and press along the edge with your thumb to seal the two crusts. Make a pretty edge; cut 3 to 4 small slits in the top crust; brush the top with the egg glaze.

9. Bake the tart on the center oven rack until the crust is golden, about 1 hour. Allow the tart to cool completely on a rack before serving.

Makes 8 to 12 servings

Raspberry Chiffon Pie

Unlike most chiffons, this pie has a very strong and tart raspberry flavor. It makes a good dessert for the warm summer months.

INGREDIENTS

1 recipe Cookie Crumb Crust made with chocolate wafers, graham crackers, or vanilla wafers (page 178), baked, or 1 single-crust recipe Basic Pie Crust 1 or 2 (page 175 or 176), fully baked (page 167)

FILLING
12 ounces raspberries, fresh or thawed and drained frozen

7 tablespoons sugar

1 tablespoon unflavored gelatin

3 tablespoons fresh orange juice

1/2 cup heavy (whipping) cream, chilled

1/8 teaspoon salt

2 tablespoons fresh lemon juice

2 large egg whites, at room temperature

1/2 recipe Whipped Cream (page 86)

12 fresh raspberries

1. Make the pie crust and cool the baked shell.

2. For the filling, combine the raspberries and 4 tablespoons of the sugar in a small bowl and let stand for 30 minutes.

3. Process the raspberry mixture in a food processor to a purée, 20 seconds. Transfer the purée to a large bowl.

4. Sprinkle the gelatin over the orange juice in a cup or small bowl and let stand at least 2 minutes to soften.

5. Using an electric mixer on medium-high speed or a hand-held whisk, beat the cream in a small mixing bowl to firm but not dry peaks. Set aside.

6. Place the cup of gelatin in a larger bowl filled half-way with hot water and stir. When the gelatin has liquified, stir it into the raspberry purée.

7. Stir the salt into the lemon juice and add this mixture to the purée as well. Let the raspberry purée stand until slightly thickened, about 3 minutes.

8. Meanwhile, using an electric mixer on medium-high speed, beat the egg whites until frothy, about 15 seconds. Gradually add the remaining 3 tablespoons sugar and beat to soft peaks, 15 to 30 seconds more.

9. Fold the whipped cream into the purée, then fold in the egg whites. Pour this chiffon into the crust. Allow it to set for 6 hours in the refrigerator.

10. Before serving, top the pie with whipped cream and crown it with the fresh raspberries.

Makes 8 to 10 servings

Chocolate Chiffon Pie

*B*efore I started Rosie's, I thought that chiffon pies all came out of boxes of Jell-O brand instant something. Then I learned about homemade chiffon, and scales fell from my eyes. This pie calls for a vanilla cookie crust, but you can substitute a chocolate cookie crust if you prefer.

INGREDIENTS

*1 recipe Cookie Crumb Crust made
   with vanilla wafers (page 178),
   baked, or 1 single-crust recipe
   Basic Pie Crust 1 or 2 (page 175
   or 176), fully baked (page 167)*
2 ounces unsweetened chocolate
*1 tablespoon instant coffee or espresso
   powder*
3 tablespoons cold water
2¼ teaspoons unflavored gelatin
6 tablespoons boiling water
3 large eggs, separated
9 tablespoons sugar
1½ teaspoons vanilla extract
*¾ cup heavy (whipping) cream,
   chilled*
*½ recipe Whipped Cream (page 86)
   for topping*
*½ ounce unsweetened chocolate
   for shaving*

1. Make the pie crust and cool the baked shell.

2. Melt the chocolate in the top of a double boiler placed over simmering water. Transfer it to a large bowl and set aside.

3. Dissolve the instant coffee in the cold water. Then sprinkle the gelatin over the coffee and let stand at least 2 minutes to soften.

4. Pour the boiling water into the chocolate and stir with a wooden spoon until the mixture is smooth.

5. Add the gelatin mixture to the chocolate mixture and stir quickly until it dissolves.

6. Lightly beat the egg yolks together with a fork, then quickly add them along with 5 tablespoons of the sugar and the vanilla to the hot chocolate mixture and mix until smooth.

7. Beat the heavy cream in a small bowl on high speed until stiff.

8. Place the bowl with the chocolate mixture slightly into a bowl of ice water and whisk constantly until the mixture begins to thicken, 2 to 4 minutes.

9. Beat the egg whites in a medium-size bowl on medium-high speed until frothy, about 30 seconds. Gradually add the remaining 4 tablespoons sugar and continue beating until the whites are stiff but not dry, 60 seconds more. Immediately fold in the whipped cream.

10. Pour this chiffon into the crust. Refrigerate immediately and allow it to set for 6 hours.

11. Before serving, spread the whipped cream topping over the pie so that the outside edges of the chiffon are visible. Cover the cream with chocolate shavings (page 33). Eat within 1 day of making.

Makes 8 to 12 servings

Chocolate Mousse Pie in a Toasted Pecan Crust

A rich, dark mousse encased in a sweet nut crust that's glazed with semisweet chocolate.

INGREDIENTS

CRUST
2 cups chopped pecans
1/2 cup (lightly packed) light brown sugar
5 tablespoons unsalted butter, melted
3/4 cup semisweet chocolate chips

FILLING
4 ounces semisweet chocolate
2 ounces unsweetened chocolate
1 teaspoon instant coffee powder
4 large eggs, at room temperature
1/2 teaspoon vanilla extract
1 1/2 cups heavy (whipping) cream, chilled

1/2 ounce unsweetened chocolate for shaving

1. Preheat the oven to 375° F.

2. Toast the pecans on a cookie sheet until they are golden in color, about 5 minutes.

3. Place the nuts, sugar, and butter in a medium-size bowl and toss with a fork or your hands. Pat the mixture evenly over the bottom and up the sides of a 9-inch pie plate.

4. Bake the crust on the center oven rack until the butter and sugar begin to caramelize, 8 to 10 minutes.

5. Distribute the chocolate chips evenly over the crust, return it to the oven, and bake until the chips are softened, 1 to 1½ minutes. Remove the crust from the oven and spread the chips over the bottom and sides with a frosting spatula. Refrigerate the crust while you prepare the filling.

6. For the filling, melt both chocolates with the coffee in the top of a double boiler placed over simmering water. Then vigorously whisk in the eggs and vanilla until the mixture is smooth. Transfer this mixture to a medium-size bowl and cool for at least 5 minutes.

7. Using an electric mixer on medium-high speed, beat the cream until it forms firm peaks. Fold two-thirds of the cream into the chocolate mixture and spread the mousse in the crust.

8. Refrigerate the pie until ready to serve, 6 to 8 hours. Store the remain-ing whipped cream in a small bowl covered with plastic.

9. Before serving, spoon the cream onto the center of the pie and spread it, leaving a 1½-inch border free. Cover the cream with chocolate shavings (page 33).

Makes 10 servings

Crucheon's Fudge Pie

*W*hen I was a student at Berkeley, I was a regular at a little restaurant called Crucheon's, mostly because it had desserts I was prepared to die for. It seems appropriate that a fudge pie would be one of my college experiences because fudge first caught on about 150 years ago at women's colleges, where students made it as an excuse to stay up late and talk. I didn't need an excuse. I kept working on this recipe until I was able to create the dark, chocolaty filling in its butter crust. I dedicate the results to Crucheon's. Serve each slice with whipped cream.

1 single-crust recipe Basic Pie Crust 1 or 2 (page 175 or 176), lightly baked (page 167)
4 ounces unsweetened chocolate
8 tablespoons (1 stick) unsalted butter
3 large eggs, at room temperature
1 cup plus 2 tablespoons sugar
½ recipe Whipped Cream (page 86) for topping

1. Make the pie crust and cool the baked shell.

2. Preheat the oven to 375°F.

3. Melt the chocolate and butter in the top of a double boiler placed over simmering water. Cool until the mixture is tepid.

4. Using an electric mixer on medium speed, beat the eggs and sugar in a medium-size mixing bowl until the mixture is thick and light yellow, about 80 seconds.

5. Add the chocolate mixture and mix on medium speed until blended, about 30 seconds. Scrape the bottom and sides of the bowl with a rubber spatula and mix for 15 seconds more.

6. Cover the edge of the pie crust with a strip of aluminum foil so that it won't burn and pour the filling in.

7. Bake the pie on the center oven rack until the filling is set and forms a crust and a tester inserted in the center comes out with moist crumbs, 35 to 40 minutes. Remove the foil from the crust after 30 minutes of baking.

8. Serve the pie warm with whipped cream.

Makes 8 to 12 servings

Chocolate Berry Tart

I don't remember when I first tasted chocolate fondue, although I do remember someone ordering it for me and saying, "This'll knock your socks off." An understatement. I think of this pie as a less messy version of that fondue, and I'd like to propose a toast to the marriage of two of the world's most distinguished tastes — fresh berries and rich chocolate. May they thrive and prosper.

INGREDIENTS

1 single-crust recipe Shortbread Tart Crust (page 177), fully baked in 9-inch tart pan (page 167)

FILLING

1 ounce unsweetened chocolate, cut into 4 pieces

1/2 cup plus 2 tablespoons semisweet chocolate chips

1/4 cup plus 2 tablespoons milk

1/2 cup plus 2 tablespoons heavy (whipping) cream

1 1/2 large egg yolks (see Note), at room temperature

1 teaspoon vanilla extract

1/2 teaspoon instant espresso powder

TOPPING

1/3 cup heavy (whipping) cream, chilled

1 pint ripe strawberries, rinsed and hulled, or raspberries (not necessary to rinse)

1. Make the tart crust and cool the baked shell.

2. Chop both the chocolates to fine flakes in a food processor, about 20 seconds.

3. Heat the milk and cream in a small saucepan over low heat just to boiling, about 5 minutes. Remove it from the heat.

4. Add the egg yolks, vanilla, and espresso powder to the chocolate and process about 8 seconds.

5. With the processor running, pour the hot cream and milk through the feed tube and process until the chocolate is melted. Scrape the bowl with a rubber spatula and process several more seconds.

6. Let the mixture cool to lukewarm, 10 to 15 minutes, then spread it in the tart shell.

7. Chill the tart at least 4 hours in the refrigerator.

8. Before serving, whip the cream (for topping) until it forms firm peaks and spread it over the surface of the tart, starting at the center. Distribute the berries evenly over the cream.

Makes 8 to 12 servings

Note: Crack the second egg yolk into your palm. Use a knife to gently cut through the center of the yolk, then slide one half of the yolk into a cup along with the first whole yolk. Put the extra half yolk in a container in the refrigerator and scramble it into your kids' eggs the next morning.

Chocolate-Crusted Peanut Butter Pie

*S*tart with a crust so deli-
ciously crunchy that it
would make a great candy bar,
fill it with the flavor of peanut
butter and the lightness of
whipped cream cheese, and you've
got yourself a dessert that's
dangerous to have around the
house.

INGREDIENTS

CRUST
2 cups coarsely chopped unsalted dry-
roasted peanuts
¼ cup granulated sugar
4 tablespoons (½ stick) unsalted
butter, melted
¾ cup semisweet chocolate chips

FILLING
8 ounces cream cheese, at room
temperature
½ cup plus 2 tablespoons peanut
butter (smooth or crunchy)
¾ cup plus 2 tablespoons confec-
tioner's sugar
½ cup milk
1 cup heavy (whipping) cream,
chilled

½ ounce unsweetened chocolate
for shaving

1. Preheat the oven to 375°F.

2. Place all the ingredients for the
crust in a large bowl and toss them
together with your hands or a wooden
spoon.

3. Pat the mixture firmly into a 9-
inch pie plate with your fingers, push-
ing it as far up the sides of the pan
as possible.

4. Place the crust on the center oven
rack and bake for 10 minutes. Place
it in the freezer to cool completely,
15 minutes.

5. For the filling, using an electric
mixer on medium speed, cream the
cream cheese, peanut butter, and
confectioner's sugar together in a
medium-size mixing bowl until light
and fluffy, about 1½ minutes. Scrape
the bowl with a rubber spatula.

6. With the mixer on low speed,
gradually add the milk and mix until
it is incorporated, 10 seconds. Scrape
the bowl and mix several seconds more.

7. Whip the cream in another mixing
bowl to soft peaks and fold it into the
peanut butter mixture.

8. Scoop the filling into the pie shell
and freeze the pie for at least 6 hours.

9. Two hours before serving, move
the pie from the freezer to the refrigerator. Shave chocolate over the
top right before serving.

Makes 8 to 10 servings

Lemon Cream-Cheese Pie

*M*y version of a cream-cheese pie has quite a tart filling to enhance the variety of flavors. I've added a sour cream topping and graham cracker crust.

(page 178)

INGREDIENTS

1 recipe Cookie Crumb Crust made with graham crackers (page 178), baked

FILLING
9 ounces cream cheese, at room temperature
½ cup sugar
1½ teaspoons grated lemon zest
½ cup sour cream, at room temperature
1 large egg, at room temperature
5 tablespoons fresh lemon juice
1 teaspoon vanilla extract
2 tablespoons all-purpose flour

TOPPING
1 cup sour cream, at room temperature
3 tablespoons sugar
1 pint fresh raspberries or rinsed and hulled strawberries

1. Make the crumb crust and cool the baked shell.

2. Preheat the oven to 325°F.

3. Using an electric mixer on medium speed, cream the cream cheese, sugar, and lemon zest in a medium-size mixing bowl until light and fluffy, about 1 minute. Scrape the bowl halfway through and at the end.

4. Add the sour cream and mix on medium-low speed until the mixture is smooth, about 30 seconds. Scrape the bowl.

5. Beat in the egg, lemon juice, and vanilla on medium speed until blended, 30 to 45 seconds. Scrape the bowl.

6. Add the flour and mix just until blended, about 8 seconds. Pour the filling into the crust.

7. Bake the pie on the center oven rack until the top is rounded and springs back to the touch, 45 to 50 minutes. (A tester inserted in the center will not come out dry.) Small cracks may form on the surface.

8. Allow the pie to cool on a rack for 20 minutes.

9. Meanwhile, prepare the topping: Stir the sour cream and sugar together, and spread it over the cream-cheese filling. Return the pie to the oven for 5 minutes.

10. Allow the pie to cool to room temperature, then refrigerate it for 4 hours. Cover the top with whole fresh raspberries before serving.

Makes 8 to 12 servings

Strawberry Cream-Cheese Tart

*S*trawberries and cream have probably been keeping company since the first cow wandered into a berry patch. So herewith is my contribution to that excellent combination: a crunchy, buttery tart shell holding a sweet cream-cheese filling topped with whole strawberries. It's an elegant version of the classic New York cheesecake, and I like to display it on a cake pedestal for full effect.

INGREDIENTS

1 single-crust recipe Basic Tart Crust (page 176), lightly baked in 9-inch tart pan (page 167)

12 1/2 ounces cream cheese (1 1/2 large packages plus 1 tablespoon), at room temperature

1/4 cup sour cream, at room temperature

1/2 cup sugar

1/4 cup fresh lemon juice

2 large eggs, at room temperature

1 to 2 pints fresh strawberries, rinsed and hulled

1/2 cup strawberry or red currant jelly

1. Make the tart crust and cool the baked shell.

2. Preheat the oven to 350°F.

3. Cream the cream cheese, sour cream, sugar, and lemon juice in a food processor until thoroughly blended, about 30 seconds. Scrape the bottom and sides of the bowl with a rubber spatula.

4. Add the eggs and process for 10 seconds. Pour the filling into the tart shell.

5. Bake the tart on the center oven rack until the filling rises in the center and a toothpick inserted in the center comes out clean, about 40 minutes.

6. Cool the tart on a rack at least 2 hours. Top the tart with the strawberries arranged in concentric circles.

7. Heat the jelly in the top of a double boiler placed over simmering water until liquified. Glaze the berries by brushing the jelly over them with a pastry brush. Let the glaze set for 15 minutes. Serve the tart at room temperature.

Makes 8 to 10 servings

Linzertorte

*O*riginally from Vienna, the Linzertorte has become an extremely popular dessert in America. This beautiful lattice-topped tart is made from cookie dough rich in the flavor of ground almonds and fragrant spices. Layered between the crusts is a filling of raspberry preserves.

INGREDIENTS

CRUST
8 ounces almonds
1 cup (2 sticks) unsalted butter,
    at room temperature
³/₄ cup sugar
¹/₄ teaspoon salt
1 teaspoon ground cinnamon
¹/₄ teaspoon ground cloves
1 teaspoon grated lemon zest
1 teaspoon grated orange zest
1 large egg
2 teaspoons vanilla extract
1¹/₂ cups all-purpose flour
1 tablespoon unsweetened cocoa
    powder

FILLING
1¹/₄ cups raspberry preserves (18-ounce jar)
2 teaspoons fresh lemon juice

¹/₄ cup finely chopped almonds for sprinkling

1. Preheat the oven to 400°F. Lightly grease an 11-inch tart pan with butter.

2. For the crust, process the almonds in a food processor until finely chopped, about 15 seconds. Set aside.

3. Using an electric mixer on medium speed, blend the butter, sugar, salt, spices, and citrus zests together in a medium-size mixing bowl just until the butter is incorporated, 15 to 20 seconds. Stop once to scrape the bowl with a rubber spatula.

4. Whisk the egg in a small bowl until blended; add 2 tablespoons of the egg to the butter mixture. Set aside the remaining egg for the glaze. Add the vanilla to the butter mixture and mix until they are incorporated, about 15 seconds. Scrape the bowl.

5. With the mixer on high speed, add the flour and the cocoa and beat just until blended, about 15 seconds. Scrape the bowl. Add the almonds on low speed and mix until blended.

6. Remove the dough from the mixing bowl and work it a bit with your hands so that it holds together. Break off about one-third of the dough, cover it with plastic wrap, and refrigerate it.

7. Press the remaining dough evenly over the bottom and up the sides of the prepared tart pan with your fingers. Wrap a strip of aluminum foil around the top edge of the pan and fold it over the very top of the crust to keep it from burning.

8. Bake the tart shell on the center oven rack until the dough loses its sheen and is golden, about 15 minutes. Cool the tart shell on a rack. Turn off the oven.

9. While the tart shell is baking and cooling, remove the dough from the refrigerator and place it between two pieces of plastic wrap or waxed paper. Roll it out to a rectangle about 12×8 inches. Slip this dough, still sandwiched between the plastic, onto a platter or cookie sheet and refrigerate it for 2 hours.

10. After 2 hours, preheat the oven to 400°F.

11. Remove the foil from the tart shell and set the foil aside.

12. For the filling, stir the raspberry preserves and lemon juice together in a small bowl. Spread the mixture evenly over the bottom of the baked tart shell.

13. Remove the chilled dough from the refrigerator and prepare the lattice. Peel off the top piece of plastic wrap and cut the dough lengthwise into 9 strips about ¾ inch wide.

14. Using a frosting spatula, carefully remove the first 4 strips from the paper one at a time and place them across the top of the tart. Pinch the edges of the strips down onto the top of the baked edge and save any extra dough. Then place the next 5 strips at right angles to the first 4 across the tart. Use the scraps to fill in the

spaces along the edges of the crust between the lattice strips.

15. For the glaze, brush the remaining egg over the lattice strips with a pastry brush. Sprinkle the crushed almonds over the entire surface of the tart.

16. Replace the foil around the top edge of the tart and place the tart on the center rack of the oven. Bake it until the top is shiny and golden and the jam is bubbling, about 30 minutes.

17. Remove the tart from the oven and allow it to cool completely on a rack.

Makes 12 to 16 servings

Almond Raspberry Tartlets

*F*or these miniature tarts, I fill a butter crust with an almond paste mixture and accent it with raspberry preserves.

*1 single-crust recipe Basic Tart Crust
    (page 176), dough refrigerated
    but not rolled out*
2½ ounces almond paste
5 tablespoons sugar
1 large egg, at room temperature
*1 tablespoon plus 1 teaspoon
    all-purpose flour*
2 teaspoons melted unsalted butter
¼ teaspoon salt
2 to 3 tablespoons raspberry preserves

1. Preheat the oven to 425°F. Have
ready 2 mini-muffin tins (twelve 1¾-
inch cups per pan).

2. Pinch off 24 rounded tablespoons
of the tart dough and press them into
the cups with your fingers so that
the dough forms a rim about ⅛ inch
above the top of the pan. The shells
should be about ³⁄₁₆ inch thick. (There
will be dough left over. This can be
wrapped and frozen for future use.)
Refrigerate the shells for 15 minutes.

3. Bake the shells on the center oven
rack until golden, about 10 minutes.
Cool on a rack. Reduce the heat to
350°F.

4. While the shells are baking, beat
all the remaining ingredients except
the raspberry jam in a small mixing
bowl with an electric mixer on
medium-high speed until thoroughly
mixed, about 1½ minutes.

5. Place ¼ teaspoon raspberry jam in
the bottom of each tart shell, then
spoon a rounded teaspoon of almond
filling over the jam.

6. Bake the tartlets until the tops are
golden and a tester inserted in the
center comes out dry, about 15 minutes. Cool for 2 hours before removing
the tartlets from the pans.

Makes 24 tartlets

Apple Brown Betty

*A*mong the important ques-
tions that will go unan-
swered in this book are who was
Betty and how did her name get
attached to this crumble, which
isn't particularly brown. It's
something you'll want to ponder,
no doubt, as you work your way
through its scrumptious pecan
crumb topping to the apples underneath. You may also find yourself pondering whether you even
need the apples with a crust this
good. Serve Apple Brown Betty
with vanilla or other favorite ice
cream.

INGREDIENTS

FILLING
5 to 6 medium-size Granny Smith
apples, peeled, cored, and cut into
³⁄₈-inch-thick slices (7¹⁄₂ cups)
5 tablespoons granulated sugar

TOPPING
²⁄₃ cup all-purpose flour
²⁄₃ cup (lightly packed) light brown
sugar
²⁄₃ cup finely chopped pecans
¹⁄₂ teaspoon ground cinnamon
5 tablespoons plus 1 teaspoon (¹⁄₃ cup)
unsalted butter, at room temperature, cut into 5 pieces

1. Preheat the oven to 350°F. Generously grease an 8-inch square baking
pan with butter.

2. Place half the apple slices in the
prepared pan and sprinkle them with
the granulated sugar. Layer the remaining apples over the sugar.

3. For the topping, place the flour,
brown sugar, nuts, and cinnamon in a
large bowl and stir them together with
a wooden spoon. Work the butter into
the mixture with your fingertips until
it is evenly distributed. Spread the
topping evenly over the apples.

4. Bake the betty on the center oven
rack until the topping is crunchy and
golden and the apples are bubbling,
55 to 60 minutes. Serve hot.

Makes 9 servings

Caramel Apple Casserole

*E*ven my cousin Kate Dooley,
who ingests 750 milligrams
of lecithin every day instead of
other fats, couldn't resist this
dessert. I felt a little guilty about
tempting her when I made it
with the Vermont apples we had
picked that day—but not very
guilty because even virtuous
people need an occasional treat
to remind them of how virtuous
they're being.

INGREDIENTS

PASTRY
3 cups all-purpose flour
3 tablespoons granulated sugar
¹⁄₂ teaspoon salt
1 cup (2 sticks) unsalted butter,
chilled, cut into 16 pieces
3 large egg yolks, at room temperature
2 tablespoons ice water

APPLE FILLING
5 medium-large apples, peeled, cored,
and cut into ¹⁄₄-inch-thick slices
(6 cups)
1 cup (lightly packed) light brown sugar
2 tablespoons fresh lemon juice
¹⁄₄ teaspoon salt

CARAMEL
8 tablespoons (1 stick) unsalted butter
¹⁄₂ cup granulated sugar

1. Preheat the oven to 375°F. Grease a 2-quart soufflé dish with butter.

2. To make the pastry, process the flour, granulated sugar, and salt in a food processor for 20 seconds. Add the butter and process until the dough resembles coarse meal, about 30 seconds.

3. Stir the egg yolks and water together in a cup. With the processor running, pour this mixture through the feed tube and process until the dough comes together, 35 seconds.

4. Remove the dough from the processor and knead it for several turns. Divide the dough into quarters and shape each piece into a thick round disk.

5. Roll each disk ⅛ inch thick between 2 pieces of plastic wrap (see page 165 for rolling instructions). Trim each disk to fit the soufflé dish. Stack the pancakes on a plate with plastic wrap between each layer and place them in the refrigerator while you prepare the filling.

6. Place all the ingredients for the filling in a large bowl and toss to evenly coat the apples. Set aside.

7. For the caramel, melt the butter in a small saucepan and stir in the granulated sugar. Bring the mixture to a boil over medium heat, then simmer for 2 minutes.

8. Pour two-thirds of the caramel into the prepared dish. Fit one pastry circle in the bottom over the caramel.

9. Place a third of the apple mixture (2 cups) over the pastry and top with a second pastry circle. Add another third of the apples, top with the third pastry circle, then the remaining apples and the fourth pastry circle.

10. Pour the remaining caramel over the top and spread evenly with a frosting spatula.

11. Cover the top of the dish with aluminum foil and pierce the foil in several places with the tip of a knife.

12. Place the dish on the center oven rack and put a cookie sheet on the rack below to catch any drips. Bake the casserole for 30 minutes. Remove the foil and continue baking until the top is golden and the apple mixture is bubbling, 30 to 35 minutes longer.

13. Remove the dish from the oven and cool on a rack. Serve warm or at room temperature.

Makes 8 servings

CHAPTER SIX

The Old
Smoothies

The recipes in this chapter have the odd distinction of being defined mostly by what they aren't: no flour, crust or icing, neither pie nor cake, square nor cookie. What's left over are custards, puddings, and chilled and whipped confections, the foods of childhood and old age. They're soothing and I like to think of them as a kind of culinary tribute to the roundness of life.

That leaves five other ages of man, and when I was growing up, we spent those eating Jell-O. Remember Jell-O? The dessert there's always room for, the thing you could count on finding at family restaurants, the only salad you'd eat and only then if your mother mixed it up with canned fruit and those little marshmallows that look like pussy willows? (My mother would never forgive me if I didn't note that marshmallow ne'er touched Jell-O in her kitchen, but I ate enough at friends' houses to know all about this concoction.)

It's likely that Jell-O is one of those things you put away with childhood and, with all due respect, that's probably for the best. But sophisticated as our palates may now be, that slithery, creamy texture, that flavor bursting onto our tongues almost as an afterthought provide the same familiar pleasure whether we're eating pudding, Bavarian, or crème brûlée—which are, after all, only fancy versions of the shimmery food we grew up on.

Apparently, food smoothness is a universal craving because puddings and custards show up in cooking almost everywhere in the world. Try out this richness on your tongue: mousse, charlotte, chiffon, coeur à la crème, tiramisù, baked Alaska, Persian cream, blancmange, blote kage, tapioca, meringue, weinschaum, zerde, zabaglione. And that's not even counting the wonderful names the English have for their puddings, like Poor Knights of Windsor and Grateful Pudding and, my favorite, Kiss-Me-Quick.

Now if you have a list of names a mile long for a single food, that says something about where it stands in your pantheon of pleasures, and, in fact, the British use "pudding" to signify all dessert. The children of my former neighbors would politely ask me what's for pudding when I invited them over for a meal, and it took me months to admit my cross-cultural clumsiness and ask their mother what they were talking about.

To me, pudding is custard, a fancier version of Beechnut baby food, though lighter and richer. I think of puddings and other chilled creations as the most seasonal of desserts (with the possible exception of pies before frozen fruit became passable). Chills and whips are the ideal dessert in the sultry summer months when you crave something sweet, but not ponderous. Others, such as Indian or bread pudding, are creatures of the autumn harvest months, and chocolate and butterscotch puddings are to me what sacrifices to the gods were for the ancients when the winter dark made them fear the sun would never return.

Pudding It all Together

These desserts are perhaps the most delicate of all to make because they demand precision and seldom allow for a middle ground. They don't usually take too long, though, and you'll find that once you're familiar with a few basic recipes, whole worlds of mousses, crèmes, and trifles will open to you. I've divided the recipes in this chapter into three categories in order to explain some of the preparation techniques.

Stove-Top Puddings

For puddings that contain liquid, sugar, cornstarch, and eggs, it is usually best to dissolve the cornstarch in a portion of the liquid and to stir in the eggs with a whisk. The remaining liquid should be heated with the sugar in a heavy saucepan over medium-low heat just to the boiling point. Then give the cornstarch mixture a final stir (it tends to settle as it sits) and add it in a stream to the boiling mixture while stirring vigorously with a whisk. The mixture is then brought to a second boil while stirring constantly and usually boiled for 10 to 30 seconds more to ensure proper thickening. It is essential for cornstarch to be brought to a boil in order for it to "clear," that is to lose its chalky taste and become less cloudy in appearance.

After the pudding has cooked, pour it into a large bowl. Let it sit for 10 minutes, stirring occasionally with a wooden spoon. Then cover the surface of the custard with plastic wrap that has been punctured several times with a knife or skewer to release steam and refrigerate.

Curdled eggs are the biggest problem that can occur with these puddings. If this starts to happen, you can do one of two things. Either pour the mixture immediately from the pot into a cool bowl and stir it vigorously with a whisk (you can strain it to check for evidence of cooked eggs), or pour the mixture into a blender and blend on medium-high speed for 5 to 10 seconds until it's smooth. The second process is more reliable for making your pudding smooth, but it also tends to loosen it.

Baked Custards

These desserts, which include such delights as Noodle Kugel, Pumpkin Caramel, and Baked Chocolate Custard, occasionally call for some stove-top cooking, but regardless of preliminaries, they're all baked in a large baking dish or individual ramekins after the ingredients have been stirred together in a mixing bowl.

I bake my custards in a water bath, which allows them to cook more evenly and gently. To make a water bath, put the custard dish or dishes in a shallow pan on the center rack of the oven, and pour enough hot water into the pan to come about two-thirds of the way up the sides of the custard baking dish.

For more delicate puddings, such as Chocolate Almond Custard, Peaches 'n' Cream Custard, and Baked Chocolate Custard, I find that individual ramekins allow the custard to bake more evenly than a large baking dish. Hearty puddings, such as the bread puddings, Noodle Kugel, and Indian Pudding, can be baked in large dishes with no problem.

Test if baked puddings are done by inserting a tester close to the center but not directly in it. If it comes out clean, the pudding is done. The center will continue to cook after the custard comes out of the oven. Remove the custard from the water bath as soon as it leaves the oven and allow it to cool to room temperature before refrigerating.

Mousses and Gelatin Desserts

Mousses are soft and creamy, sometimes frothy desserts which derive their lightness from egg whites and/or whipped cream. A classic chocolate mousse is made by folding whipped cream and/or beaten egg whites gently into a mixture of egg yolks and melted chocolate. I loosen the chocolate mixture by stirring in one-third of the egg whites with a whisk first, then completing the folding process with a rubber spatula.

Fruit mousses and chiffons are made by mixing fruit with juice and sometimes egg yolks, then adding gelatin to thicken the mixture slightly before folding in whipped cream and/or beaten egg whites.

Gelatin, if used properly, is a great enhancer, but too much of it can make a dessert tough and rubbery. I've found that most recipes call for too much. The chocolate in chocolate mousses gives them enough firmness, so they seldom require gelatin, though you can use it in conjunction with whipped cream or beaten egg whites. You can also use it with sour cream, heavy cream, cream cheese, or fruit juice for other desserts, such as fruit mousses, which need the gelatin to help them set so that they don't separate.

Before folding egg whites or whipped cream into a mixture that contains gelatin, let the gelatin mixture set enough first so that it forms a very loose mound when dropped from a spoon.

To unmold a gelatin dessert, moisten a chilled plate slightly and have it ready. Then run the point of a knife around the edge of the mold, turn it upside down over the plate, and put a hot, damp cloth over the bottom of the mold for several seconds. Shake it lightly to loosen the dessert onto the plate.

Pudding on the Ritz

*7*he desserts in this chapter vary greatly from hearty winter fare to the light, fruity gossamers that make a perfect end to a summer meal. Of the latter, fruit mousses and Bavarians are particularly lovely accented with fruit sauces. I like to serve each portion on a dessert plate and surround it with a pool of sauce that contrasts in both color and taste. Several slices of kiwi or whole strawberries make an attractive garnish. Add a couple of butter cookies on the side!

Bread pudding, Indian pudding, chocolate mousse, and traditional puddings, such as Daddy's Oedipal Chocolate Pudding and Butterscotch Pudding, are stick-to-your-rib sweets and are best served piled generously in a dessert bowl with whipped cream and in some cases a heavier bourbon or vanilla sauce.

The beauty of nearly all these desserts is the ease and speed with which they're made. Because so many of them call for ingredients you're likely to have around the house, you can literally whip up a little something at a moment's notice. And all that froth and shimmer make them look more impressive and less filling than they have a right to. Up until not so long ago, fancy restaurants would serve anything before they would use the word "pudding" on a dessert menu. It sounded so—heaven forbid—family style. But now they've learned what smart cooks knew all along— the proof is in the pudding.

Daddy's Oedipal Chocolate Pudding

*M*y father, the champion dessert eater, has never been much of a dessert maker, but this pudding is all his own. For those who prefer their comfort food on the rich, indulgent side, this one's for you!

INGREDIENTS

3 ounces unsweetened chocolate
1½ cups heavy (whipping) cream
2¼ cups milk
½ cup plus 2 tablespoons sugar
¼ cup cornstarch
2 large egg yolks
2 tablespoons unsalted butter,
    cut into 2 pieces
1 recipe Whipped Cream (page 86)
    for serving

1. Melt the chocolate in the top of a double boiler placed over simmering water.

2. Pour the cream, 1½ cups milk, and the sugar into a large saucepan. Heat over medium heat, stirring twice during this time, until scalded, about 5 minutes.

3. Meanwhile, in a medium-size bowl, dissolve the cornstarch in the remaining ¾ cup milk. Then whisk in the egg yolks.

4. Whisk the melted chocolate vigorously into the scalded mixture. Cover and heat over very low heat to blend, about 2 minutes. Uncover the saucepan and whisk again vigorously until the mixture is uniform in color and all specks of chocolate have disappeared.

5. Raise the heat to medium-low. Remove about 1 cup of the chocolate mixture from the pan and pour it in a stream into the egg yolk mixture while mixing vigorously with a whisk. (If the mixture should curdle, place it in a blender and blend it on low speed until smooth, 5 to 10 seconds.)

6. Bring the chocolate mixture remaining in the saucepan just to the boiling point and add the egg yolk mixture to it in a stream while mixing vigorously with a whisk. Mix constantly until the mixture thickens and forms loose mounds when dropped from the whisk back into the pan, 30 seconds.

7. Strain the pudding into a medium-size bowl and gently fold in the butter until it is completely incorporated.

8. Allow the pudding to sit for 5 minutes, stirring it gently several times to release steam. Puncture a piece of plastic wrap in several places with a knife or skewer. Lay it directly on the surface of the pudding. Leave the pudding at room temperature for 10 minutes. Then lift the plastic wrap and stir the pudding gently again.

9. Place the plastic wrap back on the surface of the pudding and refrigerate the pudding until chilled, 4 to 6 hours. Serve piled in a bowl topped with whipped cream.

Makes 8 to 10 servings

Butterscotch Pudding

*I*t must have been sometime during my high school years that I indulged myself almost daily with butterscotch pudding. This is an especially creamy version of that adolescent pleasure.

INGREDIENTS

2 cups milk
1 cup heavy (whipping) cream
1 cup plus 2 tablespoons (lightly packed) dark brown sugar
⅛ teaspoon salt
¼ cup plus 2 teaspoons cornstarch
2 large egg yolks, at room temperature
3 tablespoons unsalted butter, cut into 3 pieces
1½ teaspoons vanilla extract

1. Pour 1¼ cups of the milk, the cream, sugar, and salt in a heavy medium-size saucepan. Heat over medium heat, stirring twice during this time, until scalded, about 5 minutes.

2. In a small bowl, dissolve the cornstarch in the remaining ¾ cup milk. Whisk in the egg yolks.

3. Remove about 1 cup of the cream mixture from the pan and pour it in a stream into the egg yolk mixture while mixing vigorously with a whisk. (If the mixture should curdle, place it in a blender and blend it on low speed until smooth, 5 to 10 seconds.)

4. Bring the cream mixture remaining in the saucepan just to the boiling point over medium-low heat. Then add the egg mixture in a stream while stirring vigorously with the whisk. Cook, stirring constantly, over low heat until the mixture thickens and forms loose mounds when dropped from the whisk back into the pan, 1½ minutes.

5. Strain the pudding into a medium-size bowl and gently fold in the butter and vanilla until they are completely incorporated. Allow the pudding to cool for 10 minutes, stirring it gently several times to release the steam. Puncture a piece of plastic wrap in several places with a knife or skewer. Lay it directly on the surface of the pudding. Refrigerate the pudding for at least 6 hours before serving.

Makes 4 to 6 servings

Creamy Stove-Top Rice Pudding

(for Eliot)

7his recipe took a lot of attempts to perfect, for it had a penchant for curdling. The method that I came up with, to my relief, is foolproof. The custard is cooked first so that if it curdles it can be put in the blender and made smooth again before adding the rice. Eliot, my business partner, is such a devotee of my rice pudding that he would drive miles to my house to eat it each time I tested the recipe.

INGREDIENTS

1³/₄ cups plus 2 tablespoons water
¹/₂ cup plus 3 tablespoons long-grain
    white rice
¹/₂ teaspoon salt
2 tablespoons unsalted
    butter
¹/₂ cup raisins
1 cup milk
1 cup heavy (whipping) cream
4 large eggs
7 tablespoons sugar
1 teaspoon ground nutmeg
1¹/₂ teaspoons vanilla
    extract

1. Bring the water, rice, and salt to a simmer in an uncovered, medium-size saucepan over medium-high heat. Cover the pan and simmer over low heat until the rice is tender, about 15 minutes. The water should be completely absorbed by the rice.

2. Remove the pan from the heat and stir in the butter and the raisins. Cover the pan and allow the rice to sit while you prepare the custard.

3. In a heavy large saucepan, vigorously whisk the milk, cream, eggs, sugar, and nutmeg until well blended.

4. Cook the mixture over low heat, whisking constantly, until it is thick enough to coat the back of a wooden spoon, 10 to 15 minutes. (The time may vary considerably depending on the pan and the stove.) Immediately remove the pan from the heat, stir in the vanilla, and then add the rice by large spoonfuls, stirring gently after each addition. (If the pudding should curdle before adding the rice, place it in a blender and blend on low speed until smooth, 5 to 10 seconds. Then pour the custard into a large bowl and add the rice.)

5. Allow the pudding to sit for 30 minutes, then cover and refrigerate until ready to serve. It can be served warm or cold.

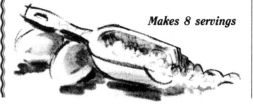

Makes 8 servings

Chocolate Almond Custard

*L*ight and delicate, this custard is topped with a brownielike meringue.

I N G R E D I E N T S

CUSTARD
2½ *cups milk*
½ *cup heavy (whipping) cream*
¼ *cup sugar*
3 *tablespoons cornstarch*
Pinch of salt
2 *large egg yolks,*
    at room temperature
1 *teaspoon almond extract*

TOPPING
1¼ *ounces unsweetened chocolate,*
    chopped
3 *tablespoons heavy (whipping) cream*
2 *large egg whites,*
    at room temperature
2 *tablespoons sugar*

1. Preheat the oven to 325°F. Lightly grease 6 ramekins with butter.

2. For the custard, scald 2 cups of the milk and the cream in a heavy medium-size saucepan over medium-low heat.

3. In a small bowl, combine the remaining ½ cup milk, the sugar, cornstarch, and salt and stir until the cornstarch is dissolved.

4. Stir the cornstarch mixture into the scalded milk and cook, stirring constantly, over medium-low heat until it boils, about 6 minutes. Remove the pan from the heat.

5. Gently stir the egg yolks with a fork in a small bowl. Gradually add one-third of the hot milk mixture to the yolks while whisking vigorously. Pour this mixture back into the remaining milk mixture, stirring constantly. Bring the custard to a boil while stirring constantly over medium-low heat and boil for 2 minutes.

6. Remove the pan from the heat and stir in the almond extract.

7. Fill each prepared ramekin two-thirds full with the custard.

8. Prepare the topping: Melt the chocolate with the cream in the top of a double boiler over simmering water. Mix it with a spoon, then pour it into a medium-size bowl.

9. Beat the egg whites with an electric mixer on high speed until frothy, about 30 seconds. Gradually add the sugar and continue beating the whites to form soft peaks, 30 seconds. Stir one-third of the whites into the chocolate rapidly with a whisk, then fold in the rest of the whites with a rubber spatula. The chocolate will be quite stiff, making the folding process somewhat difficult.

10. Top each cup of custard with 2 heaping tablespoonsful of the chocolate mixture.

11. Place the cups in a shallow baking pan on the center oven rack. Pour enough hot water into the baking pan to come two-thirds of the way up the sides of the ramekins.

12. Bake until the custard is loosely set and a tester inserted close to but not in the center comes out dry, about 45 minutes.

13. Remove the ramekins from the water bath; the custard will set further as it cools. Serve at room temperature.

Makes 6 servings

Baked Chocolate Custard

A dense, dark custard, this is great served hot or cold with whipped cream on top.

2 cups heavy (whipping) cream
¾ cup milk
1 cup semisweet chocolate chips
½ ounce unsweetened chocolate, cut into 4 pieces
6 large egg yolks, at room temperature
2 teaspoons vanilla extract
1 recipe Whipped Cream (page 86) for serving

1. Preheat the oven to 325°F. Lightly grease 6 ramekins with butter.

2. Combine the cream, milk, and both chocolates in the top of a double boiler. Heat over simmering water, whisking occasionally, until the chocolate is melted, 8 to 12 minutes. Then stir the mixture very briskly with the whisk until any specks or strands of chocolate are dissolved and the liquid is uniformly brown. Turn off the heat.

3. Using the whisk attachment of an electric mixer on medium-high speed, beat the egg yolks in a medium-size mixing bowl until thick and pale in color, 3 to 4 minutes.

4. Gradually add the chocolate mixture to the egg yolks, stirring rapidly with a whisk. Blend in the vanilla.

5. Pour the mixture through a sieve or strainer into the prepared ramekins. Place the ramekins in a shallow baking pan on the center oven rack. Pour in enough hot water to come two-thirds of the way up the sides of the ramekins.

6. Bake the puddings until a tester

inserted close to but not in the center comes out dry, about 1 hour 20 minutes.

7. Remove the ramekins from the water bath and serve warm or cold with whipped cream.

Makes 6 servings

Peaches 'n' Cream Custard

A rich and flavorful baked custard topped with fresh peaches that have been lightly sautéed in bourbon. It is best to prepare the topping right before serving. If you prepare it earlier, heat it slightly before spooning it over the custard.

I N G R E D I E N T S

CUSTARD
2¼ *cups milk*
¾ *cup heavy (whipping) cream*
1 *cup plus 2 tablespoons (lightly packed) light brown sugar*
5 *large egg yolks*
3 *large eggs*
2¼ *teaspoons grated lemon zest*
1¼ *teaspoons vanilla extract*
½ *teaspoon salt*
¾ *teaspoon ground cinnamon*

TOPPING
4 *medium-size peaches, pitted and cut (with peel) into ½-inch-thick slices (about 4 cups)*
2 *tablespoons (lightly packed) light brown sugar*
3 *tablespoons fresh orange juice*
Pinch of salt
2 *tablespoons plus 2 teaspoons bourbon*

1. Preheat the oven to 350°F. Lightly grease 8 ramekins with butter.

2. Place all the ingredients for the custard in a large bowl and stir vigorously with a whisk until completely blended.

3. Pour the custard mixture into the ramekins. Place them in a shallow baking pan on the center oven rack. Pour enough hot water into the baking pan to come two-thirds of the way up the sides of the ramekins.

4. Bake the custard until it is loosely set and a tester inserted close to but not in the center comes out clean, about 35 minutes.

5. Allow the custard to cool to room temperature, then cover with plastic wrap if you plan to refrigerate it. The custard should be at room temperature when served.

6. To prepare the topping, place the peaches, sugar, orange juice, and salt in a medium-size skillet. Bring to a simmer over medium-high heat; simmer until most of the liquid is absorbed but the peaches still hold their shape, 2 to 3 minutes.

7. Remove the skillet from the heat, add the bourbon, and toss gently.

8. Spoon the peaches on top of each custard and serve.

Makes 8 servings

Pumpkin Caramel Custard

*T*his smooth custard with a mild taste of pumpkin and a caramel glaze makes a nice surprise at the end of a winter holiday meal.

<hr>

I N G R E D I E N T S

PUDDING
4 whole large eggs
3 large egg yolks
1½ teaspoons vanilla extract
2 cups milk
⅔ cup sugar
*1 tablespoon plus 1 teaspoon
    ground ginger*
1 teaspoon ground nutmeg
1 teaspoon ground cinnamon
1 teaspoon ground allspice
⅛ teaspoon ground cloves
½ teaspoon salt
½ cup canned pumpkin purée

CARAMEL
½ cup sugar
2 tablespoons water

1. Preheat the oven to 350°F. Arrange an oven rack just below the center. Grease a 6-cup soufflé dish with butter.

2. For the pudding, vigorously whisk the eggs, egg yolks, and vanilla in a large mixing bowl until blended. Set aside.

3. Place the milk, sugar, spices, and salt in a medium-size saucepan and set aside.

4. Place the sugar and water for the caramel in another medium-size saucepan and heat to boiling over medium heat without stirring. As soon as it boils, swirl the pan and continue swirling over the heat until the mixture turns a rich amber, 4 to 5 minutes.

5. Remove the caramel from the heat and immediately pour it into the prepared soufflé dish. Tilt the dish from side to side to evenly coat the bottom. Place the dish in a shallow baking pan. Pour enough hot water in the baking pan to come two-thirds of the way up the side of the soufflé dish. Set aside.

6. Bring the milk mixture just to a boil over medium heat. While whisking vigorously, pour the milk mixture in a thin stream into the egg mixture. Strain the mixture into a large bowl and whisk in the pumpkin, blending thoroughly so that there are no lumps.

7. Pour the pumpkin mixture into the soufflé dish and place it, with the baking pan, in the oven. Reduce the heat to 325°F and bake the custard until it is firm and a tester inserted close to but not in the center comes out clean, about 1¼ hours.

8. Remove the dish from the water bath. Cool the custard on a rack, then refrigerate it for 4 to 6 hours or overnight.

9. To serve, run a thin knife around the sides of the dish. Invert a serving dish on the soufflé dish and flip the custard carefully onto the serving dish.

Makes 8 servings

Truffle Soufflé

*I*n a book of recipes notable for their richness, this one probably takes the cake. It's loaded with butter and chocolate, and although it's flourless, you can slice it into pieces like a cake. But it works better scooped out like a pudding.

INGREDIENTS

4 ounces unsweetened chocolate, chopped
4 ounces semisweet chocolate, chopped, or ⅔ cup chocolate chips
1 cup sugar
2 teaspoons instant espresso powder
½ cup boiling water
4 large eggs, separated
2 teaspoons vanilla extract
1 cup (2 sticks) unsalted butter, melted and cooled to tepid
1 recipe Whipped Cream (page 86) for serving

1. Preheat the oven to 300°F. Lightly grease a 6- to 8-cup soufflé dish with butter.

2. Place both chocolates, ¾ cup of the sugar, and the espresso in a large bowl. Add the boiling water and stir until the chocolate melts. Cool the mixture to tepid.

3. Whisk the egg yolks and the vanilla together in a small bowl. Add the butter and whisk until the mixture is silky and smooth, about 10 seconds.

4. Using an electric mixer on medium-high speed, whip the egg whites in a medium-size mixing bowl until frothy, about 30 seconds. Gradually add the remaining sugar and continue beating until the whites form firm peaks, 1 minute.

5. Add the egg yolk mixture to the chocolate mixture and stir, then fold in the egg whites.

6. Pour the soufflé batter into the prepared dish and place the dish in a shallow baking pan on the center oven rack. Pour enough hot water into the baking dish to come two-thirds of the way up the sides of the soufflé dish.

7. Bake the soufflé until the top rises up and cracks, about 1½ hours. (A tester inserted in the center will not come out dry. When checking for doneness, be sure to open and close the oven carefully.) Turn the oven off and allow the soufflé to set for 1 hour in the water bath, in the oven. Serve the soufflé hot or warm, garnished with whipped cream.

Makes 6 to 8 servings

Chocolate Bread Pudding

*C*ertainly not your average bread pudding, this is more of a rich chocolate dessert with bread in it. It is great served hot or cold with whipped cream or vanilla ice cream. I like to use challah, which makes it a bit more special, but croissants or buttered French baguettes work well too.

INGREDIENTS

1½ cups milk
1¾ cups plus 2 tablespoons heavy (whipping) cream
6 tablespoons sugar
1½ cups semisweet chocolate chips
⅛ teaspoon salt
3 large eggs, lightly beaten with a fork
3 cups cubed (1-inch) challah, 3 croissants cut into ½-inch cubes (3 cups), or ⅓ French baguette, split lengthwise, generously buttered, and cut into ½-inch cubes (3 cups)

1. Heat the milk, cream, sugar, chocolate chips, and salt in a medium-size saucepan over low heat, whisking occasionally, until the chocolate is completely melted and all the chocolate specks are gone, 3 to 4 minutes. Remove the pan from the heat.

2. Briskly whisk in the eggs.

3. Place the cut-up bread in a large bowl and pour the chocolate mixture over the bread. Toss, then refrigerate the pudding for 2 to 3 hours, tossing the mixture occasionally with a large spoon to make sure all the bread is soaked. You can pull a few pieces apart with your fingers to check.

4. Fifteen minutes before baking, preheat the oven to 350°F. Generously grease a 6- or 8-cup soufflé dish with butter.

5. Scoop the pudding into the prepared dish. Bake on the center oven rack until the top is crisp, about 40 minutes. Then lay a piece of aluminum foil loosely over the surface of the pudding and bake until the pudding is set and a tester inserted close to but not in the center comes out dry, 30 minutes more. Cool slightly before serving.

Makes 8 to 10 servings

Bourbon Bread Pudding

*T*his dessert melts in your mouth from its crunchy topping down through its custard filling, with or without the sauce. You can make it with crusty French bread, but I think that croissants make it extra special. Serve it warm on the first day and right out of the refrigerator thereafter.

INGREDIENTS

1 cup heavy (whipping) cream
1 cup whole milk
4 large eggs
1 teaspoon vanilla extract
¼ cup bourbon
½ cup plus 2 tablespoons sugar
¼ teaspoon ground nutmeg
¼ teaspoon salt
3 to 4 croissants, cut into ½-inch cubes (4 cups), or ⅓ to ½ French baguette, split lengthwise, generously buttered, and cut into ½-inch cubes (4 cups)
⅓ cup dark raisins
Bourbon Sauce (recipe follows; optional)

1. In a large bowl, vigorously whisk the cream, milk, eggs, vanilla, bourbon, ½ cup of the sugar, nutmeg, and salt until blended. Add the bread cubes and toss to ensure even saturation.

2. Refrigerate the pudding for at least 2 hours, tossing the mixture with a large spoon occasionally to make sure all the croissants are soaked. You can pull a few pieces apart with your fingers to check.

3. Fifteen minutes before baking, preheat the oven to 350°F. Grease an 8-inch square baking dish with butter. Scoop the pudding into the baking dish. Sprinkle the remaining 2 tablespoons sugar over the top of the pudding.

4. Bake the pudding on the center oven rack until the top is crisp and golden and has risen in the center, about 50 minutes.

5. Allow the pudding to cool 30 minutes before devouring or, if you wish, while you make the sauce.

Makes 8 servings

Bourbon Sauce

INGREDIENTS

½ cup sugar
2 large egg yolks
5 tablespoons bourbon
4 tablespoons (½ stick) unsalted
    butter, cut into 4 pieces

1. Pour ¾ inch water in the bottom of a double boiler and bring it to a simmer over medium-low heat.

2. Place the sugar and egg yolks in the top of the double boiler (not yet over the simmering water) and stir vigorously with a whisk until light in color.

3. Whisk in the bourbon and place the top of the double boiler over the simmering water. Cook, whisking vigorously, until the mixture is hot and slightly thickened, 3 to 4 minutes.

4. Pour the mixture through a fine strainer into a small bowl, add the butter, and stir until it melts.

5. Serve the sauce warm over the bread pudding. If you prepare the sauce ahead of time, reheat it in a double boiler over hot water.

Makes ¾ cup

Apple Bread Pudding with Vanilla Sauce

A classic pudding accented with tart apple chunks and vanilla sauce.

INGREDIENTS

1 cup heavy (whipping) cream
1 cup milk
2 whole large eggs
2 large egg yolks
⅓ cup (lightly packed) light brown
    sugar
¼ teaspoon salt
1 teaspoon vanilla extract
2¼ teaspoons ground cinnamon
3 to 4 croissants, cut into ½-inch
    cubes (4 cups), or ⅓ to ½ French
    baguette, split lengthwise, gener-
    ously buttered, and cut into
    ½ inch cubes (4 cups)
2 cups cubed (½-inch) peeled tart
    apples (about 3), such as
    McIntosh or Granny Smith
⅓ cup golden raisins
1 tablespoon plus 1 teaspoon
    granulated sugar
Vanilla Sauce (recipe follows)

1. In a large mixing bowl, vigorously whisk the cream, milk, eggs, egg yolks, brown sugar, salt, vanilla, and ¼ teaspoon of the cinnamon until blended.

2. Add the croissant cubes, apples, and raisins, and toss several times with a large wooden spoon to ensure even saturation.

3. Refrigerate the pudding for at least 2 hours, tossing the mixture occasionally with the wooden spoon to make sure the bread is soaked. You can pull a few pieces apart with your fingers to check.

4. Fifteen minutes before baking, preheat the oven to 350°F. Grease an 8-inch square baking dish with butter. Scoop the pudding into the baking dish. Mix the granulated sugar and the remaining cinnamon together and sprinkle it over the bread pudding.

5. Place the baking dish in a shallow baking pan on the center oven rack and pour enough hot water into the larger pan to come two-thirds of the way up the sides of the pudding baking dish.

6. Bake the pudding until the top is golden and crisp and has risen in the center, about 50 minutes.

7. Remove the pudding from the water bath and allow it to cool for 30 minutes while you make the sauce.

Makes 8 servings

Vanilla Sauce

INGREDIENTS

*½ cup plus 2 tablespoons heavy
    (whipping) cream*
½ cup plus 2 tablespoons milk
¼ cup sugar
¼ teaspoon salt
1 tablespoon cornstarch
*3 tablespoons unsalted butter,
    cut into 3 pieces*
1½ teaspoons vanilla extract
½ teaspoon ground nutmeg

1. Scald the cream, all but ¼ cup of the milk, the sugar, and salt in a heavy medium-size saucepan over medium heat.

2. Dissolve the cornstarch in the remaining ¼ cup milk in a small cup. Stir it into the cream mixture.

3. Bring the mixture to a boil over low heat, whisking constantly. Continue boiling and whisking until the sauce thickens, about 3 minutes.

4. Remove the pan from the heat and stir in the butter, vanilla, and nutmeg. Allow the sauce to cool slightly before serving.

Makes 1¼ cups

Indian Pudding

*T*he Puritan women learned how to make this dark, spicy dessert from the Indians, and it has remained a New England favorite ever since, probably because it warms the cockles and sticks to the bones during those long winters. My partner Eliot can't get enough of it. He likes it served warm with vanilla ice cream or heavy cream spooned over the top, so this recipe is for him.

INGREDIENTS

2 cups milk
1 cup heavy (whipping) cream
½ cup yellow cornmeal
½ cup (lightly packed) light brown sugar
½ cup molasses
1 teaspoon salt
2 teaspoons ground cinnamon
¼ teaspoon ground nutmeg
¼ teaspoon ground cloves
¼ teaspoon ground ginger
4 large eggs
4 tablespoons (½ stick) unsalted butter, cut into 4 pieces

1. Preheat the oven to 325°F. Lightly grease a 6- or 8-cup soufflé dish with butter.

2. Scald the milk in a medium-size saucepan over medium-low heat.

3. While the milk is heating, pour the cream into a medium-size bowl and stir in the cornmeal, sugar, molasses, salt, and spices.

4. Add the cornmeal mixture to the scalded milk and cook, whisking constantly, over medium-low heat until the pudding has thickened to the consistency of syrup, about 5 minutes. Remove it from the heat.

5. Beat the eggs in a small bowl with a whisk. Add ½ cup of the hot cornmeal mixture to the eggs while whisking rapidly. Then vigorously whisk the egg mixture into the remaining cornmeal mixture. Add the butter and stir until it melts.

6. Pour the pudding into the prepared baking dish, and place the dish in a shallow baking pan on the center oven rack. Pour enough hot water into the larger pan to come two-thirds of the way up the sides of the pudding baking dish.

7. Bake the pudding until it is set and a tester inserted close to but not in the center comes out clean, about 1¼ hours.

8. Remove the pudding from the water bath and cool slightly. Serve the pudding warm.

Makes 10 servings

Noodle Kugel

*A*lthough this pudding traditionally accompanies a plate of brisket, I always find myself continuing to indulge in it long after the meat is gone. So I've sweetened the basic recipe and serve it as a dessert, warm or cold.

INGREDIENTS

8 ounces enriched broad egg noodles
2 cups sour cream
8 ounces whipped cream cheese
8 ounces small- or large-curd cottage cheese
½ cup plus 4 teaspoons sugar
2 teaspoons grated lemon zest
¼ teaspoon salt
4 large eggs
8 tablespoons (1 stick) unsalted butter, melted
¾ cup golden raisins
2 teaspoons ground cinnamon

1. Preheat the oven to 350°F. Lightly grease a 13 × 9-inch baking pan with butter.

2. Cook the noodles in a large pot of boiling water until tender but still slightly firm, about 7 minutes. Drain and set aside.

3. Place the sour cream, cream cheese, cottage cheese, ½ cup sugar, the lemon zest, and salt in a food processor and process until blended, about 20 seconds.

4. Add the eggs and butter and process until incorporated, about 5 seconds more.

5. Pour the cream cheese mixture over the noodles in a large bowl, add the raisins, and toss the pudding together with a large spoon.

6. Spread this kugel evenly into the prepared pan. Mix the remaining 4 teaspoons sugar and the cinnamon and sprinkle it over the top.

7. Bake the pudding on the center oven rack until the top is crisp, the center is firm and has risen, and a tester inserted in the center comes out dry, 45 to 50 minutes. Cool at least 30 minutes before serving.

Makes 10 to 12 servings

Chocolate Mousse

*T*hough it may verge on culinary cliché by now, I've found a good chocolate mousse to be one of the mainstays of dessert making. Part of the reason is that it's easy to make, but considered a major accomplishment—kind of like having mastered the soufflé.

This recipe imparts a no-nonsense, full-bodied taste from the first spoonful to the last.

INGREDIENTS

9 ounces semisweet chocolate

3 ounces unsweetened chocolate

2 large eggs, at room temperature

4 large eggs, separated, at room temperature

2 tablespoons rum, or 2 tablespoons strong brewed coffee, or 1 tablespoon each rum and coffee

1¼ cups heavy (whipping) cream, chilled

2 tablespoons sugar

1 recipe Whipped Cream (page 86) for serving

½ ounce unsweetened chocolate for shaving

1. Melt both chocolates in the top of a double boiler placed over simmering water.

2. Whisk the 2 whole eggs and 4 egg yolks together in a large bowl until blended. Whisk in the rum and/or coffee.

3. Add the chocolate to the whole egg mixture and whisk very vigorously so the eggs don't curdle. Cool just to room temperature.

4. Meanwhile, using an electric mixer on high speed, beat the cream in a medium-size mixing bowl, until soft peaks form, 1 minute. Chill in the refrigerator.

5. In a separate bowl, beat the egg whites until frothy, about 15 seconds.

Gradually add the sugar and continue beating until the whites form soft peaks, 30 seconds more.

6. Add one-third of the egg whites to the chocolate mixture and whisk to loosen the mixture, then fold in the rest of the whites. Fold in the cream.

7. Spoon the mousse into a 2-quart serving bowl or 8 individual dessert cups. Refrigerate immediately for at least 6 hours. Serve with whipped cream and chocolate shavings (see page 33). Eat within one day of making.

Makes 8 servings

Chocolate Cream-Cheese Mousse

*W*hen I realized that most of my chocolate desserts have a bittersweet flavor, I set out to find something that was pure sweetness, and this is it. The taste is like a Hershey's Kiss, and the texture like a dense mousse because of the cream cheese.

INGREDIENTS

MOUSSE

3 ounces semisweet chocolate
3 ounces unsweetened chocolate
8 ounces cream cheese, at room
   temperature
¾ cup sugar
3 large eggs, separated
1½ teaspoons vanilla extract
1½ cups heavy (whipping) cream,
   chilled

BOURBON CREAM

1 cup heavy (whipping) cream
2 tablespoons sugar
3 tablespoons bourbon

½ ounce semisweet or unsweetened
   chocolate for shaving

1. Melt both chocolates in the top of a double boiler over simmering water.

2. Process the cream cheese and ½ cup of the sugar in a food processor until smooth, about 10 seconds. Scrape the bowl with a rubber spatula.

3. Add the egg yolks and vanilla and process until smooth, about 5 seconds. Add the hot chocolate and process until the mixture is velvety, about 10 seconds. Transfer it to a large mixing bowl.

4. Using an electric mixer on high speed, whip the cream in a medium-size mixing bowl just until the peaks are firm, 1¼ minutes.

5. Whip the egg whites in a separate bowl on medium-high speed until frothy, 15 seconds. Gradually add the

remaining ¼ cup sugar and continue beating until the whites form soft peaks, 30 seconds more.

6. Whisk about one-third of the whites into the chocolate mixture to lighten it, then fold in the rest of the whites.

7. Fold in the whipped cream.

8. Pour the mousse into a 2-quart serving bowl and refrigerate at least 8 hours or overnight.

9. Just before serving, prepare the bourbon cream: Using an electric mixer on high speed, beat the cream, sugar, and bourbon in a medium-size bowl until soft peaks form, 1 minute.

10. Scoop out small portions of the mousse and serve each portion with a dollop of the bourbon cream. Shave chocolate over the cream (see page 33). Eat within one day of making.

Makes 12 to
16 servings

Coeur à la Crème

*T*his rich dessert is surprisingly delicate in taste, perhaps because it's not too sweet. It takes its name from the heart-shaped mold, and I find that it's a wonderful accompaniment to peeled and sliced peaches and plums, or fresh or frozen strawberries and raspberries. Toss the fruit with a bit of sugar before serving.

INGREDIENTS

1 cup small- or large-curd cottage cheese, at room temperature

8 ounces cream cheese, at room temperature

½ cup sour cream, at room temperature

½ cup heavy (whipping) cream, at room temperature

½ cup plus 2 tablespoons sugar

1. Line a 2-cup coeur à la crème mold with a double layer of cheesecloth that overhangs all sides and place the mold on a larger plate.

2. Process all the ingredients in a food processor until smooth, 20 to 30 seconds.

3. Use a rubber spatula to scoop the cream cheese mixture into the mold and smooth the surface. Fold the excess cheesecloth over the top and refrigerate at least 8 hours or overnight.

4. To serve, unfold the cheesecloth. Invert a serving plate over the mold and flip the crème onto the plate. Gently remove the mold and the cheesecloth.

5. Serve small portions along with fruit, if desired.

Makes 8 servings

Orange Cream-Cheese Bavarian

*J*ust when you think your Thanksgiving menu will never change, along comes this Bavarian that mixes the flavors of orange and cranberry with the smooth richness of cream cheese, and *voilà!* — the perfect and unexpected dessert.

INGREDIENTS

BAVARIAN
¼ cup cold water
1 envelope unflavored gelatin
1 cup heavy (whipping) cream
8 ounces cream cheese
1 can (6 ounces) frozen orange juice
    concentrate
¼ cup sugar
1½ teaspoons vanilla extract
1 tablespoon fresh lemon
    juice

CRANBERRY SAUCE
1¾ cups cranberries
1½ cups fresh orange juice
5 tablespoons sugar
½ teaspoon grated orange zest

Fresh mint leaves and cranberries
    for garnish

1. Grease a 4-cup mold or bowl
lightly with vegetable oil.

2. Put the water and gelatin in a
food processor and process for 5
seconds.

3. Heat the cream just to the boiling
point, then pour it into the food processor. Process to dissolve the gelatin,
about 10 seconds.

4. Add the cream cheese, orange
juice concentrate, sugar, vanilla, and
lemon juice and process another 10
seconds.

5. Pour the mixture into the prepared mold and refrigerate until set,
3 to 4 hours.

6. Meanwhile prepare the sauce:
Place the cranberries and ½ cup of the
orange juice in a small saucepan. Simmer covered over medium heat until
the berries crack and become soft, 2
to 3 minutes. Remove the pan from
the heat and stir in the sugar and
orange zest.

7. Pour the cranberry mixture and
the remaining 1 cup juice into a food
processor and process to a purée.
Strain the purée into a small bowl and
cover with plastic wrap until ready to
serve.

8. To serve, remove the Bavarian
from the mold (see page 217). Slice it
and spoon the sauce around the slice
on a small dessert plate. Garnish each
plate with several mint leaves and
whole cranberries.

Makes 12 servings

Smooth as Silk with Raspberry Sauce

A slippery smooth Bavarian
with a hint of lemon, ac-
cented with a raspberry sauce.

INGREDIENTS

BAVARIAN
1½ teaspoons unflavored gelatin
½ cup water
1 cup light cream
½ cup plus 1 tablespoon sugar
1½ teaspoons grated lemon zest
1¼ teaspoons vanilla extract
1 cup sour cream

RASPBERRY SAUCE
2 pints fresh raspberries
⅓ to ½ cup sugar
2 tablespoons fresh lemon juice or
 orange juice

1 kiwi, cut into 6 slices, for garnish

1. Stir the gelatin into the water to soften in a small bowl. Set aside.

2. Place the cream and sugar in a medium-size saucepan over low heat, stirring frequently until the sugar is dissolved, 3 to 4 minutes.

3. Add the softened gelatin to the cream mixture and stir until it is dissolved. Remove the pan from the heat, stir in the lemon zest and the vanilla, and cool the mixture to room temperature.

4. When cool, add the sour cream and stir until completely blended. Pour the mixture into 6 dessert cups or wine glasses and refrigerate for 4 hours.

5. To make the sauce, purée the raspberries with the sugar in a food processor for about 10 seconds.

6. Strain the mixture into a small bowl, add the lemon or orange juice, and stir.

7. Just before serving, pour the sauce over each Bavarian. Garnish with a slice of kiwi.

Makes 6 servings

Index

A

B

Butter, 12
 bars, Dutch, 158–59
 cake, Desert Island, 66–67
 cookies, Rosie's, 123–24
 –glazed nutmeg mounds, 114–15
 shortening vs., 171
 sponge method, 23–24
Buttercreams:
 mint, 137
 mocha, 86
 Rosie's, 85–86
Buttermilk chocolate cake, 40–41
Butterscotch:
 cinnamon icebox cookies, 120–21
 Congo bars, 142–43
 Dagwoods, 141–42
 pudding, 219

C

Cake flour, 12
Cakelike drop cookies, 94
Cake pans, 13, 19–20
Cakes, 17–88
 almond pound, 62–63
 apple, 54
 applesauce-raisin, 54–56
 baking, 25–26
 banana, 56–57
 berry sponge, 67–68
 bittersweet orange, with a lemon glaze, 52–53
 Boston cream pie, 49–50
 breakfast coffeecake, 59–60
 carrot-pineapple layer, 51–52
 chocolate buttermilk, 40–41
 chocolate custard sponge roll, 71–73
 chocolate fruitcake, 45–46
 chocolate mousse, 42–44
 chocolate nut torte, 44–45
 chocolate sour-cream layers, Rosie's famous, 36–37
 coconut-pecan oatmeal, 58–59
 cold fudge sundae, 38–39
 cooling and removing from pans, 19, 20–21
 cream cheese pound, 62
 decorating, 27–33
 Desert Island butter, 66–67
 fresh blueberry-muffin breakfast, 60–61
 fudge, 37
 golden layers, 47–48
 Harvard mocha, 49
 lemon-glazed orange chiffon, 68–69
 lemon icebox, with fresh strawberries, 76–77

lemon pudding, 75–76
 lemon-strawberry sponge roll, 73–75
 mixing batter for, 21–25
 mocha, 40
 mustard gingerbread, 57–58
 pineapple upside-down, 50–51
 poppy-seed chocolate-chip, 65–66
 poppy-seed pound, 64–65
 preparing pans for, 19–20, 21
 putting batter into pans for, 25
 queen raspberry, 38
 salvaging, 33
 serving, 33–35
 snowball, 39
 snow queen, 48–49
 sour cherry fudge, 41–42
 storing, 35
 summertime, 48
 testing for doneness, 26–27
 Texas ruby red, 39
 Tom's birthday roll, 70–71
 Velvet Underground, 37
 see also Cheesecake(s)
Caramel:
 apple casserole, 211–12
 pumpkin custard, 224–25
 –topped pecan cheesecake, 81–82
Carrot-pineapple layer cake, 51–52
Center bouquets, on cakes, 31–32
Cheesecakes(s):
 baking, 26
 brownie, 80–81
 caramel-topped pecan, 81–82
 cherry bars, 148–49
 pumpkin, 78–80
 traditional, à la Reuben's, 77–78
Cherry:
 cheesecake bars, 148–49
 sour, fudge cake, 41–42
 sour, tart, 183–84
Chiffon cakes, 20
 baking, 26
 lemon-glazed orange, 68–69
Chiffon pies, 174
 chocolate, 200–201
 raspberry, 199–200
Chocolate, 12
 berry tart, 203–4
 brownie cheesecake, 80–81
 chunky, bars, 140
 –crusted peanut butter pie, 205
 –dipped pecan logs, 122–23
 fudge frosting, 83
 hot fudge filling, 87
 melting, 24
 shavings, 33
 sunken kisses, 104–5
 topping, German, 84–85

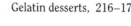

German chocolate topping, 84–85
Gingerbread, mustard, 57–58
Gingersnap crumb crusts, 79
Gingersnappers, 105–6
Glazes, 110
    almond, 63
    butter, 114, 115
    chocolate, 44, 137–38
    egg, 126, 127
    lemon, 53, 69, 113, 114
    orange, 145, 146
    spiced, 55, 56
Golden cake layers, 47–48
Graham cracker crumb crusts, 81, 82

H

Harvard mocha cake, 49
Hermits, 109–11
Honeypots, 147–48
Hot fudge filling, 87

I

Icebox cake, lemon, with fresh strawberries, 76–77
Icebox cookies, butterscotch cinnamon, 120–21
Indian pudding, 230
Ingredients, 10, 11, 12

J, K, L

Jam:
    butter cookies, Rosie's, 123–24
    Maya's pocketbooks, 127–28
    ruby gems, 124–25
    sandwiches, 155–56
Jayne Mansfields, 143–44
Jell-O, 214
Jelly-roll pans, 13
Knives, 14
Kugel, noodle, 231
Lace cookies, oatmeal, 106–7
Lattice tops, 171
Layer cakes:
    frosting, 27–29
    general directions for,
      19–20, 25, 26
    splitting layers for, 29

Lemon:
    cake cookies, 113–14
    cream-cheese pie, 206
    cream-cheese squares, 149–50
    custard filling, 88
    glaze, bittersweet orange cake with,
      52–53
    –glazed orange chiffon cake, 68–69
    icebox cake with fresh strawberries,
      76–77
    meringue pie, 194–95
    pudding cake, 75–76
    raisin pie, 189–90
    squares, tart, 152–53
    strawberry sponge roll, 73–75
Lime pie, Florida, 193–94
Linzer bars, 156–58
Linzertorte, 208–9
Loaf cakes, decorating, 32
Loaf pans, 13, 24
Log cakes, 95–96
Log cookies, 95–96
Luongo, C. P., 131

M

Macaroons, chocolate, 109
McCarthy, Karen, 147
Mandelbrot, 111–12
Marshmallow, frosting, 83–84
Maya pies, 115–17
Maya's pocketbooks, 127–28
Measuring cups, 13
Measuring dry ingredients, 24
Measuring spoons, 13
Meatless mince tart for Christmas, 187–89
Menzies, Michelle, 111
Meringue:
    chocolate drops, 108–9
    pie, lemon, 194–95
Microwave ovens, 14
Mince tart for Christmas, meatless, 187–89
Mint brownies, 137–38
Mixers, electric, 11–13, 14
Mocha:
    buttercream, 86
    cake, 40
    cake, Harvard, 49
Mousse(s), 216–17
    chocolate, 231–32
    chocolate, cake, 42–44
    chocolate, pie in a toasted pecan crust,
      201–2
    chocolate cream-cheese, 232–33
    –filled pies, 174
Mustard gingerbread, 57–58

N, O

Nectarine:
    pie filling, 172–73
    synergy, 186–87
Noah Bedoahs, 122
Noodle kugel, 231
Nutballs, 111
Nutmeg mounds, butter-glazed, 114–15
Oatmeal:
    coconut-pecan cake, 58–59
    lace cookies, 106–7
    orange wafers, crispy, 107–8
Orange:
    birthday cake bars, 145–46
    cake with a lemon glaze, bittersweet,
      52–53
    chiffon cake, lemon-glazed, 68–69
    chocolate-chip cookies, 101–2
    cream cheese Bavarian, 234–35
    oatmeal wafers, crispy, 107–8
Ososky, Pam, 79

Pantry, 11
Parchment, 15, 19, 91
Passover desserts:
    Berry sponge cake, 67–68
    chocolate macaroons, 109
    chocolate mousse cake, 42–44
    chocolate nut torte, 44–45
    D D's, 139
    sour cherry fudge cake, 41–42
    Tom's birthday roll, 70–71
    truffle soufflé, 225–26
Pastry bags, 15, 30
Pastry cookies, filled, 97–98
    Maya's pocketbooks, 127–28
    rugalah, 126–27
Peach(es):
    'n' cream custard, 223–24
    crumb pie, 185–86
    pie filling, 172–73
Peanut butter:
    chocolate-chip bars, 144–45
    cookies, 103–4
    pie, chocolate-crusted, 205
    sunken kisses, 104–5
Pear pie filling, 172–73
Pecan:
    bars, 150–51

cheesecake, caramel-topped, 81–82
chocolate-bourbon pie, 191
coconut oatmeal cake, 58–59
crunchies, 117–18
logs, chocolate-dipped, 122–23
orange chocolate-chip cookies, 101–2
pie, 190
sweet-potato pie, 191–92
toasted, crust, 201, 202
Pie crusts, 163–69
    basic, 175–76
    butter vs. shortening in, 167
    chocolate peanut, 205
    cookie crumb, 178–79
    crumb, 169
    lattice top, 171
    lining pan with, 166–67
    mixing batter for, 164–65
    prebaking, 167–68
    problems with, 166
    rolling dough for, 165–66
    shortbread, 168–69
    toasted pecan, 201, 202
    upper, 167
Pie plates, 13
Pies, 161–212
    all-American apple, 179–80
    baking temperatures and times for,
      173–74
    banana custard, 196
    blueberry-plum crumb, 184–85
    chocolate-bourbon pecan, 191
    chocolate chiffon, 200–201
    chocolate-crusted peanut butter, 205
    chocolate mousse, in a toasted pecan
      crust, 201–2
    coconut custard, 197–98
    Crucheon's fudge, 202–3
    decorative edges for, 170–71
    deep-dish pumpkin, 193
    Florida lime, 193–94
    fruit fillings for, 172–73
    lemon cream-cheese, 206
    lemon meringue, 194–95
    lemon-raisin, 189–90
    peach crumb, 185–86
    pecan, 190
    raspberry chiffon, 199–200
    sour cream apple, 180–81
    storing, 174
    sweet-potato pecan, 191–92
Pie weights, 14
Pineapple:
    carrot layer cake, 51–52
    upside-down cake, 50–51
Plastic wrap, 15
Plum:
    blueberry crumb pie, 184–85
    pie filling, 172–73

2, R

T

U, V

W, Y